PROPHETIC EVANGELIST

The Living Legacy of Harry Denman

PROPHETIC EVANGELIST

The Living Legacy of Harry Denman

Acknowledgments

Grateful acknowledgment is made to the following who have been primarily responsible for assembling and editing this volume: Dr. Lynne M. Deming, Editor, Upper Room Books; the Reverend David L. Hazlewood, Executive Secretary, Discipleship Resources; and Dr. Craig Gallaway, Editorial Director, Discipleship Resources. Deep appreciation is also expressed to Dr. Billy Graham for writing the FOREWORD; to Dr. Joe Hale, General Secretary, the World Methodist Council, who was a member of Dr. Denman's staff, for preparing the OPENING REFLECTIONS; to Ms. Lou Dozier, Dr. Denman's longtime secretary, who wrote her personal recollections and edited PART ONE: MEMORIES; to Dr. Robert F. Lundy, former Bishop of Malaysia and Singapore, who edited PART TWO: WRITINGS; and to Dr. Thomas F. Chilcote, Jr., former President of Emory & Henry College and also a member of Dr. Denman's staff, who edited PART THREE: MEDITATIONS. Indebtedness is noted to United Methodist News Service, Mr. Thomas S. McAnally, Director, and to the World Methodist Council, Dr. Hale, General Secretary, for several photographs used in this volume. Gratitude is given to The Upper Room for permission to use the Warner Sallman portrait of Harry Denman on the dust jacket and to reproduce three previously published meditations by Dr. Denman. Certain articles, reports, and other writings included in this volume first appeared in *The Alabama Christian Advocate*, *Shepherds*, and *Together*.

CONTENTS

FOREWORD

Harry Denman was one of the great mentors for evangelism in my own life and ministry—and for countless others in evangelism as well. His knowledge and his vision for evangelism were worldwide, and yet he never lost his heartbeat for the individual person who did not know Christ. While a Methodist, he was ecumenical in spirit and action.

I never knew a man who encouraged more people in the field of evangelism than Harry Denman. He was always ready to share his advice and wisdom with me whenever I would ask him, and his counsel was invaluable to me on many occasions—from what cities to go to, to the organization of the Billy Graham Evangelistic Association.

He was a man of integrity and believed deeply that integrity was one of the greatest needs in evangelism and missions. He also was a man of great love and warm spirituality. He could be tough if he needed to be, but his graciousness and loving spirit will always be remembered. But the thing that people will remember above all about Harry Denman was his love of Christ and his desire to see others come to know Him. He truly was one of those rare individuals whose impact will continue for generations to come.

—Dr. Billy Graham
January 8, 1993

Opening Reflections

Why would anyone want to read a book about a man who was born one hundred years ago? When Harry Denman died in 1976, Billy Graham called him "one of God's greatest servants" and described his passing as a personal loss. No one would have expected such a memorial accolade when Harry was a teenager. In order to help his mother with the family's financial burden, he dropped out of high school to work as an errand boy for the Tennessee Coal and Iron Company in Birmingham, Alabama. Yet by the time he was twenty-eight, he was business manager for the First Methodist Episcopal Church, South, of that city and was on his way to a life's work that would reach around the globe. He not only became the most influential layperson in his denomination but was probably more widely known than most of the church's bishops. I write as one who felt the power of Dr. Denman's life firsthand.

Nearly forty years ago, at the conclusion of one of his sermons, Dr. Denman invited those present to make, and affirm after him, a series of faith affirmations. Each built upon the previous statement:

- I believe that Jesus is Christ, the Son of God.
- I believe that God has raised Him from the dead, and He is alive.
- I believe that He is able to save any person from the

law of sin and death if he will repent and believe, because of my own experience.
- I will tell it from my lips and life.

He asked those who wanted to say that to record the affirmations in the back of their Bibles and to sign what they had written. I remember that night and those affirmations, for I was one who responded. Six years later I was invited to join the staff of the General Board of Evangelism, where I was privileged to be associated with Dr. Denman for four years.

We find the roots of Harry Denman's achievements in a Christian home. He loved to recall a time in his boyhood when his congregation was struggling to meet the budget, and an appeal was made for people to bring their special offerings on a particular Sunday morning. That morning Harry watched his mother go back and forth in their home between the kitchen and a buffet in the dining room. She was obviously torn about what she should do. In the buffet were two silver spoons, family heirlooms, brought by his mother when they immigrated from England. That morning when the time came for the offering, his mother went to the altar with others who brought their gifts and placed those two silver spoons on that altar! Influences like this made Harry Denman who he was.

While Harry worked at the Birmingham church, he continued to improve himself, finishing high school in his twenties and going on to earn both the B.A. and M.A. degrees. He was elected Secretary of the Department of Evangelism of The Methodist Episcopal Church, South, in 1938, at the age of forty-five. The next year when the three major bodies of American Methodism united to form The Methodist Church, he was the natural choice to become the first General Secretary of the Board of Evangelism. He remained in that post for twenty-seven years. Under his leadership, the Department of Evangelism of The Methodist Episcopal Church, South, became the General Board of Evangelism of The Methodist Church. During his tenure, *The Upper Room*, which originated in 1935 in the Board of Missions of The Methodist

Episcopal Church, South, became the most widely read devotional publication in the world—used by ten million people daily, with editions in more than forty languages.

As the Board grew, Dr. Denman supervised the construction of a stately building in Nashville that housed the General Board of Evangelism and The Upper Room. It was widely known as The Upper Room building because its beautiful chapel housed Pelligrini's carving of *The Last Supper*. Millions of persons visited the chapel over the years to see *The Last Supper*. Persons also visited the General Board of Evangelism because Dr. Denman had become a symbol of the vision that Methodism would emerge again in modern times as an evangelistic movement.

Dr. Denman was never captive to structure, but he was skilled in working with it, proposing legislation to the appropriate General Conference committee for action by the whole church. Under his leadership the working staff grew to almost 250 persons.

Even so, he often said, "Evangelism is not done from a swivel chair in this building." He believed passionately that lay Christians should visit people in their homes and invite them to become Christian disciples. Through the Board's program of Visitation Evangelism inspired by Dr. Denman, as many as 500,000 new disciples were brought into membership of The Methodist Church in a single year.

He set the example himself. In communities across the United States, he personally visited day after day, year after year; teaming up with pastors and laypersons to go into homes, inviting mothers, fathers, and children to Jesus Christ. No one can say just how many were drawn into the faith and into the circle of God's love by these visits. He did not ask the church to do what he was unwilling to do personally. Because he boldly went to people outside the church, others tried it and found they were able too.

Those who caricatured Harry Denman as one who "buttonholed people on the street" never knew him. There was a kindness, a gentleness, and a deep consideration about his personal witness that was warm and engaging.

I went with him to visit a small-town theater owner

who had no knowledge of the church or involvement in religion. The owner felt his life was worthless. Dr. Denman so communicated such a genuine interest in, and love for, the man that the man began to feel that he *mattered*. Dr. Denman's message of the love of God was stated simply and without pretense, and the man responded.

Like Jesus, he had a way with people. Those who felt they were sinners were drawn to him. He often asked persons, "Pray for this sinner," speaking of himself. "Our business is not to condemn," he said. "Our business is to commend and to love. What this world needs today is love. All of us like to be loved. Your children like to be loved. Your husband likes to be loved, and you like to be loved. Your neighbors like to be loved. People who are in sin like to be loved."

He felt it was the business of every Christian to *be* an evangelist and not simply talk about evangelism or expect the preachers to do the evangelizing. He believed change would not happen unless changed people took the initiative to be God's witnesses. "It is the business of the Christian people to make our society. Spiritual power does not come from an organization or machinery. Spiritual power comes from God, so if we desire to have a spiritual society, then we must live it ourselves."

Though a layman, Harry Denman was famous for his "preaching." He spoke in such a way that every single individual in the audience felt he was speaking directly to him or her. He wrote out his message by hand on note paper, folded it, and put it inside his breast pocket. He did not look at these notes when he spoke. He had a powerful voice that could rise and fall and through which he communicated his message with humor, pathos, urgency and conviction, and invariably, a call for response. To hear him preach was an unforgettable experience. He drew you into the text. When he spoke about Jesus' walking along the Sea of Galilee, calling those fishermen to "follow me," you felt you were there. When he told of Nicodemus's coming to Jesus by night and Jesus' talking to him, you could hear Jesus telling *you* how to be born anew. Because Jesus was alive in his life, the living

Christ came alive to his hearers as he presented the gospel.

His preaching was Bible-centered, and most of his illustrations were found there. On one page of one sermon, I found seventeen separate biblical examples of Jesus' encounters with men and women. Dr. Denman took the message of the New Testament with utter seriousness because he had let that message transform his life.

One of his favorite methods of Bible study was to copy the scripture in longhand, thus allowing the words to make a deeper impression on his soul. During his life, Dr. Denman copied the whole Bible in this way, some of its books many times. He loved the stories of Jesus' ministry and had great insight into the scripture. Once while speaking in a seminary, as he gave out his text he was interrupted by a student who said that the verse he had just quoted did not appear in the oldest manuscripts. With good humor Dr. Denman continued, "Well, I've lost my text, so I'll have to get another scripture!"

He sometimes asked members of the congregation to repeat their favorite verses aloud. They would respond with verses that had special meaning. I remember his saying on one occasion, "There is one verse I've never heard anyone give as a favorite." The people listened to learn which one. He continued, "Judge not that ye be not judged."

The message he delivered with his lips and life was a simple one: Christ is willing to live in us; he lived in the flesh in Galilee, Samaria, and Judea; he loved with a love that led to the cross; God raised him from the dead; and he is alive now.

"I believe that Christ is anxious for me to live the Christian life so that people can see him and desire to be Christians." Again, "The love of Christ can only be seen in people. The living Christ is unable to do anything unless he has someone in whom he can live and through whom he can love all persons!"

His definition of discipleship comes through in these words from one of his sermons:

When Jesus determined how He was going to carry out prophecy, He became the suffering servant Isaiah

talks about. He was going to love God with all His
heart, soul, mind, and strength. And by doing that He
would love all people with His soul, mind, strength,
and heart. You see, person.Jesus lived the life of the
cross. He gave himself redemptively and sacrificially. I
think Jesus would have died for any person he ever saw.

So every time he looked into the face of a
person, he did not see a Samaritan; he saw a person.
He did not see a woman; he saw a person. He did
not see a publican; he saw a person. He did not see a
prostitute; he saw a person. He did not see a leper;
he saw a person. He did not see a lame man; he saw
a person. He did not see a demon-possessed man; he
saw a person. And he loved that person better than
he did his own life, and he gave himself for that person. He healed on the Sabbath, and of course, the religious people did not like it. He was a guest of a sinner,
and the religious people did not like that. I think if I
could ever write a book, the title would be, *The
Guest of a Sinner.* This was said about him when he went
to the home of Levi and to the home of Zacchaeus.

The theme of love was overpowering in Harry Denman's
messages. When he was accused of being hypnotized by the
word, he answered, "When I say *love* I mean the kind of love
Jesus talked about—not the love of family, and not the love of
friends, and not the love of a cause, and not the love of
country, but this love of sacrifice. Jesus was willing to die for
any person he ever saw, and he taught us to love that way."

But this was more than sermon material or theory to
Harry Denman, and that's why his preaching had such power.
Those who knew him well saw an example they could not
easily ignore, and even those who knew him only in passing
sensed the integrity and sacrifice that marked his life. He had
no permanent residence. A room was provided for him in the
new Board of Evangelism building in Nashville, but he slept
there only a few days a year. When this space was needed for

offices, he gave up the room. Home for him was wherever he happened to be at the time. He rode trains and buses as frequently as airlines, because buses and trains gave him better opportunities to meet and visit with people. The trademarks associated with him—such as owning only one suit and one coat and giving away things that had been given to him—were outward expressions of life lived on a deeper level than most people experience. People, not possessions, mattered most to him.

He advocated—and lived—love that was concrete. When a woman who identified herself as a "fighting Christian" wrote condemning her pastor and her denomination, Dr. Denman replied, "I don't think you are a fighting Christian. I think you mean you are a loving Christian because love is the greatest force in the world, and love brings more pressure than anything I know. The greatest argument that anyone can see from Christianity is to see the love of Christ in persons. We do not have to argue with people or say things to them. All we have to do is to live the gospel." I expected him to press his point and apply it to the angry writer. Instead, he continued, "I hope you will pray that I will do this."

Harry Denman tried to tell his generation that conflict among church factions never honors Christ or advances the cause of evangelism. When the Sunday school hymn, "The Fight Is On," was suggested as the Christian's battle cry, he replied,

> The fight is on, but it is a different fight. When the people hate, the Christian loves. When the people try to get even, the Christian gives. When the people are despondent, the Christian has hope. When the people are full of fear, the Christian has faith. When there is hate against people, the Christian hates what the other people are doing. When people desire to be waited on, the Christian serves. Where people have selfishness, the Christian sacrifices. Where people are trying to get, the Christian gives. When people get angry, the Christian has peace. When people are intemperate, the Christian is temperate. That is the

kind of fight I think we ought to be engaged in. This is what our blessed Lord did.

Dr. Denman frequently said that Jesus' harshest teachings were addressed most often to religious people who were self-righteous. This is one way his presentation of the gospel was different. He emphasized neglected elements of Jesus' message. The one trying to save his or her life must lose it. To be a leader, one must be a servant of all. To save, we give away. To live, one dies.

In 1958 he addressed a National Convocation on Local Church Evangelism in the Uline Arena in Washington, D.C. It was a masterful address, and he concluded with a story about a bishop in his home area, reading the appointments.

A church was to have a new preacher appointed as pastor. The members of that church had a beautiful sanctuary; they had a lovely educational building; they had a parking lot. I think they had air conditioning. They had a beautiful kitchen, lovely recreational facilities, an outdoor barbecue place. They had everything, even a little debt! The talk of the conference was, "Who's going to be pastor of this church? Who is the bishop going to send?" A good many were willing to go, to put themselves on the altar! The name of that church was Calvary!

He reached the climax of all he wanted to say, thundering, "Who wants to go to Calvary? Who wants to go to tell about a Savior, to tell about the good news of God, to tell about eternal life, to tell about the kingdom of God? Who wants to go to Calvary tonight?"

Dr. Denman witnessed not only by preaching and by example but through the thousands of letters he wrote each year. Wherever he was, in whatever part of the world, he dictated letters or wrote notes in longhand to be transcribed and mailed from Nashville. At one time four secretaries were working under the direction of his longtime secretary, Lou Dozier, to cover his correspondence. She had at least one helper most of the time in other years.

Dr. Denman possessed tremendous energy, often rising as early as three or four in the morning, dictating as many as 100 letters a day—many of them long and detailed responses to letters he had received. He did much of the correspondence when he was preaching three to five times a day and making evangelistic visits in homes in communities across the United States. Letters he wrote went to the highest levels of government. He wrote presidents, senators, political leaders, men, women, boys, and girls.

In 1974, many years after Dr. Denman retired, I met Robert Strauss in a hotel in Taiwan. Strauss was, and is, an important political figure in the United States. He was last assigned to serve as U.S. ambassador to the U.S.S.R. When I told him of my work in Nashville, he asked about Harry Denman. He knew Dr. Denman through the letters he had received from him!

One person wrote him so frequently that before he got a reply in the mail, another would arrive. He answered every letter. She wrote him fifteen times in one two-month period! He gently suggested after receiving more than 100 letters that perhaps "it might be well to see if you can go a week without writing a letter, and in the meantime you will be able to accomplish a good many other things!"

Like a modern Francis Asbury, who carried Christian literature in saddlebags across the frontier, Dr. Denman sent books on the Christian faith and life along with his letters to the thousands of people he met.

He took a special interest in children and parents and the responsibilities the parents had toward rearing their children. He once wrote, "The home is God's great institution, and the church is to assist the home. The parents went into the holy of holies of God and reproduced the race. The parents should go into other holy of holies to help [God] redeem the race. If parents bring children into the world, then these same parents ought to teach them about Christ and live the Christlike life in front of them."

Dr. Denman was a keen political observer. Before the airlines established the concept of regional "hubs," one might board a plane in Nashville for a flight to Cleveland, Ohio, for example, and make a number of stops along the way. I was with Dr. Denman on one such flight. He brought a newspaper on board in Nashville that he read enroute to the first stop in Louisville. As soon as we landed there, he hurried from the plane and brought back a Louisville *Courier Journal*, which he read on the way to Cincinnati. In Cincinnati he got off to buy a *New York Times*, which he read on the way to Columbus. In Columbus he got yet another paper to read on the flight to Cleveland. When he spoke that night in Cleveland, his message was built around what had been the headline story in each of those papers: the selling of the U.S. gold reserves to other countries. The editors were sensationally calling it "the gold drain." He was eloquent and provocative as he addressed the audience that evening. "We're losing our God! Our gold is leaving us." It was a contemporary word on materialism in society, God's rightful place, and Jesus' call to self-denial.

Even though he was an avid reader of newspapers, he warned against believing everything you read in the paper. When someone sent him newspaper clippings with negative stories about the church he loved, he wrote, "Many years ago when I lived in Birmingham, I would go home at night, and my mother would say she read such and such a statement in the paper. I would say, 'Mother, it did not happen that way. I was there. I know exactly what happened.' I would try to explain it to her, but she always believed what she read, not what I said." Dr. Denman always sought to put the best construction on things. "We think because we see something in print that it is true, but you must remember that newspapers always give the startling news because they desire to sell the newspapers."

He wanted the fellowship of Christ to include all Christians: "One of the things about being a Christian is that we can disagree with people without being disagreeable. When we become disagreeable, we say things we ought not to say. We can apologize and say we are sorry, but we cannot take the words back because they have already been said, and those words out on the sound waves will last forever. I cannot make people believe what I believe; all I can do is to tell them what I believe, and if I want my statement to be persuasive, then I must live it. This is what Jesus did; he lived it." We need to hear this, and see if we can live it too!

Dr. Denman had a keen social consciousness. He was a pioneer in advocating the civil rights of all people. As a Southerner born in Alabama, he supported voting rights, open housing, and civil rights for black citizens long before it became the popular thing to do in other parts of the country.

"Dr. Martin Luther King," he wrote, "had more education than I have, and I think he was a better Christian than I am, but he could not preach in some churches because his face was black. I could preach in those churches because my face was white. He could preach a better sermon, he had been to school more than I have, but just because his face was black he could not preach in certain churches. This is one thing I do not understand." He also wrote, "If we despise a man because he is a Jew, and only because he is a Jew, then we despise Christ, because he was a Jew."

One person who had been baptized by immersion in a church that limited baptism to Caucasians tried to convince Dr. Denman that he needed to be immersed. He replied, "Water does not save anyone; it is faith in Jesus Christ. Water baptism is a confession that we have repented of our sins and that we are putting our trust in the Lord Jesus Christ. I am glad that you have had immersion, but I am sorry that you were baptized by a man who only baptizes white-skinned people. I started wondering the other day if Jesus ever saw a white-skinned person. He was born in the Middle East and that is where he lived all of his life, and they are brown-skinned people."

He was equally indignant about economic exploitation. Over the years he led a number of evangelistic campaigns in Cuba, with large teams of pastor-evangelists fanning out across the island to preach in local Methodist churches. He returned from one of those campaigns where he had seen workers in the sugar cane fields, observed their living conditions, and been told about the very low pay they received. As we were having dinner, he said to me, "After seeing what I've seen in Cuba, I can't look at sugar!"

Harry Denman was a world citizen. In his excellent biography,* Harold Rogers says that in one year he made 407 addresses in nineteen countries. He preached on every continent and on many of the islands. Often his international visits seemed providential.

Dr. Denman visited Estonia at a turning point in its history in 1956. No Methodist had been able to visit Estonia since 1939. Dr. Denman, accompanied by Upper Room editor J. Manning Potts, arrived in Tallinn just after the head of the church, Alexander Kuum, had been released from a five-year imprisonment in Siberia. When Dr. Denman and Dr. Potts arrived, the conference was in session in Haapsalu. This was the first conference Kuum had presided over in five years. They were taken from Tallinn to attend the sessions.

Dr. Denman's words of greeting triggered an outpouring of pent-up emotion. He said, "We were not able to visit you, but in all these years we have prayed for you, and we have never forgotten you." The people were so overcome with emotion that they began to sob audibly. They had not heard a Christian voice from outside for seventeen years! I understand Dr. Denman was overcome with emotion also.

His ties with Korea are well-known. He was a close friend of Dr. Helen Kim, president of the great Ewha Women's University in Seoul. She introduced him to Korea, inviting Dr. Denman to lead an evangelistic crusade in the university. At the close of one campaign in 1961, 1,289 persons were baptized in a single service. Dr. Kim reported on the great revival that had swept across the campus: "Literally thousands of our young men and women and girls and boys have come into contact with the person of Christ. They have been challenged to his way of life and have committed themselves to his cause. We have seen some of these wonders and miracles performed on our campus as well as on other campuses throughout Korea."

Dr. Denman and Dr. Potts were invited repeatedly to return to Korea with teams of laypersons. This work continued over several years. It was during this time that the idea of the International Prayer Fellowship was born. When it was organized, a layman from the team, Jimmy Davis, was elected to be the first international president. In this period of expansion "to the whole world," Dr. Denman also conceived and established an auxiliary support organization, the Foundation for Evangelism, "to diffuse the blessings of the gospel of Jesus Christ throughout the nation and the world."

Dr. Denman believed in prayer and practiced the life of prayer. Before speaking he would say, "Let us pray." The prayer that followed was a silent one. He believed and taught that prayer should be more our listening than our speaking to God. His prayers were personal; every day he prayed by name for every bishop of the church. I wonder if anyone does so today.

On Friday, November 22, 1963, several of the evangelism staff members were eating lunch in the Board of Evangelism cafeteria when the switchboard operator was called to the phone. She returned to the table shaken and said the President of the United States had been shot. We ran to tell Dr. Denman. He called the staff to gather in The Upper Room Chapel, and it was soon filled to capacity. He led in prayer and invited two or three of us to pray. We were interrupted by the announcement that the President was dead. Dr. Denman's prayer that day in the chapel was one of the most sensitive and moving I have ever heard.

Dr. Denman never married. When the people of Birmingham wanted to name a church for him, he would not consent to it, suggesting that they name it for his mother, Hattie Denman. When he died on November 8, 1976, he was buried in Elmwood Cemetery next to his mother and beside Sig Bower, a Jewish friend with whom he had worked in civic projects in Birmingham and whom he considered one of his closest friends. Mr. Bower had been a newspaperman and at the time of his death had no family. Dr. Denman made provision for his burial in the family plot.

The one who was perhaps closest to him and the nearest he had to family, Lou Dozier, his longtime secretary and coworker, invited me to sit with her and with the Board of Evangelism General Secretary, Rueben Job, at the funeral. When we left the cemetery, Lou asked me to accompany her to the Fair Haven Manor, where he last lived, to gather Dr. Denman's belongings. In the apartment we found two chairs, a few pairs of socks, some underwear, and a shirt. We also discovered almost 500 letters he had written but had not mailed. Some were ready to be posted; others had incomplete addresses and needed a street address or post office box number that only Lou could supply. She completed each address and mailed them all. For people receiving them, it was like the verse in the Bible: "He being dead, yet speaketh."

To those who heard, knew, and loved him, the message of his life remains clear and compelling. To all who meet him for the first time through this book, the good news of God revealed in Jesus Christ, greater than the messenger, surfaces with freshness and immediacy, as does his passion that evangelism should be reborn in the church he loved.

In life, Harry Denman chose to be an instrument of God's love and a herald of his coming kingdom. That which he affirmed abides. His work endures because with John the Baptist, he could truly say, "I must decrease but He must increase."

—*Joe Hale*

Harry Denman: A Biography by Harold Rogers, was published by The Upper Room in 1977. It was reprinted by the Foundation for Evangelism, by arrangement with The Upper Room, in 1991. Copies are available from the Foundation Office, P.O. Box 985, Lake Junaluska, NC 28745. The price is $10.00 for the hardback edition or $5.00 for paperback, postpaid. Another biography entitled *Love Abounds: A Profile of Harry Denman, A Modern Disciple*, by Asbury Smith and J. Manning Potts, also published by The Upper Room, is out of print.

INTRODUCTION

Why is Harry Denman remembered so vividly almost twenty years after his death?

In a day of enveloping secularism and religious pluralism, when the leadership of the institutional church often has come under vigorous attack, this simple yet complex native of Alabama who witnesses persistently and winsomely for Jesus Christ across decades still enjoys unquestioned respect throughout United Methodism and beyond. The celebration of his one-hundredth birthday, even when his admirers know that he probably would resist such a celebration, is eloquent evidence that the church senses a deep need to recapture the impact of his ministry. Why is this so?

Perhaps we find the best answer in the man himself and the various roles he played with such consummate skill throughout a long lifetime.

He was an *ecclesiastical statesman*. His spiritual vision was always bifocal. He was at his best when telling the story of Jesus and salvation to an individual, something he managed to do every day of his mature life. Yet he always kept in mind and heart the needs and opportunities of the whole church in its wider mission. Harry Denman's vision grew out of his conviction that it was possible, in God's time, for the whole world to turn to our Lord. He believed that his job was to do what he could to bring that about, one person at a time.

He was a master in designing strategies that had the capacity to alter priorities and programs throughout the larger Christian community. The General Conference of our denomination is one of the great legislative bodies of the Western world. To see Harry Denman operate in one of its committees, to listen to his conversations with its leaders, and to observe the subsequent approval of his recommendations became an exciting adventure in the study of those group dynamics that control public forums.

Again and again, this remarkable man swayed the mind of Methodism and caused its elected representatives to enact policies and shape programs that he was convinced, usually as the result of prayer, would produce a better church. But his involvement was always that of a statesman, never a precint politician; and it was invariably biblically based.

Whatever else he was doing, Harry Denman was constantly serving as a *personal witness* to the saving grace of the Lord Jesus Christ. He did this everywhere. He was as much at home talking gently and sympathetically to inmates in a prison as he was when he would plead with the clergy at a district preachers' meeting to be more Christ-centered and sacrificial in their ministry. He always found a graceful way to talk with a clerk in a store about his or her soul. He took advantage of every opportunity to speak to business leaders, airline pilots, bartenders, and hotel porters about their personal relationship to God. This man who had no family of his own, deeply and sincerely loved all people, and his innate respect for every person enabled him to hone his personal evangelism efforts into a fine art. He kept his theology simple and close to the Bible, and the delicate sensitivity with which he approached individuals rarely turned them off and often resulted in the commitments he sought. As he asked people to pray for him, he communicated the message, "I am praying for you."

His constant wooing of adults and children to the Lord was the source of his greatest delight and remains the practice for which he is most clearly remembered. For Harry Denman, evangelism was not one of several things the church ought to do. Evangelism was where the church began its relationship with people. It was the end of the congregation's efforts as well as its beginning. In between he trusted that if people were in Christian community, God would change them, and they would live differently.

Harry Denman was an *organizational genius*. The manner in which he built, virtually by himself, the General Board of Evangelism from one man and his secretary at work in a small, Spartan-like office to an organization of 250 individuals occupying a vast headquarters building costing millions of dollars is one of the amazing sagas in the story of contemporary Christianity. His administrative methods, often unorthodox, succeeded in developing an almost fierce loyalty among both professional and support staff.

He integrated his leadership of one general board into the whole pattern of denominational and ecumenical mission, yet always contrived to stay close to the local church whether in some large metropolitan center or in a remote rural area. He was a program man, a team player, an inveterate letter writer, and both an efficiency expert and a budget craftsman. His theory of structure was always pragmatic. He demanded hard work from his associates but always worked harder himself. He had an organization to run, which he could have stayed home to do. He chose to be out where the people were—helping them develop a working knowledge of what God did in Christ.

Harry Denman was a *lovable person*. His innumerable eccentricities were delightful and almost delicious. He deplored materialism and both preached and taught against it constantly. The almost unbelievable limitations that he imposed upon his wardrobe and other earthly possessions have become part of both his legacy and his legend. Yet he was a memorable conversationalist, an exquisite guest and always, even to those who were never with him very much, a treasured friend. Kindness was his hallmark. Little children loved him, and he knew them by name. He prayed for every bishop of the church and many other leaders daily. His remarkably well-furnished mind, always kept up-to-date on current themes and events, attracted leaders in the academic and political worlds. One of the extraordinary friendships that emerged during his latter years was with Dr. Helen Kim, the Korean educator and president of Ewha Women's University in Seoul, who shared his passion for evangelism. During the lengthy time he spent at Lambuth Inn, Lake Junaluska, North Carolina, following his official retirement, many who encountered him were amazed to experience at once his broad general concerns about the Christian community and the sharp focus of his interest in little, often obscure, details related to the life of a friend. This man, virtually without living relatives, was taken into the homes and hearts of thousands who found his disarming appeal irresistible.

Harry Denman, as the title of this book suggests, was a *prophetic evangelist*. Some leaders of our church have said that he was the most radical person they ever knew in his social understanding of the Christian gospel. His position on race was uncompromising, even when his was a voice crying in the wilderness and in a part of the country traditionally and historically conservative on this issue. In 1964 a strong opponent to the abolition of the Central Jurisdiction was heard to say, "Ours is a lost cause, and one of the biggest reasons is Harry Denman!"

He supported Dr. Martin Luther King, Jr., and often wrote to him. His strong advocacy of racial justice dated from earlier days when he was a member of the board of education in an Alabama county. His membership was in a black church in Nashville, and he saw to it that Holy Communion in The Upper Room Chapel was served by representatives of all races, with all races welcomed to the Communion table. From the beginning, all facilities in the building he erected were open to all races, although a "no smoking" sign was posted prominently. His concept of racial justice embraced all peoples, including the Jews. One of his lifelong friends was Jewish and, by invitation of Harry, is buried in the Denman cemetery lot in Birmingham.

Substantial evidence indicates that Harry Denman believed in the equal distribution of property among all persons, a principle that appeared in the early church. He practiced a philosophy of possessions akin to this ideal without compromise in his own life, and its articulation emerges at least occasionally in his writings and public utterances.

The most astounding thing about Harry Denman's social interpretation of the gospel is that it occurred during a period when the conscience of the church was often recalcitrant on such issues, and yet his churchwide influence never seemed to diminish because of his outspoken, unapologetic proclamation of social holiness. Indeed, he was a prophet before his time.

Growing up in a simple neighborhood in Birmingham, Alabama, Harry became a giant in simplicity. In his community, he learned as a child to believe what you were taught, to test it for yourself, and then to decide if you would believe and act on it the rest of your life. Harry was taught and he believed that God loves us in Christ. He acted that belief out in his life.

While Harry Denman appeared to be a simple person, his biographer suggests that his was a "complex simplicity." He literally traveled millions of miles across the earth, was at ease in any of the world's cultures, and often socialized with distinguished leaders. He was adored by plain people and respected by the mighty. He organized world conclaves of evangelism and rode Greyhound buses to speak in tiny black churches. He built serviceable and enduring structures in his own denomination and helped Billy Graham design the remarkable organization that he has used with effectiveness across the years. He made bold proposals to politicians and statesmen, worked constantly to help bright young people from all over the globe secure education in American institutions, and demanded that the church acquire a world mind as it charted its course for future years.

Perhaps the reason Harry Denman is remembered with such affection and gratitude is because, far more than most of us, he was able to develop and exhibit in his own life and career those qualities that characterize the whole gospel of Jesus Christ.

For his own era, and perhaps for ours as well, Harry Denman was the *quintessential* Christian.

Ezra Earl Jones,	*Earl G. Hunt, Jr.*
General Secretary	President
The General Board of	The Foundation for
Discipleship	Evangelism

Part One

MEMORIES

INTRODUCTION

When someone mentions the name Harry Denman, the response is, "Oh, yes, I remember Harry." The person then proceeds to tell of his or her own experience with Harry Denman or stories he or she has heard about him. Part of this book is an attempt to gather these stories into a lasting testimony for future generations so they will have a deeper insight into the real Harry Denman.

Since I worked with Dr. Denman as his personal secretary for thirty-two years, I was assigned the task of gathering stories, testimonies, anecdotes, and remembrances from people who knew him. I sent a "Letter to the Editor" of all United Methodist general publications. I wrote personal letters to the staff who worked under his leadership and to friends who are still living.

The response to my request has been wonderful. I have received about ninety letters, tapes, or phone calls. They came from thirty-two states and Poland. Many told the same stories, so we have arranged these stories in several categories, printing only one version of each story.

At least ten letters mention his one suit, one pair of shoes, and only a briefcase in all his travels. His trademark phrase, "Pray for me," brought about ten stories also. Almost every letter mentioned something about his prayer habits and the unique ways he had of witnessing to everyone he met.

Five or six letters shared his interest in children and

youth, especially high school and college students. Testimonies of personal help, both spiritual and monetary, came from four students.

Almost every person mentioned how he or she was helped by his witness—either through prayer, visitation, or his actions. Two families told of his special concern for them in times of special need.

At least six letters recounted experiences with Dr. Denman on evangelistic missions to other countries. Many remembered his aversion to publicity and personal recognition of any kind.

Several remembered his sense of humor, and then the staff provided stories of all kinds.

*   *   *

Harry Denman was born in Birmingham, Alabama, September 26, 1893. His parents, William Henry and Hattie Leonard Denman, were born in Gloucestershire, England. They immigrated to Birmingham, where they met and married. William Denman worked as a molder in one of the foundries. According to those who remember, his father "just up and left" when Harry was nine years old.

Some years later Harry Denman learned that his father had gone to Pittsburgh, Pennsylvania, where he followed his trade as a foundry worker. Naturalization papers recorded there give April 22, 1911, as the date when William Henry Denman, aged fifty-seven, became a United States citizen. Dr. Denman never mentioned this to me, but some believe the father probably had some contact with his wife and son in Birmingham. But apparently he never returned. Additional records indicate that his father died September 11, 1927, and was buried in Pittsburgh. His mother died in 1937 in Birmingham at the age of seventy-two and was buried in Elmwood Cemetery, where Harry Denman is also buried.

Harry Denman made numerous attempts to locate any relatives he might have in England. He recalled having been to England with his mother when he was six years old and remembered a little about the house where his grandparents lived. In his search he was able to locate the house and the graves of his grandparents but was not able to locate any living relatives.

When his father left home, Harry Denman dropped out of school and went to work as an errand boy for the Tennessee Coal and Iron Company. He later worked in other capacities for this company. In 1915 he resigned to become the secretary of the Birmingham Sunday School Council for thirty dollars a month. With this salary he supported himself and his mother and, with some small assistance from other sources, paid his way through preparatory school and two years of college. In 1919 he became business manager for the First Methodist Episcopal Church, South, in Birmingham. He continued to study at Birmingham Southern College, receiving a B.A. degree in 1921 and an M.A. degree in 1930. In later years he was awarded two honorary doctorates, one from Athens College, Athens, Alabama, and the other from Ewha Women's University, Seoul, Korea.

Harry Denman held the position of business manager at First Methodist Church until he was elected secretary for the Department of Evangelism of the Board of Missions of The Methodist Episcopal Church, South, and came to Nashville, Tennessee, June 1, 1938.

He retired as general secretary of the Board of Evangelism, March 31, 1965, but kept preaching and writing letters until shortly before his body died, November 8, 1976.

—Lou Dozier

I REMEMBER HARRY

As plans for the centennial celebration of Harry Denman's birth begin to develop, my thoughts turn to my days of working as his secretary.

I remember the first time I saw Dr. Harry Denman (I never called him Harry as long as he lived). He came to Nashville in 1938 to work with Dr. Grover C. Emmons in the Department of Evangelism of the Board of Missions of The Methodist Episcopal Church, South, located in the Doctors' Building on Church Street in downtown Nashville.

I was working as a bookkeeper for *The Upper Room*, which was also part of the Board of Missions, Methodist Episcopal Church, South. *The Upper Room* offices were in one big room, shared with the Women's Division of the Board of Missions on the street level. The executive offices were on the sixth floor. We did not see much of the executives except for Dr. Emmons, our editor. Word of a new person's coming on the staff spread quickly, and we all eagerly awaited the arrival of this man. We worked five and one-half days a week at that time. One Saturday morning I got on an elevator to go to Dr. Emmons's office on the sixth floor when this strange man also walked on. The elevator operator, Robert, knew everybody by name who worked in the building. When the stranger got on the elevator, Robert said, "Good morning, Mr. Denman." Of course, my ears perked up, and I looked him over—"the new man."

Somewhere between the first and sixth floors, the elevator stopped and another passenger got on to whom Dr. Denman said, "Good morning."

The person responded, "What's good about it?"

Dr. Denman said, "Well, it's Saturday, and you can take a bath tonight."

Time passed as it does when we were busy. I did not know much about what was going on except in my own job, which kept me more than busy, for we kept books with pen and ink. The circulation of *The Upper Room* was growing rapidly during this period.

Changes began to take place in our cozy little world. The 1938 General Conference voted to merge with The Methodist Episcopal Church and The Methodist Protestant Church. The merger was in 1939 at a special Uniting Conference.

I just kept posting ledger sheets and doing what I was told, not knowing any of the inner workings. One day the news came that the Board of Missions would be moved to New York to merge with the Methodist Episcopal Board, and The Upper Room would become a part of a new Commission on Evangelism in the newly formed Methodist Church. Grover C. Emmons would remain editor of *The Upper Room* and become co-general secretary of the new Commission with Harry Denman.

We moved to several different locations and kept sending out more and more *Upper Rooms*. In April, 1944, we were all shocked by the unexpected death of Grover Emmons. Many more changes took place, including a new editor and a new business manager. Roy H. Short was the editor, and Harry Williams was business manager.

In mid-September of 1944, Harry Williams called me to his office and surprised me beyond words when he offered me the position of secretary to Harry Denman. My goal was to be an accountant, not a secretary. I told Dr. Williams I was not interested in making a change. He would not accept my answer and told me to think and pray about it for a few days and that we would talk some more.

Little did I know what a big change it would be in my life when I finally agreed to assume the job of secretary to Harry Denman! I moved into the new office on October 1 and worked with the former secretary for five days before she left.

I remember the first time Dr. Denman came in after I became his secretary. I had not had much time to learn about the office, and I was scared to death at the thought of his coming in. I had talked to him several times on the phone, but he had not been in the office. He arrived at the appointed time, said "Good morning," and went into the cramped quarters he called an office. After what seemed an eternity to me, he called me to come into his office. I remember the words as if it were only yesterday, "Miss Dozier, I am happy to have you in my office. You can do anything you want to except talk. Take a letter." We used shorthand for dictation in those days, so he dictated several letters, and I went out to my typewriter to see if I could read my shaky shorthand notes.

I remember another surprise that same day. When Dr. Denman came in from lunch, he had two cards from the bank where he had a checking account. He asked me to sign them, which authorized me to sign checks and handle all of his financial affairs. From that day on he never signed a check, paid a bill, or knew how much money he had. It was such an unheard of thing to do. Any *man* who would completely turn all his financial business over to a *woman*, much less a secretary he had known only a few days, must be out of his mind! But Harry Denman did! It was my privilege to be able to take care of all his business as long as he lived and to close out his estate after his death. Closing the estate was no big task, for he gave all his material possessions away throughout his life.

I remember that Dr. Denman told me to open all of his mail, even if it was marked *Personal*. This was hard for me to do at first, and several times I would send him an unopened envelope marked *Personal*. He sent it back for me to open, saying he wanted me to read *all* his incoming and outgoing mail and to sign his name to the letters he dictated. This practice was a source of irritation to some of his lady friends who wanted a handwritten reply to their letters!

I remember that Harry Denman never carried a calendar of his future schedule with him. When he was approached in the field about an engagement, he would tell them to write to his secretary at the office. This too was a source of irritation for many, because they wanted an answer right then.

Early one morning, while I was still asleep, my phone rang. I sleepily answered to hear the most pathetic voice say, "Lou, where am I going?" He was in the airport at Dallas, Texas, on his way to one of the nearby towns. Someone was supposed to meet his plane and take him to the right town. Because of a schedule change in the flight to Dallas, he missed his party and had no idea where to go. He had spent the night in the airport. Needless to say, he never left for another engagement without a card with all the details clearly written out!

I remember Harry Denman's great concern for the wives and children of the staff, especially those who traveled extensively. Each year at the Valentine season he would have a luncheon and invite only the wives. He would always have a small corsage or gift for them. On these occasions he would tell the women how much he appreciated what they were doing and the sacrifices they were making at home to make it possible for the men to do their jobs better. I say *men* because there were no women on his administrative staff. In later years three women were at the assistant secretary level.

I remember his remarkable administrative ability. By that, I mean the confidence and trust he placed in his staff. He believed in working as a team, with each person assigned a specific role. In staff meetings he always listened as each person contributed. Once a course was decided, everyone was expected to follow through individually.

Harry Denman did not look over his shoulders or check to see what was being done. His staff members knew they were responsible for their own assignments. Because of his trust, all of us were eager to do our best—not that we were perfect. At one time or other, we all made mistakes, but Harry Denman was ready to assume the blame and help correct the errors.

I remember that he never had a desk in his office, just a chair, a table with a center drawer, a telephone, and a dictating machine. A picture of his mother hung on the wall along with a few other pictures of bishops or children of his closest friends. His table was never cluttered with trinkets.

I remember he gave no apparent thought for himself. Over my protest, he would accept engagements that he knew would require travel and preparation with no time for sleep or rest. Sometimes he would go for thirty-six hours without going to bed, catching a nap in an airport or on a plane or on a bus instead. When in the office, he would often sleep two or three hours and spend the other twenty-one or -two answering mail or doing his desk work. He believed that evangelism could not be done in an office but had to be taken to where the people were. He devoted his whole being to this task as long as he was physically able until only a month before his death.

I remember Harry Denman never sought publicity. He played down the man Harry Denman and exalted Jesus Christ. He would never allow anyone to send out his picture or biographical material for publicity purposes. Occasionally someone somewhere would maneuver to get a picture, perhaps as he arrived on a plane or was leaving a meeting, and run a news story. But such publicity was never developed with his consent. He preached to large crowds in churches, auditoriums, stadiums, and camp meetings, but he would pour out his heart and soul with equal fervor to the few gathered in a remote village or at a storefront church.

I remember the time the wives of the staff planned a party for everybody in the building to celebrate Harry Denman's birthday. They had decorated the dining area and made delicious goodies for the occasion. The appointed time came, and the crowd gathered—but no Harry Denman. I was pleading with him in his office to go to the party. Finally, after much persuasion from me and other members of staff, he made an appearance. He just did not want any special attention.

I remember when the time came for him to retire as general secretary of the Board, March 31, 1965. He was so concerned that there would be some big affair in his honor that he left for India on December 31, 1964, and was gone four months. Wilson Weldon has shared a letter he received from Harry Denman, which tells exactly how he felt about it. (See p. 62.)

I remember that he almost always closed his letters with the words, *Sincerely your friend, Harry Denman*. One time the staff had had a particularly trying day of meetings. To close they joined in prayer. At the conclusion of his prayer, instead of the traditional amen, he said, "Sincerely your friend, Harry Denman."

I remember when we moved the Board offices into some old residences during the time the new building at 1908 Grand Avenue was under construction. We were crowded into small rooms, and more than one staff person shared an office. One man was very unhappy with this arrangement and insisted that he have a private room. The space simply was not there. So Harry Denman devised a plan that the women's restroom on the second floor could be converted into an office for this person, and the men and women would share the restroom on the first floor. Needless to say, a great uproar ensued and no further mention was made about a private office.

I was always aware of the compassion Harry Denman had for the individual—the rich, the poor, the sick, the well, the child, the aged, the government official, the garbage collector. He saw each person as a child of God; he took every opportunity to assure each of God's love. Taxi drivers in Nashville often referred to him as "the man who talked to me about Christ." They might not have known his name, but they knew he loved Christ and he loved them. This response also came from waitresses, elevator operators, bellhops, skycaps, cashiers, hotel clerks, pilots, stewardesses, and the typists and janitors in his office.

I remember that letters came daily from young people

who poured out their joys and troubles and sought his advice and prayers. In the day of the generation gap, when youth were rebelling against the establishment, he continued to get mail from young people all over the world. They asked him to speak at their assemblies, camps, retreats, and church meetings. He answered every piece of mail and accepted as many invitations as time would allow. Mail kept coming for ten years after his so-called retirement. In going through his mail after his death, I found other young peoples' letters that he had not answered. They had arrived after he became too ill to write.

I remember his great love and concern for children. He always paid special attention to children, often inviting them to come to the front of the church. He would ask them questions such as, "Who said grace at your breakfast table this morning?" Sometimes there were embarrassed parents in the background! He would ask them for their names and addresses. He would write them letters and send them books, according to their age. I remember how the secretaries that assisted me dreaded the deluge of letters to be written following each engagement, especially when he was preaching in a local church.

I remember Harry Denman had a world mind, and he was a world traveler. The miles he traveled can be stated only in terms of millions. He was as much at ease with the people of Asia, Africa, or India as in his own office. He ate their food, stayed in their homes, preached in their churches, witnessed to them in their fields and shops, and loved them as his own. Many of them he called his "spiritual children." It was his dream to take a group of ministers from the United States to conduct evangelistic missions in other countries. He was able to make this dream come true; and over a period of years led, along with Dr. J. Manning Potts and other staff members, missions to many countries.

I remember the evangelistic revivals at Ewha Women's University in Seoul, Korea, and the deep spiritual relationship he had with Dr. Helen Kim, president of Ewha University from 1931 to 1961. At the invitation of Dr. Denman and Dr. Potts, Dr. Helen came to Nashville during one of her visits to the United States. We had three parties for her in one day—a luncheon, an afternoon reception, and a dinner in the evening. Then the men left town and Mrs. Potts, Dr. Potts's secretary, Clarice Winstead, and I had the privilege of entertaining her for another day. She was delightful and fun to be with in an informal setting. She wrote Harry after returning home that she enjoyed her visit to Nashville, but it was the first time she had ever been entertained by proxy!

(Find the detailed story of the Denman-Kim relationship printed in *Harry Denman: A Biography* by Harold Rogers, 1977.)

I remember Harry Denman was an excellent dictator most of the time, but there were times when he would be in a hurry or very tired. Then he would not always be clear in what he said. In such instances, he told me and the other secretaries to "say what I meant to say and not what I said." I usually knew what he was trying to say, but it was not always easy for some of the less-experienced secretaries.

I remember how Harry Denman copied the Bible by handwriting several verses—sometimes several chapters—every morning. He copied the entire Bible at least once. He said this discipline led him to new insights into the scriptures.

I remember that in the late fifties, for a period of about two years, Dr. Denman would have a luncheon each month for all persons in the building who had celebrated a birthday that month. He paid for these from his personal funds. This was a time when he could talk personally with each one and find out about the families, children, and grandchildren. One statement that he frequently used with the staff and others he met was, "You are very rich." He used this when referring to children and grandchildren. Perhaps there was a bit of nostalgia that he never had a family, other than his mother. The participants always appreciated these celebrations.

I remember Harry Denman's prayer life. He did not just talk about prayer; he prayed. He customarily rose early every morning and spent several hours reading and studying the Bible and praying. Every day he prayed by name for each member of his staff, for the bishops of The United Methodist Church, and for many who requested special prayers from time to time. Seldom did persons come into his office that he did not share prayer with them before they left. His farewell was not good-bye but a sincere "pray for me." I can still see the amazement on some of those faces.

He planned his life and work through prayer. When we were the busiest in our office, he would often ask that we stop and have a prayer for the plans, the work, the tight schedule, or some special situation. He believed in listening to God as well as beseeching God. He never ceased this habit. In his final illness, he prayed with the visitors who came to the hospital to see him. As I left his hospital room the last night of his life, I heard him pray that I would have a safe trip home.

These and many other memories of Harry Denman enrich my life and continue to inspire me to keep the principles by which he lived alive. That I will share the heritage that is mine is now my earnest prayer.

—*Lou Dozier*

Prayer

This story came from a woman who was a member of a little church somewhere in Kentucky. Harry was going to preach in their little town church on a Sunday afternoon. It was pouring rain, but the church was filled. They had come to hear Harry, but no Harry had appeared. They sang and sang. At long last Harry appeared at the door of the church with a bag of popcorn, which had been his lunch. His shoes were covered with mud because he had been out visiting from house to house, up and down the streets. He walked down that beautiful carpet, leaving mud with every step. Then he went to the altar and knelt, showing those big, muddy shoes to the congregation. He made his prayer to the Lord before he went to the pulpit to preach. She said he had already preached the sermon by what he did.

—Berlyn V. Farris

While working at the Board of Evangelism, I became engaged to a soldier who was stationed in the Air Force at the Galápagos Islands. He was injured seriously in a bomb truck accident. He was so near death that his grave was blasted in the sand along with the grave of another soldier, who was killed. Everyone tried to comfort me with their prayers. Dr. Denman prayed that God would give the doctors and nurses unusual

47

skills as they cared for Tommy. These prayers must have been answered as Tommy did fully recover and was able to come home within the year.

During those days of slow recovery, I always tried to remember that Dr. Denman said, "God always answers all our prayers with a yes, no, or wait awhile." Soon after Tommy returned, we married and moved to New England.

In the years that followed, Dr. Denman continued his interest in my family. We exchanged many letters and had a few brief visits with him. My husband has died, my boys are married, and I have four wonderful grandchildren. They all know who Harry Denman was. We all give thanks for his life and cherish his memory.

—*Katy Thomas*

I remember warmly when a group of us were eating with Harry in a restaurant. Our waitress was a vivacious little girl.

Harry spoke to her and asked, as he often did, "Will you pray for me?"

She looked at him and responded, "Sure, brother, what's your problem?"

I remember the times when Harry called me on the phone and asked me to take his place in a weekend conference or in a week-long revival meeting. I was scared to death, but thankfully God carried me through each experience victoriously. I knew Harry was praying for me, and that gave me courage.

—*Eugene E. Golay*

I dearly cherish memories of Dr. Harry Denman in our own church, at area campgrounds, at Lake Junaluska, as well as our letters through the years. Could even our wonderful Lord keep account of all the friends Dr. Denman prayed for, encouraged, and asked to pray for him? I daresay the prayers we prayed for him, to the four corners of the world, did us more good than they did him.

—*Betty Brown Carter*

We remember Harry Denman as our "modern-day apostle Paul." He preached in our Flat Rock, Michigan, church in the early 1970s. On the first Sunday of a week of evangelistic services, he invited about a dozen youngsters in the 8:30 A.M. service to come forward. He met them in the middle aisle at the first pew and asked them to make a circle. He put his hands on each of their shoulders and asked, "Who said grace at your house before breakfast this morning?" They didn't know what to say. There was dead silence for about a minute. No one stirred in the congregation. Then he asked slowly, "Did *you* do it?"

A brother and sister said, "We didn't have breakfast!"

Another said, "We ate separately." One by one each answered . . . no one had grace before breakfast. Dr. Denman's closing words were a prayer for the youngsters and their homes.

—*Ron Carter*

I remember when I had the privilege of becoming personally acquainted with Harry Denman. It was in 1963 when he came to Asbury United Methodist Church of Prairie Village, Kansas, to conduct a week-long "Spiritual Life Clinic."

As chairman of the Membership and Evangelism Committee, it was appropriate for me to meet him at the Kansas City airport. As Harry proceeded into the terminal, I recognized him from his photograph. I introduced myself while noticing that he carried a bowling ball bag. I asked if he had other luggage to pick up. He said, "No, I have all my worldly possessions in this bag."

We talked while driving to Prairie Village, and he alluded to my comment about the bowling bag. He said, "You know, the first prayer I pray ever morning is, 'Lord, don't let me become a Pharisee.' "

—*John R. Watts*

Harry addressed the opening of an Ashram I attended in New Hampshire. He began by saying, "Let us pray," which was followed by several minutes of silence. Afterward he explained that he seldom prayed out loud anymore because he was afraid he would unconsciously speak to the audience instead of God. It left a lasting impression on me.

—*Conway Keibler*

Dr. Harry Denman always had time for the boys and girls who worked at Lambuth Inn. We looked forward to his stay at the hotel. He always set aside time during his stay to have devotions with us. He seemed genuinely interested in each one of us; he radiated such a Christian spirit. He often would take me aside and ask me about my future plans. From time to time he would slip me a little money to help with my college expenses.

—*Kitty Mann*

My father suffered a stroke on July 5, 1937. When the church was notified of his condition, Dr. Denman immediately came to our house. He went in to see my father, came back out on the porch where I was sitting, and asked me, "Frank, do you know how to pray? Your father is a very sick man."

I was not quite seventeen at the time, and I told him, "I say my prayers every night."

He said—and I will never forget this, "I don't mean that. Do you *really* know how to pray?"

His words have remained with me for more than fifty years, and I do not know any individual who was more able to demonstrate to everyone he met the importance of prayer. I can't remember a single occasion when I was with him that he did not end our conversation with these sincere but profound words: "Pray for me." All who knew him were blessed [for having known him over the years].

—*Frank Dominick*

I journeyed to Leesburg, Florida, for a Methodist Men's Retreat in the late fifties. It was hot weather and old buildings. Fans were everywhere but ineffective. Harry Denman led the group of 500 men who were crowded into the old hall adjoining the dining room. It was a most moving experience, with 500 men on their knees. Following the service someone said to him, "That was a most wonderful sermon; it meant so much to me." Harry Denman's answer was simple and memorable to me. He simply said, "Pray for me."

—*Willard E. Bronson, Jr.*

Dr. Denman would pray at the drop of a hat. We picked him up at the airport, and he offered a prayer for us. We went to a nearby restaurant to eat. When the waitress came to serve us, he offered a prayer on her behalf. When we left the restaurant he insisted on taking a cab back to the airport. When the cab arrived, he offered another prayer for the cab driver and for my wife and me for our evangelistic efforts. He impressed me with his gentle manner and spirit.

—*James Fraggos*

Harry Denman practiced what he preached, which made the gospel he wanted known carry a lot of weight. One of my most treasured memories is a private time of prayer with him, kneeling at the altar in the International Prayer Room at Lake Junaluska, North Carolina.

—Mary Jo Harrison

The Salina District Conference was held in the Sams Chapel on Kansas Wesleyan University Campus at Salina. Dr. Denman was the featured speaker. Those of us from Luray, including our youth, sat as close to the front as possible. When it was time for Dr. Denman to speak, he announced, as we had come to hear him do so many times before: "Let us listen to the Lord." Everyone bowed in prayer, and our young daughter told us later that she had "peeked." She said Dr. Denman had taken tooth powder from his pocket, taken out his teeth, powdered them, put them back in, and proceeded as usual! We certainly appreciated Dr. Denman's ministry: his humor and wit but also his message and his philosophy—Why do I need two suits when some people don't have any?

—Mr. & Mrs. Richard Krenz

Harry was a man of prayer. Ed Lewis, pastor in the Baltimore Conference, told me about accompanying Dr. Denman to the Holy Land. Early in the morning, Ed followed Dr. Denman to the shore of the Sea of Galilee. Dr. Denman bent down, scooped up water in his hand, and let it fall back into the lake. Ed heard Dr. Denman pray, "Our Father, Who art in heaven, hallowed be Thy Name. Thy kingdom come, thy will be done...through me, Lord, through me."

—Charles D. Whittle

I recall Dr. Denman's sharing that he arose about 12:30 A.M. each morning, studied the scriptures by copying them, and prayed during the night. Mr. D. E. Jackson, business manager for the General Board of Evangelism, told about rooming with Dr. Denman. He awoke during the night, and Dr. Denman was reading the Bible by flashlight so as to not disturb Mr. Jackson. Dr. Denman said he prayed for every bishop by name from memory. He said, "I lump the district superintendents together, because there are so many of them."

—*Charles D. Whittle*

Touring the Holy Land—through Palestine, over into Jordan, atop Mt. Nebo, and into Syria and Damascus—we made our trips by limousine to selected places we wanted to see, along with what the driver-guides showed us. As we stopped at places where the Bible told of some interesting event, we would walk about, repeat the story, and then have prayer. In Damascus we visited a small church-chapel built on what had been the home of Ananias, the Christian in that city whom the Lord asked to go visit Paul just after Paul's experience on the Damascus Road. Ananias has always been a hero of mine because his visit with Paul completed his "conversion experience." Anyway, how thrilled I was as we stood in this little chapel for Dr. Denman to call out, "Ross, lead us in prayer."

—*Ross A. Fulton, Sr.*

LEADERSHIP

Dr. Denman usually liked to have full staff meetings the week preceding Christmas. At this time churches were involved with special programs and activities, and most of the "field staff" were in Nashville. At one of these pre-Christmas meetings, some of the staff members were complaining that they would like to have more time at home with their families since they were away so much of the time during the year. Dr. Denman listened to the complaint and accepted the validity of what his "family" members were saying. That year and thereafter, staff meetings continued to be held in December, but they concluded a day or two prior to Christmas Day.

—*Russell Q. Chilcote*

Not everyone related to Harry's blunt and direct style of personal evangelism. His critics could be blunt, even ruthless. Once he came back to Nashville after having been on a preaching mission to a Kansas City suburban church. We were in a staff meeting, and the staff could tell that he was upset about something. Then he told us that while he was teaching personal evangelism in this church, the associate pastor interrupted to blurt out: "You are a hypocrite!"

Then Harry said to me, "Howard, I want you to go to this church for me and see what went wrong." So he wrote the pastor and made an engagement for me to preach and meet with his evangelism group, including the associate. I found out that the young man just wasn't on Harry's wavelength. Harry was using the conventional approach to evangelism that he understood and practiced. It included paying attention to the children and trying to create an environment favorable to his sharing with others the Christ that he knew. The associate pastor thought that was manipulative. I told him that Harry would agree with Dwight L. Moody, who told one of his critics: "I like the way I am doing evangelism better than the way you are not doing it!"

—*Howard W. Ellis*

I was director of the Central Department of Evangelism of the National Council of Churches. My Board consisted mostly of the Directors of Evangelism, of which Harry was one, of the member denominations. That was my first relationship with him. Every now and then he would suggest to me that I might be better off working for The Methodist Church. Periodically, when he was in New York, he would mention my coming on the staff in Nashville. He made that offer one time when a combination of circumstances made me seriously consider his offer, and that is how I came to Nashville.

People all over the country knew him as a rather homespun type of speaker and loved him for that, but I doubt if many people really knew that he was one of the best administrators in the church. He turned his staff members loose to do their work, but he was aware of everything that was happening. I had always known when I was in the National Council that I could get a response to a letter more quickly from him than from any other evangelism director. Then when I came on the staff, I learned that he returned every telephone call and answered every letter that had come that day.

—*Berlyn V. Farris*

Yes, Harry Denman was a dynamo, a dynamo for Jesus
Christ. Never before or since have I met such a magnetic
personality. He drew people unto him for our God, the Christ.
From that special week when Mr. Denman led our Christmas
revival, until his death, we corresponded often. His answers
were always prompt, interesting, and straight to the point
when a question was asked or a subject was discussed. I
treasure these letters and get them out now and then to
reread. This man was truly an apostle of Christ.

—Polly Garris

When I was a student at Asbury Seminary, Dr. Harry Denman
came to speak to the students. He made quite an impression
on many of the students because he stood in line with the
students to get food in the cafeteria instead of exercising the
privilege that faculty and guests had of getting at the head of
the line and not waiting their turn. He visited with the
students as he waited in line and then sat at a table with
students instead of the faculty table.

—Carl Halverson

One of the staff had been traveling with Harry, and they
shared a hotel room. He said Harry "slept like a cat." He was
up every hour or so doing something. This staff member
awakened one time to see Harry sitting by the window to get
a glimmer of streetlight, with his pad and pencil out, writing
a letter.

—Berlyn V. Farris

I enjoyed transcribing Harry Denman's letters from the old-
fashioned dictaphone cylinders. Every letter was always

answered promptly. He loved everyone regardless of color or race. In his eyes we were all God's children.

—*Katy Thomas*

I remember that Dr. Denman committed much of his thinking to what became typescripts, and I was one of the editors to whom some of them were directed for editing. One day his secretary brought me yet another typescript when I had several others of his on my desk. I felt swamped. I already had enough regular editorial work on my desk to outlast the work hours of any given day. So with the latest Denman typescripts in hand, I went to the office of Dr. J. Manning Potts and asked what I should do. "Russ," he said, "Dr. Denman is in charge. What he asked you to do will have to be worked in along with your regular work." With patience and to the best of my ability, I edited Dr. Denman's type-scripts. I did so with the satisfaction and confidence of know-ing that he appreciated the help I gave him—that good man with a warm heart and grateful spirit.

—*Russell Q. Chilcote*

I remember Dr. Denman was a person of strong conviction about many things, not the least of which was how something should be done or how he wanted it done. Harry Williams was also such a person, and many times long conversations ensued as each one tried to get his point across. Neither gave in easily. I always felt that both men admired this trait in each other, although often it seemed that neither cared for the other. When an evangelistic mission was being planned for the city of Philadelphia, Harry Williams was there, and Dr. Denman was in Nashville. Telephone conversations often stretched into hours rather than minutes as each tried to convince the other that his idea was best. Convictions were a strong part of each of their lives, and compromises did not come cheap.

—*Madelyn Lazenby*

I remember when Harry invited me to go with him to a big, downtown, city-wide, week-long mission in Toronto. It was an ecumenical effort with sixteen or more churches involved. Since I was in Chicago on Sunday, I could easily make it to Toronto for the Monday night session. When I got to Toronto, I checked into the Twin Tower Hotel and was assigned to a luxurious room in the newer section of the twin towers. It was wonderful. The staff seldom got to stay in such fine quarters. I gave Harry a call.

"Howard, where are you?" I told him. He replied, "Please get over here to this old tower right away."

I moved, but I didn't know why. I had almost a roomful of art equipment. I began wondering why he asked me to come. He did not schedule me for any action in the evening services. I soon learned. His schedule called for him to be in Philadelphia for a meeting on Thursday, and he was planning to fly there and back in time to preach on Friday. He didn't tell any of the preachers in charge, but I began to realize why he wanted me. I was to substitute for Harry on Thursday and probably Friday, the closing night. Our hosts were expecting him back; but knowing plane schedules, I was sure there was no way to fly to Philadelphia, attend a meeting all day, and get back to preach the closing two nights.

It was up to me to tell our hosts what only I knew: that Harry would not get back and that he intended for me to substitute. I had tried it a few times, but no one could substitute for Harry Denman, especially when you were not expected! It didn't happen; it wasn't my congregation. It was Harry's, and I couldn't get them back.

But the closing night was different. It was made clear that Harry would not be back, that I was the man of the hour, and that they were to celebrate the gospel in art with me.

I understood midweek why he insisted we occupy one hotel room instead of two. But I never understood why he didn't tell me and others what was going on. I remember Harry and some of his strange ways.

—*Howard W. Ellis*

I remember a personal favor. My wife, two young sons, and I moved from Pittsburgh, Pennsylvania, to Nashville, Tennessee in August 1946. In doing so I resigned a secondary school teaching position and gave up graduate studies at the University of Pittsburgh. I had completed all but six credit hours toward a master's degree.

About two years passed, and the thought of completing the halted studies surfaced anew. I corresponded with the University of Pittsburgh. They informed me that the remaining six credits could be earned at Vanderbilt University, where I soon was accepted as a graduate student. What splendid news! I was elated at the prospect made possible by the cooperation of these two universities.

Now I needed another kind of cooperation: authorization to attend school. I approached my department head. He offered me no encouragement to attend school while having a full-time job in his department. This I could understand.

I decided to approach Dr. Denman about the opportunity that lay before me. He responded favorably with words of encouragement. I used my vacation time to attend classes, completing studies in 1949. The University of Pittsburgh conferred the Master of Letters degree on me at the June 14, 1950, commencement.

I doubt that I would have obtained this degree had Dr. Denman not sanctioned and encouraged me to complete in Nashville the academic work I had so far advanced in Pittsburgh.

—*Russell Q. Chilcote*

I was blessed to have participated in the Florida Conference MYF Evangelism Workcamp, September 5–12, 1949, at the Methodist Youth Camp at Leesburg, Florida. Dr. Denman was our special resource person. It was a wonderful experience for us to get to know Dr. Denman. He inspired us all to go out and serve the Lord. He encouraged us to share our faith. I will always recall his saying, "Pray for me."

As a lay delegate to the Florida Annual Conference this year, I saw many there—both clergy and lay—who had taken part in that Workcamp experience. I know that having the opportunity to know and learn from Dr. Harry Denman was a factor in the lives of the many people whose lives have been influenced and enriched by him over the years. He was "one of a kind." I am grateful to God for having the opportunity to know Dr. Harry Denman.

—*Margie Lou Dunaway*

For several years the Presbyterians at Massanetta Springs would have a pledge service at the annual Bible conference. Dr. Denman was the favorite fundraiser. He always gained more cash and pledges for the following year's Bible conference than anyone else. He would come up with quips of all kinds and lay it on heavy about our special obligation to the Lord and about those who would benefit from the following year's Bible conference.

Then you would pass Dr. Denman along the sidewalks at Massanetta Springs and say hello to him. He would say hello and add, "Please pray for me."

—*A.J. Schrader*

Harry Denman was an inspiration to me—the kind of witnessing Christian I wanted to be. Enclosed is a copy of a letter from him dated Nov. 6, 1964, after Bishop Gerald Kennedy had asked me to chair a committee on recognition. It shows a typical response about his real self—so different from many in the church and in political life.

—*Wilson Weldon*

Dr. Wilson Weldon
302 W. Market Street
Greensboro, North Carolina

Dear Wilson:

I notice in the Minutes of the Executive Committee that you were appointed chairman of a special committee of the Board of Evangelism "to plan a fitting recognition for Harry Denman."

May I say a few words about this plan. I do not need or want any kind of recognition. I have had too much recognition. The Methodist Church has done more for me than I can ever do for it. I have had too many honors. I do not need a television set, a briefcase, or a car. I would give them away. I certainly do not want a book of letters. Those who love me will write on their own initiative. This is being done now. I do not want a dinner because that would cost a thousand dollars or more. I would rather that money be spent in other ways. If I were married and had children and grandchildren, I think it would be nice to have a dinner and let them hear what was to be said. I hear too much now. It is embarrassing to me and I do not desire to hear any more.

I do not want to be General Secretary-Emeritus. This is superfluous. I have seen too many such persons. I wish to be Harry Denman, servant of the Lord Jesus Christ. I do not intend to quit working. I will go on proclaiming the Gospel as long as I am physically able and have money in the Harry Denman Travel Fund.

I do not need a watch. A good friend sent to Switzerland for a very expensive watch for me. I must either give it back to him or give it to someone else. Someone sent me a suit of clothes and accessories. I must give these away. I have one suit.

I am not retiring. As soon as my successor is elected, I am going to start accepting invitations which I hope will keep me busy.

Please ask the Committee to forget the Recognition. I thank the Board for thinking of this. The Board gave me too much recognition by having my portrait painted by Warner Sallman.

I have had a wonderful time during the past years and hope to continue having a good time.

Please pray for me.

Sincerely your friend,

Harry Denman

CC: Bishop Gerald Kennedy
    Dr. Truman Potter
    Dr. J. Manning Potts

I remember Harry Denman as always warm, open, friendly. He had a view of evangelism that was anything but narrow. While he subscribed to most of the traditional methods of evangelism—including revivals and personal witness—he was open to many other methods, some new and experimental.

On more than one occasion he said to me, "Ed, you are an evangelist." He said that because of my work with the media on behalf of the church. I had never thought of this work as evangelism; but he named it that, and I felt honored (and humbled) that Harry regarded me as an evangelist.

O.B. Fanning, who headed the Nashville Office of Methodist Information, told how he got a photograph of the legendary Harry Denman. Believing that having his picture published was unacceptable vanity, Dr. Denman refused to have a photo made. Fanning teamed up with Bob Bell, religion writer for *The Nashville Banner*. During a meeting O.B. engaged Dr. Denman in conversation while Bell slipped up with a camera. Bell called, "Harry" and snapped. It turned out to be an excellent picture and was distributed widely to the press—with no complaint from Denman.

—*Edwin H. Maynard*

I was not fortunate enough to know Dr. Harry Denman, but Glenn "Tex" Evans told me this story that is still very vivid in my mind. "Tex" was on the staff of the Board of Evangelism. The occasion was Harry Denman's eightieth birthday party, being held at the Upper Room.

Tex and Harry were sitting in the corner talking about world evangelism as the festivities were going on around them when Harry made this statement, "I don't understand why Christians in the United States are so afraid of the Russians taking over this country. Just think what a marvelous opportunity that would be to spread the gospel of Jesus Christ!"

Harry Denman knew, long before any of the rest of us could see, that the power of the gospel would be stronger than the evils of the Communist system.

—*James M. Robinson*

I shall never forget our staff meetings and Harry's deep commitment to evangelism as the supreme task of the church. He set the churches on fire, and we had the greatest years in evangelism in the history of modern Methodism. Methodism today needs a voice like his to stir the Council of Bishops, the General Conference, and the annual conferences to a revitalized thrust in dynamic evangelism. He was God's man everywhere and at all times. He made a tremendous impact upon my life and helped to fashion the direction of my ministry.

—*Eugene E. Golay*

We all remember the meeting in the Arena in Washington, D.C., in the hottest weather ever experienced there. There was no air conditioning in the Arena, and the staff and delegates complained as loudly as we could to one another about selecting a unair-conditioned building in the middle of the summer in Washington, D.C. But there sat Harry, at every session of every meeting, with his black coat on and his black tie, acting as if he were never more comfortable. As I recall, it was a very successful meeting.

Harry's real genius was his ability to sell evangelism to the whole church. The lay visitation movement was never done before and has never been done on a churchwide basis since. Every bishop was in on it.

I was in Oregon when it was at its height. Gerald Kennedy was our bishop. This was something he had never related to in his whole career, but he was in this with both feet. Harry knew that if he could get the bishops behind something, then the superintendents would follow, and then the pastors. No one in the board has ever done that since.

People will say, "Well, this is a different day." But The Methodist Church wasn't too strong on evangelism when all this started. The routine revival meeting had almost dried up. At least it was not producing new people in the church. This was something new, and it had to be sold to the church. He put Guy Black on the road to every conference; but behind that promotion, someone was selling a massive program to the whole church, and Harry is the one who did it. He put out a free magazine that told the story of what could be done in evangelism and sent it to every pastor. He paid for it by selling materials.

The people who saw him only as a popular preacher were probably not aware of the administrator who changed the nature of the whole Methodist Church.

—*Berlyn V. Farris*

I was hired by Dr. J. Manning Potts, editor of *The Upper Room*, in early 1950. My title was editorial associate, but my job was to do whatever needed to be done that I could do. This afforded me many occasions to be in the company of the great man, Harry Denman.

I remember he would have a Christmas dinner for all the staff and their wives, not families. We also had staff meetings at that season. The staff meetings were long, and some of the staff wanted to spend more time with their families. Nobody reminded them that the staff was Dr. Denman's only family, and he also wanted to be with his family at Christmas.

—*Brooks B. Little*

On one occasion Dr. Denman had breakfast in Dallas, Texas; lunch in New York; and dinner in Chicago. Whether this is true or is just a rumor is not certain. What is certain is that if he were invited to speak by groups interested in evangelism, he would be there if humanly possible.

Before the days of computers, airlines used a printed Official Airline Guide to know what planes were going where. Dr. Denman carried his personal copy of this guide. On a plane he would plan his next trip. He knew when, where, and how to travel. When he went to the ticket counter, he told the attendant where he wanted to go and gave the exact flight number and time of departure. At least once he was told it was not possible to do what he had presented. Dr. Denman took the guide and showed the attendant how it was possible.

—Brooks B. Little

I remember Harry's clever way of handling his staff—having the bills sent to him on the road after they had been paid, and then writing the staff member about any item that concerned him.

—Bishop Roy Short

I remember when one of the staff bought a Cadillac car. The purchase was discussed in staff meeting. The owner said it made a statement—when you arrived in a Cadillac, you had arrived! I don't know what was said, but in a relatively short time the Cadillac was traded for a less expensive car.

—Brooks B. Little

When Harry Denman interviewed me for a job and invited me to come, I asked him for a job description.

"I can give it to you in one sentence: Help make the Methodist Church an evangelistic movement."

Then I asked him to be more specific—how he wanted me to do it.

He replied, "Just keep on doing what you have been doing, only do it with us."

—Lawrence L. Lacour

No one had more sensitivity as to certain social proprieties than Harry Denman. Whenever we had dinners for the staff and their spouses, Brother Harry would always have a corsage for each wife.

Our staff meetings were a joy. Although Harry was prepared to make decisions and take responsibility as our leader, he was not an authoritarian.

—*Lawrence L. Lacour*

We had flown through the night and through a terrible storm down the Burma Peninsula out of Rangoon, landing in Singapore at dawn on Saturday. We were all groggy. We caught about four hours sleep and a shower and gathered at a church up by Trinity College about 10:50 A.M. to be briefed on our work in Singapore. Bishop Amstutz was there and D.S. Hang and other Methodist leaders from there.

As I recall, D.S. Hang was outlining all the bus tours for that afternoon and sightseeing in the area, when Dr. Denman broke in to say, "Now Brother Hang, we didn't come to Singapore to drink tea—we came to preach Christ, so we'd better forego the sightseeing, get our assignments to the churches, and go to work." And that's what we did.

—*Ross A. Fulton, Sr.*

SIMPLICITY

I had a conversation with Dr. Denman following his return from India. I had heard that he had been given a cashmere coat while in India. Upon Dr. Denman's arrival in Nashville, I was quick to go to his office and welcome him home. As we talked about his travels, I found the opportunity to share the news that I had heard regarding the coat he had received. When Dr. Denman asked why I was concerned about the coat, I mentioned that we were about the same height and that, inasmuch as he always gave items away, I would be most pleased to receive the cashmere coat.

Dr. Denman stood and smiled. As he placed his hand on my shoulder, he said in his deep voice, "This morning, Maurice, I gave the coat to a fellow down on Fifth Avenue. He didn't have a coat. You have a coat. You can only wear one at a time. You only need *one* coat." Then he said, "Brother Maurice, let's have a prayer."

—*W. Maurice King*

I remember being so impressed to learn that most of his worldly possessions consisted of what he was wearing on his back! He had no need for material gifts.

—*Kitty Mann*

Dr. Denman stayed with my husband and me during a speaking engagement. We noticed that his overcoat was in pretty bad shape. I found out where he stored it in the summer. I knew he wouldn't accept a coat outright as a gift. Toward the end of summer I bought a coat for him in Asheville and took it to the dry cleaners where his old coat was stored. I asked the owner to give him the new one when he came to pick up his coat. I didn't tell the owner who I was. I just said to tell Dr. Denman that my husband and I loved him and wanted him to have a new coat.

From what I learned later, Harry at first refused the coat, saying it was not his. He figured out who we were from the owner's description. I think he took the coat, but I do not know whether he kept it or not. He told me later it was too "fine" for him. I told him to wrap his feet up in it on some long cold trips, and it wouldn't be "fine" very long. He laughed.

—*Mary Jo Harrison*

My wife, Mary Wingate, worked for the Kansas City Cokesbury bookstore. It was 1944, and General Conference was meeting in Kansas City. Harry Denman came into the store, dressed in his usual rather shabby manner, and asked Mary to cash a check. She had to have checks approved by her superior, who looked over her glasses and said, "I don't know him." Mary explained he was the head of the Board of Evangelism. Embarrassed, the superior reluctantly okayed the check for what to her appeared to be little more than a bum off the streets.

—*Neil Heidrick*

When I think of humility incarnate, I think of Harry Denman. I worked with him for twenty years on the evangelism staff of The Methodist Church. He was an apostle Paul, a Francis of

Assisi and a Francis Asbury reincarnated. He never drew his full executive salary. He was a bachelor, married to Lady Poverty. Though he had never taken the vows of chastity, poverty, and obedience, he lived humbly. He never owned a watch. He had only one suit at a time. He carried his toiletries in a paper bag in his single briefcase to save space in packing.

—*Howard W. Ellis*

Another story that supports all the stories about Harry Denman's having no extra clothing—just bare necessities—is this: Roy and I were in the dry cleaning business, and Roy always wanted to do the visiting minister's cleaning as a favor. One day when Roy was leaving the noon service, he said to Dr. Denman, "Let me dry-clean a suit for you today."

He replied, "Brother Roy, I'd have to go to bed." Roy told him that was all right; he needed to rest anyway. He did allow Roy to go to the motel with him and *take the suit*. He was going to take a nap or read his Bible. The suit was returned later in the afternoon because Roy didn't want Harry to miss church that night!

—*Polly Garris*

In the early 1960s, Betty and I were driving Harry Denman to the Detroit Metro Airport to fly to Nashville. He asked us to mail some cassette tapes on which he had dictated some letters to be typed. Before we had a chance to ask him why, he said, "I want to be sure these letters get to Lou, so I send them separately in case something happens to me!"

We'll always remember the famous duffel bag, packed with all his personal belongings, as we waited with him on Main Street in Flat Rock, Michigan, for the Greyhound to take him to his next engagement.

—*Ron Carter*

My family was in the clothing business, and it was obvious that Dr. Denman could use another suit of clothes. One of my uncles tried to give him a new suit from the store, but he wouldn't accept it. He preferred instead to travel light and get by with what he had with him. I learned later that was his style. Dr. Denman wrote him a letter in 1948. He has this letter framed, hanging in his den at home.

—H. John Cribb, Jr.

J. Manning Potts, editor of *The Upper Room*, told me that one time he and Harry Denman were together in Hong Kong. Harry traveled light—he never packed another suit! Harry discovered to his dismay that his pants had a rip in them. You will remember that Dr. Denman was over six feet tall, and Dr. Potts was five feet five. But Dr. Denman persuaded Dr. Potts to lend him a pair of pants so he could make his evangelistic calls while his pants were being repaired.

—Bruce C. Mosher

When I was superintendent of the Oklahoma City District, Harry Denman stayed in our home a few times. He had only one tie, which bore its share of gravy stains. I tried to give him one of my ties. I had the clip-on style that I told him would save many precious minutes. We traded ties—which he did reluctantly—but the next day he asked for his own tie back. He felt more comfortable with his "old friend."

—Irving L. Smith

I have heard of the fact that some layperson would give Harry Denman an overcoat in the winter, only to see him go down the street to a vendor who had no coat and give it to him. Then Harry would walk on down the street without a coat.

—*Alfred T. Sprouse*

As many others had done, the members of a congregation presented Harry with a new suit, knowing full well that he would have the joy of giving it to someone who needed it more than Harry Denman.

—*Fawn Summers*

I remember Harry Denman as being a sharing man. I give two personal examples. One Christmas he received, among many other remembrances, a large bag of oranges. He chose to pass these oranges on to a young man working in the Service Department of the Board of Missions. The young man was just starting out. He had a family to support, and the fruit was a very acceptable gift. The young man was my nephew.

Then one day I was visiting with Harry's secretary, and in the course of the conversation, she told me that someone had sent him a nice suitcase as a token of appreciation. She also told me that Dr. Denman did not need the suitcase and that he did not know just what to do with it.

My reply was, "Just tell him to give it to me; I can use it."

I really was not serious, so I was surprised to get a call the next day from the secretary saying, "Dr. Denman says to come on over and get the suitcase." I did, and I used it for years.

—*Eddie Lee McCall*

On several occasions I shared speaking assignments with Dr. Denman. One summer in the late sixties we were the speakers at summer camp in southern Indiana. On a free afternoon we went into the small town near the camp. Harry took every possible occasion to involve people in conversation as we walked about the town and in the stores. The owner of the men's clothing store was Mr. St. Angelo, a devout Christian and father of a promising young minister in the conference. After a brief conversation, Mr. St. Angelo led Harry over to the tie counter and told him to pick out any tie as a gift. Harry thanked him but declined. The perplexed owner, obviously wanting to give Harry a tie, again urged him to choose one. This time Harry turned and said, "Thank you very much, but you see, I already have one." That was Harry. He could not possibly be encumbered with two neckties!

I think of Harry as God's most unencumbered servant. Joseph Wood Krutch has remarked that a person's security is to be measured, not by what he or she owns, but by what he or she can do without. Few people have traveled the world with so little physical baggage as Harry Denman. He is a layman; but if God ever called a man to be an evangelist, He called Harry Denman. He is one of God's rare gifts to the church.

—*Bishop Wayne K. Clymer*

BOLDNESS

One evening at a meeting, Harry pointed out that a large portion of the city's population was unchurched. He then said pointedly, "They aren't bad; they're just poor."

—*Glenn H. Barney*

Dr. Denman could be strong-minded and stand firm. He could also listen to the viewpoints and suggestions of other persons and react by making reasonable decisions to viable suggestions.

—*Russell Q. Chilcote*

Dr. Denman served as business manager of First Methodist Church, Birmingham, Alabama. Dr. Denman, having spent several days in a hospital, saw a church member one day on the street.

The church member said, "I am sorry I did not have the chance to come to see you when you were in the hospital, but I just didn't have the time."

Whereupon Dr. Denman responded in his usual forthright manner, "You don't mean you didn't have the time, but you mean you didn't choose to spend your time visiting me."

—*Frank Dominick*

Unpredictability was a characteristic of Dr. Harry Denman. In the course of his sermonizing, he called children to the chancel and began talking with them about prayer. To the surprise of my pastoral heart, I learned that one of my leading families did not have grace before meals. I wonder how the parents felt as they listened to their exposure!

—*Eldon and Beth Boggs*

One day another experience indicated that Dr. Denman's top priority was the church's ministry. I received the following note from him one Easter: "I noted that you had fifty lilies on your altar Easter Sunday in memory of the dead. How many souls were saved in honor of the living?"

—*Wallace Chappell*

Dr. Denman didn't go into much detail in his letters, but he touched all the important bases. Lou Dozier shared an experience with me. Dr. Denman had gotten a letter that had called him every name that one "Christian" could call another, relative to something he had said on the race situation. He was way ahead of the pack in race relations. Lou told me about Harry's answer to the letter. He said, "I know I make many mistakes. Keep praying for me." If we could all remember those words when someone is on our backs, we would all be better off.

Let me mention another thing on race. Dr. Denman was speaking somewhere. He reached into his breast pocket and brought out a little New Testament. He called it a Bible in that endearing way he always used when he spoke the word *Bible*. He said, "I am mighty proud of this Bible because of who gave it to me." Then he opened it up to the front page and read, "Your friend, Martin Luther King." We have come so far since then that it is hard to realize how those words were like throwing gasoline on the fire. But Harry was one of the leaders of the movement of racial understanding without ever really making speeches about it or belonging to a committee to promote it. And he paid a price for it.

—*Berlyn V. Farris*

I remember Harry Denman during the period of 1944–45. I was seventeen years old. Ours was a neighborhood church in Jackson, Tennessee. Our pastor invited Harry Denman to preach a series of sermons for one week. One story I remember well came from his walking around the court square in Jackson. As you may know, that was a time of racial segregation. Harry Denman told our congregation that he had seen a strange thing. All of the benches around the court square stated that they were "white," but they looked green to him!

Later, after I became a pastor, Dr. Denman was speaking to a group of us pastors and proposed what was then a radical idea. He said that churches in large cities might have to consider having worship on weeknights after midnight for people like taxicab drivers.

—*Jerry Bell*

In the early seventies, Dr. Denman held a series of meetings in Russell County, Kansas, at the Otterbein United Methodist Church in Russell. We were pastoring in Luray, Kansas, about twenty-five miles away. We were so blessed with Dr. Denman's message that several carloads of us would drive the distance almost every night to attend his meetings. Among those loving him the most were our youth. He always referred to Bunker Hill as "Bunka Heights." No Saturday evening service was scheduled, and out of the blue, he announced that "the people from Luray have been so faithful to drive over every night, that Saturday night we are all going over there for a service!" And they did.

—*Mr. and Mrs. Richard Krenz*

In the seventies in Cincinnati, going Greyhound meant that you embarked or debarked in a substandard bus station. I met Harry Denman at the Greyhound station around 11 P.M. on Saturday night. He was to be my guest speaker the next morning. I had heard him speak once and on that basis had invited him to my suburban city church.

I saw him standing all alone in the middle of that dismal bus station waiting room—a big man, standing in a slumped position holding on to a brown paper grocery bag. One look and I groaned inwardly, "What have I brought to my people?" *Where to get this strange guest a bite to eat at so late an hour:* The thought became an uttered quest.

"Why not here?"

"Here!" was my horrified response.

"And why not?"

So we sat in that desolate place late on Saturday night— this great man of God whom I would discover on the morrow and my own quaking person.

Many years later and in a different church, I received a 4 A.M. call from a young man in the former church. He said he needed to talk to someone. He described Harry Denman, whom he had seen in that church in the seventies. I sadly told him that the man he sought was dead. He then spoke to me of his need.

—*Eldon and Beth Boggs*

Speaking to a crowd of us ministers in Iowa, Harry Denman asked if we had taken rooms in poor boarding houses for the conference. Then did you talk with the maid who came to clean the room? ask her about her faith? And after breakfast in their dining facility, did you go out into the kitchen to ask the cook about his or her faith? Harry did.

—*Pierce Johnson*

One of the Drew professors was a personal friend of Harry's and told this experience in class. It seems he and Harry were traveling together by bus to a speaking engagement. A group of rowdy young men in the back of the bus was disturbing all the other passengers. Since the driver was doing nothing about it, Harry got up from his seat and went back to them. The professor said to himself that Harry was walking into trouble. But in just a few moments, Harry Denman had won them over and was even making a Christian witness to them. He had that unique ability.

—*Conway Keibler*

During the summer of 1941, I traveled with Dr. Harry Denman as his evangelistic singer. I never knew a more Christlike man than Harry Denman. My association with him greatly influenced my Christian life. When we got into a city or town, we always checked into a hotel. Harry would never stay in homes, because he wanted to be free to come and go at his will. After checking in, the first place we visited was the jail. Harry would talk to the inmates, and I would sing and lead them in a few old hymns. If he saw the need, he would linger and talk with individuals.

The next place we would visit was the lowest dive or beer joint in town. Harry would go around to the different tables and talk about Christ. Doing this was as natural to him as breathing. He never asked me to sing in these places, but I would go with him. I always felt the place was changed for his having been there. Harry would talk to people on the street—

not about the weather or politics or business or crops—but about Christ. He said and he believed that this was the most important topic of conversation in the world. The summer I spent with him as his singer greatly blessed my life.

—*R. Ross Dowden*

I was at Iowa State University, Ames, Iowa, visiting my son for Mom's Weekend, probably in 1967. When my son and I left for church that Sunday morning, I suggested that we attend Collegiate Methodist Church on campus instead of going to the church he normally attended, which was Evangelical United Brethren in Ames. In response my son simply said, "No, we'll go where I always go." I immediately agreed.

I'm quite ashamed of the thoughts that went through my mind momentarily when I saw the speaker get up to give the morning sermon. It was Dr. Denman, not appearing to be either young or snappy. I thought, *This will be a real drag.* Was I ever wrong! We heard the best sermon on the good Samaritan I had ever heard, or that I've heard since. I think of him and that sermon every time I hear the story mentioned or preached on. I'm sixty-eight years old and have heard lots of good sermons, but few have impressed me or stayed with me as this one. One thing in particular he said of the Samaritan was, "If he had been in our Methodist Church today, he would have had to call a committee meeting before doing anything." I feel this is too true!

From hearing and seeing him only that one time, I felt it was obvious that he was, without a doubt, completely focused on doing business for the Lord and only the Lord. He also had the unique ability or gift of presenting and handling an altar call in a most effective way. These two things are all but gone in our church today. That morning he gave an altar call, and before it was over "wall to wall" people were in the front of the church, about five or six deep. Outside of a Billy Graham Crusade I never witnessed such a response, which was a most blessed thing to see and be a part of. I have ever been grateful for my son's insistence that we go to his usual place of worship that Sunday morning.

—*Mrs. Edward Wiederstein*

Dr. Harry Denman has been described in many different ways—all complimentary in every way. No one name or descriptive word could ever be said or written to tell what a great personality he was. His personality was unique in every sense of the word. He drew people to him. I remember when he came to our Hardy Memorial Methodist Church, Texarkana, Texas, for a revival during Christmas week, 1957. I was chair of the Membership and Evangelism Commission, and our pastor, the Reverend Harold Fagan, had contacted Dr. Denman about coming to our church. The reply was that Christmas week was the only time he could come. Since Reverend Fagan was in the hospital at the time of the commission meeting, he gave me the job of selling the commission on the idea of a Christmas revival. I was scared to death, but from what Mr. Fagan had told me about the man and from some research I did on my own, I was excited about the possibility of having him come to our church. I told the commission about this Godlike man: the consecration of his own life, his deep dedication and concern for each person's soul: how he preached, how he lived and went about his daily caring and talking with people on the street in his own unique way of witnessing for Christ. It was unanimously voted that we should invite Dr. Denman to come. The meeting was wonderful—we are still talking about it. The house was packed every night with our church people and others from the Arkansas-Texas area. His first sermon on Sunday was stimulating, thought-provoking, and soul-searching.

Dr. Denman jolted us when he said, "Do you know that there are people walking the streets of Texarkana today starving for attention, starving for love and friendliness... starving just for someone to care? Today is the birthday of

Jesus Christ. I bet your Christmas trees are laden with Christmas gifts. What are you doing for His birthday? These lonely, sad, hungry, and desperate people are God's people too."

—*Polly Garris*

I remember one occasion when I was with Dr. Denman in Detroit, Michigan, where there had been a series of meetings at various churches. The culminating presentation was at Metropolitan Church across the street from Wayne State University. The sanctuary was filled to capacity, and I was sitting on the front pew when Dr. Denman came in and sat next to me. He turned and said, "Wake me up when they introduce me." We went through the entire liturgy of the service: the singing, the praying, the announcements, the celebrations. Dr. Denman sat with his head bowed. I am sure most people thought he was praying (and who knows, maybe he was). When the district superintendent stood up to begin his introduction of Dr. Denman, I nudged him. He immediately lifted his head and listened to the words, then walked to the platform and preached. As he started to the platform, he turned to me and said, "I will be leaving at the end of the prayer and already have a pastor who will take us to the airport. So don't bow your head at the closing prayer; watch and follow me." When he finished preaching and had given a basic invitation, he asked one of the pastors to have the closing prayer. I watched as he left the platform, and I followed him out. Our bags were near the exit we had selected. We got into a waiting car where a young preacher, fresh out of seminary and in his first appointment, was going to take us to the airport. Dr. Denman sat next to him in the front seat. Joe Hale and I were in the back seat.

All the way to the airport, this young preacher kept asking questions of Dr. Denman, and Dr. Denman answered them graciously. When we got to the airport the young preacher said he would come in with us. That was fine with us. So we parked and proceeded to make our way to the ticket counter to check in for the late evening flight to Nashville. As we were leaving the ticket counter, Harry turned to the young preacher and said in his customary way, "Pray for me." The young preacher was caught off guard, so he responded, "Please pray for me." Instinctively, Dr. Denman grabbed his hand and began praying out loud in the midst of persons at the ticket counter. He prayed that a revival might occur in Detroit and that this young preacher would lead it. This young preacher, head bowed and feeling very uneasy and embarrassed, wanted to fall through the floor because everyone had stopped to watch this scene. I noticed as I was walking away that Harry was still praying for the young preacher. With his free hand, the young preacher took the collar of his coat and put it up around his neck, seemingly to hide his face. I imagine this young preacher never asked anyone to pray for him again in a public arena.

—*Ed Beck*

A church in Indiana told the story about Dr. Denman's coming to that church several years before. He was coming by train. The pastor had gone to pick Dr. Denman up from a midafternoon arrival. According to the story, Dr. Denman did not get off the train. The pastor was concerned and upset and spent a good deal of the afternoon trying to locate Dr. Denman. The church service proceeded with a packed house that evening. About the time that the pastor was going to have to do something in the nature of preaching himself or ask a visiting pastor to do so, Dr. Denman walked in, came down the center aisle, and took his seat on the platform. With a sigh of relief, the preacher celebrated Dr. Denman's arrival and then introduced him. Dr. Denman stood up and said to the people that he had arrived on the train but had gotten off on the other side, rather than on the platform, and had walked to the nearest neighborhood and had been visiting people. Then he asked that those people attending the service who had been invited personally by him that afternoon to stand. A third of the congregation stood. Then Dr. Denman asked how many had invited others to attend.

Dr. Denman was an inspiration in my life and had a great impact on me as he did so many others in so many ways. He loved the church, believed in it emphatically, and gave his life for it sacrificially. I am so grateful that God allowed me the opportunity to work under his leadership for six years.

—*Ed Beck*

When Dr. Denman moved to Nashville, he joined a Negro congregation. He said, "If you believe in integration, don't just invite folks to your church; you go to theirs!"

—*Charles D. Whittle*

When Harry preached on the statement that people made at John the Baptist's birth, "What shall become of this child?" he would say that what this child becomes depends on the parents and the Sunday school teachers. Then he would invite boys and girls, twelve and under, to come and stand before the altar. Then he would invite their parents to come and stand behind them. He would move down the line, asking each child his name. "What is your name, son?" Then he would lay his hand on the child's head and say, "What shall become of this child?" They never forgot that experience and neither did their parents.

—*Charles D. Whittle*

Dr. Gerald Harvey conducted numerous workshops in Christian education during his stay in Korea. He spoke of his concept of the church as being that of a wet nurse: a servant who gets messed upon and puked upon but is loved eventually for what the nurse has given to the development of the child. That concept appealed to me. When I mentioned it to Dr. Denman, he couldn't have disagreed more. To him the church's role is that of a midwife: bringing new babies, so to speak, to birth. When I tried to talk to him about the necessity of nurture following birth, he was not interested. "The church must evangelize!" was his concern. I didn't convince him, and he didn't convince me, but I still felt that he was truly a saint.

—*Charles H. Harper*

HUMOR

My favorite memory of Dr. Denman is when he would be preaching: He would pull himself up to full stature, throw out his chest and stalk across the pulpit area, saying, "I've quit preaching and gone to meddling." We knew he was going to "step on toes."

—Madelyn Lazenby

While working as secretary in the office of Dr. Harry Williams, I have remembrances of Dr. Harry Denman. I will share only a few.

When Ruth Ann Tate began working in the accounting department of *The Upper Room*, she had no idea who Dr. Denman was. That very afternoon, while walking through the offices, he stopped at Ruth Ann's desk and asked, "What are you doing?"

Looking up at him she replied, "Darned if I know." Dr. Denman smiled and said, "At least you're honest" and went on his way.

For several years the Board of Evangelism sponsored an evangelistic training program for theological students called the 70-E Program. Each year at the close of the two-week session, Dr. Denman would give the closing message. At the close of his message, in his usual manner, he would give an altar call. All seventy of the students and the staff crowded into the area, knelt to the floor, and bowed their heads in silent prayer. We knelt, and we knelt, and we knelt—waiting for Dr. Denman to close the altar time. Almost forty minutes passed. Finally one of the staff persons looked up. Dr. Denman was nowhere to be seen. Without our knowing, he had arranged for someone to pick him up at the back door of the chapel at an appointed time. Leaving everyone on their knees in prayer, Dr. Denman was off to another appointment in his busy schedule.

—*Madelyn Lazenby*

Dr. Denman had a good sense of humor. Occasionally when he was in town, he would take two of his secretaries to lunch, always in twos. Since he was a bachelor, he didn't want to start any rumors!

—*Katy Thomas*

Dick and I remember when we first met Harry Denman. It was in October 1958. He and Manning Potts had come to lead a week's evangelistic training for local pastors in the Khanewal area. They arrived in Khanewal earlier than planned, and they finally found their way to a house, taking a horse-drawn, two-wheel cart, "tonga," from the rail station. Harry went to the small veranda, peered in a window and shouted, "It's all right, Manning. Come on. Missionaries live here—there's a refrigerator and a Bible." So Dr. Denman and Dr. Potts were brought to our house—a big place built around a large court-yard. Right then Harry wanted to "go to the people," meaning to get on out to the village where we were to live for the week.

Being the Martha-type, I pleaded that we stay until morning as planned so I could get the meat and groceries laid in. I had the groceries, but meat was a problem. With no freezer, and with a butchering in the village only once a month, I had to take meat with me from Khanewal. Finally Dick and I worked out in our minds how to make the extra trips. Manning really wanted to stay put in Khanewal overnight. By the time we had gathered the basic essentials and opened the living room door to cross the courtyard, a sudden dust storm had come up. You couldn't see even the south wall of the courtyard across the way!

Manning took one look, gasped, and said, "Harry, the Lord has spoken; we stay here for the night."

"Well, all right," said Harry, and with that he went to an easy chair by the fireplace and went sound asleep!

The whole week was just as picturesque—how could we forget!

—*Dorothy Lockman*

I remember this story Harry Denman told: A woman's husband died and was buried. His best friend and a former suitor escorted the new widow from the grave to her car.

"Mary," he said, "I know this is a bit premature, but I have always loved you. Will you marry me?"

Not allowing her irritation to be seen, she answered, "I'm sorry, but I just promised the undertaker as he shoveled the last dirt on the grave that I would marry him."

Then there was the Methodist woman who went to her pastor and reminded him of her husband's heart problem.

"He has just been left a hundred thousand dollars by a wealthy uncle," she said. "Could you tactfully break the news to him?" The minister visited the heart patient. They discussed various subjects such as the economy, the weather, and sports.

At length, the minister asked, "John, what would you do if you had a hundred thousand dollars?" He replied, "I would give half of it to the church." The minister promptly dropped dead of a heart attack.

—*Wallace Chappell*

An ice cream social was planned after services. Harry said he had never had all the ice cream he wanted because he was always given the dasher to lick clean. That night he had plenty of ice cream plus the dasher.

For our family, Harry exemplified the spirit of Jesus in such a humble way. It was as if the Master himself was present in our home and at our table.

—*FayDel Sewell*

Brother Harry's sharp sense of humor only enhanced his spiritual impact on the lives of this congregation. Pretending to lose his New Testament while in the pulpit was delightful comedy.

—*FayDel Sewell*

About a week before Harry Denman died, Kel and I stopped by Birmingham to see Harry. He was in the hospital, and we visited him there. As we were leaving for Florida, I asked Harry to have a family prayer with us. He turned in the Bible to the scripture about the wife who tendeth to her "spindle." He read this with a wicked gleam in his eye since I had not tended to my spindle for quite a while! Then he prayed a prayer that was so wonderful that it made me cry. A week later he died.

Once we were lamenting the fact that we almost never got to be together and he said, "Well, when I die, I'll come to see you sometime." He did this one time; it was unbelievably natural, and we had a good time!

—*Mary Gatewood Banks Kelley*

I remember having the privilege, along with my family, of sitting under his evangelistic ministry two different years. He shared dinner in our home, and we transported him to hotel, camp meeting, and so forth. He was truly a man of God and followed Jesus' teachings as closely as anyone I ever knew. He had a definite opinion about what to do if a neighbor or friend was disgruntled. He would say, "Bake them a pie." He would bring this into his messages over and over again.

—Mary Morrison

When I was a student at Drew Seminary in the early 1950s, Harry Denman convulsed the student body when he spoke during the morning chapel service. The anecdote I remember was his giving advice to the theological students on personal relationships. He said that as pastors you can expect that parents will want to proudly present their babies to you. He warned that often it would be impossible to determine whether the baby was a boy or girl. So he said to always say, "Now *that's* a baby!" I have had to use his sage advice.

—Conway Keibler

I remember Harry Denman when he was in Montreal, talking to a truck driver and inviting him to attend the revival service.

"My clothes are terrible; I can't go to the service," the trucker said.

"But mine are worse," said Harry, "and I'm preaching."

—Pierce Johnson

"Anyone here named Tom?" The voice of Harry Denman was strong in that meeting in the Hartwell United Methodist Church in Cincinnati in the seventies. A hand went up, and Tom was invited to the chancel.

"How about Dick. Anyone here named Dick?" the

strong voice urged. Another hand and another man responded. Now in front of the altar we had standing Tom, Dick, and Harry. Harry turned to the altar rail, inviting the men to pray for him.

Tom said he could not, but Dick said he would. "O God, I have never met Harry before. . . ." He continued in prayer for Harry. Before the end of the event, Harry had ascertained that Dick could sing, and he asked him to do so. Without announcement, the words of the song, "He Touched Me," sung in a mellow tenor voice, sustained the pleasant drama of the moment.

—*Eldon and Beth Boggs*

When I was a student pastor back in the forties, Dr. Denman conducted an evangelistic campaign in Lancaster County, Pennsylvania, where my church was located. At the first session an elderly, well-respected pastor was called on to pray—and pray he did. After some minutes Harry Denman broke into the prayer and said, "While our brother continues his prayer, let us turn to hymn so-and-so and sing—The Methodist Church is a praying church *and* a singing church. We are doing both."

—*George S. Hewitt*

A friend of ours tells about meeting Dr. Denman at the airport in Asheville. His plane was very late getting to Asheville. He was scheduled to speak at a certain time at Junaluska, so she was driving a little fast to get there. He told her he would rather be Harry Denman late than the late Harry Denman, so slow down.

—*Mary Jo Harrison*

When Dr. Charles Golden was elected bishop and came to Nashville, he had trouble finding office space. Brother Harry gave him a fine office next to mine.

When what was previously the Board of Evangelism building was in the process of construction, there was a house on one lot owned by a widow. Mr. Jackson and Brother Harry paid numerous visits to the woman, trying to get her to sell. One day Brother Harry was discussing his frustration about the property with Manning Potts.

He said, "I want that property so much I'm willing to do anything to get it."

To which Manning replied, "I can tell you how to get it."

"How?"

"Marry the widow."

"I don't want the property that much."

—*Lawrence L. Lacour*

Once on boarding a flight, he asked the attendant what the meal was. When he was told it was filet mignon, he said, "Oh, then bring on the hamburger!"

—*Brooks B. Little*

I remember the first full-scale staff meeting I attended at the General Board of Evangelism.

Dr. Denman asked, "What do you think of the staff?"

I replied, "They're all different."

He chuckled. Dr. Denman thought of staff members as his family. Perhaps one reason was that he had no living relatives. Nashville was home base, and the Board building was his homeplace.

—*Russell Q. Chilcote*

As everyone who traveled with Harry Denman knew, he loved cafeterias. He would pass ten wonderful restaurants to eat at a cafeteria, because he loved to see what he was going to eat. One day Harry and I went into a cafeteria to eat our noon meal. It was a very busy establishment, and after the meal we had to wait in a long line to pay the check. The cashier was a middle-aged woman, and the rigors of life were etched on every crevice and wrinkle on her face. She had apparently lived a tough life and was a rather loud-talking, confrontational individual. As Harry was paying the check, he said to her in his customary fashion, "M'am, I hope you will pray for me."

She instantly retorted, "Ol' man, what the hell have you been up to lately?"

It was the only time I ever saw Harry Denman unable to make any kind of response. As we hit the door and were headed down the street, he turned to me and muttered something to the effect, "What did she mean, old man?"

—*Ed Beck*

When Harry was business administrator for The First Methodist Church in Birmingham, he often worked late at night, visiting persons with spiritual and material needs. His mother worried.

He would say, "Mama, don't worry about me. If I am in jail, the police will call you. If I am in the hospital, the doctor will call you. If I am dead, the mortician will call you." Later, he remarked, "That was some comfort, wasn't it!"

—*Charles D. Whittle*

Once, speaking to the Council of Evangelism in Minneapolis in 1956, Dr. Denman said, "There are five million persons coming to the United States this year. How are we going to reach them? They are babies that will be born." President George Fallon, noting that Harry was a bachelor, said "Harry's preaching but not practicing!"

—Charles D. Whittle

A few years after Harry retired, he was having lunch in the Terrace Hotel at Lake Junaluska.

A woman at his table said, "Did you know that Harry Denman died."

Harry said, "I don't believe he did."

She said, "Oh, yes, he did."

He said, "I'm Harry Denman."

She said, "I'm talking about the one that used to live in Nashville."

"Harry said, "I'm talking about him too."

On telling this story later, Harry commented, "So you see, a lot of people believe I am dead, but I've learned to live with things like that."

—Charles D. Whittle

WITNESS

During World War II I was fortunate enough to be hired as one of the secretaries in Dr. Harry Denman's office. The day came when he came to the office, and I had the pleasure of meeting him for the first time. He greeted me with an armful of *Saturday Evening Posts*. I thought he was a wonderful person, just as nice as I had been told. He soon found out that I had lost most of my family when I was only nineteen years old. Anytime he came to the office he always made me feel appreciated, that he was pleased with my work. One day we were discussing death and the hereafter. I asked him if he thought I would know my mother and father in heaven. A Presbyterian minister had told me that I definitely would not be able to recognize anyone in heaven and had quoted scriptures to support his beliefs. I just wondered what Dr. Denman thought about it. His reply to my question was, "The disciples knew Christ when He arose." It seemed like the greatest fear I ever had was gone. Just to know that if we follow in the steps of Jesus, we can see our loved ones in the Great Beyond was so comforting to me.

—*Katy Thomas*

In June 1972, Harry Denman came to First Methodist Church in Oklahoma City, Oklahoma, for a week of preaching. The caring compassionate love of this dear man touched many lives. Time spent with Harry was always special. He opened the scriptures in a unique way. It was as if you were sitting at the feet of Jesus.

—*FayDel Sewell*

One night in Cuba, I told Harry that I had found the verse in the Bible that best described him.

He said, "Where is it?"

I said, "I won't tell you, for I wish to use it at your funeral."

I did tell him the chapter but not the verse, and I did use it at his memorial service in Nashville.

—*Bishop Roy Short*

We visited him while he was living in a retirement home in Birmingham. We stopped by on our way to New Orleans, took him out to lunch, and went on our way. Early one morning we got a call from him at our motel room in New Orleans. He had tracked us down by calling our baby-sitter in Asheville. He began worrying about *why* we were going to New Orleans where there are some well-known *medical* centers. He wanted to make sure Tom was not taking me there for some special medical problem. Thankfully, he was not right, but we were moved deeply that he cared enough to track us down and call.

—*Mary Jo Harrison*

I remember Dr. Harry Denman at Massanetta Springs Camp Meetings in Harrisonburg, Virginia. One story that he told remains very vivid in my mind: He was speaking at a series of meetings at City Temple in London for Dr. Leslie Weatherhead. While in his office one day, a call came from a rundown rooming house. A prostitute who was dying had asked for a Methodist minister. The pastor asked Dr. Denman to go with him. When they arrived he asked Dr. Denman to minister to the dying woman.

Dr. Denman knelt down beside her bed, bowed his head, and prayed silently. When he finished he held the woman's hand and said to her, using her first name, which he had learned beforehand, "Mary, Papa just told me to tell you that He loves you and wants you to come home to Him." She smiled and died at that moment.

—*A.J. Schrader*

After completing my college education, I taught one year in Athens, Georgia. The year was very challenging and lonely at times. I must have shared this with Dr. Denman, because he suggested I attend graduate school at Peabody College for Teachers in Nashville. He laid some groundwork for me, and I know it was through his efforts that I received a nice scholarship that made it possible for me to attend the college.

I had a very happy year there. The environment at Peabody was so encouraging, and while there I met my future husband. At the end of my year there (1959–60), we decided to marry. We married in the chapel at Belmont Methodist Church. Dr. Denman paid for the use of the chapel and furnished the wedding cake. He was unable to be present for the wedding, but his loyal and wonderful secretary, Lou Dozier, was; and she helped with the arrangements for the wedding reception. I owe her such a debt of gratitude!

After our marriage, Jimmy and I lived in Nashville for about a year. From time to time I would stop to visit with Dr. Denman when he was in town. In time, we moved to Pittsburgh, Pennsylvania, and later to Oxford, Mississippi. Our paths did not cross again except by letters from time to time.

Then we heard about his death. How much richer my life has been for having come to know Dr. Denman—a true servant of God!

—*Kitty Mann*

Harry was preaching at a little community near Nashville during strawberry time. One night my wife, Clara Nell; our daughter, Louise; and I drove out to hear him preach. It was in a tent, as I recall, and there was a large crowd. He spied us in the congregation, and when the service was over asked us if he could ride back to Nashville with us. Evidently he had not bothered to make any arrangements to come home that night. He sort of depended on the Lord to get him where he needed to go, and he usually got there. Louise shared the backseat with him. She had some candy which she offered him. The letter of thanks we got from him (and there were always plenty of them) came not to us but to Louise. He thanked her for the candy.

—*Berlyn V. Farris*

Harry Denman taught me about humility and meekness. Here is a list of lessons I learned from him:

You can travel with one briefcase—and that's enough.

Personal automobiles are not a necessity.

You can wash handkerchiefs and dry them on the mirror overnight.

You can tell people you love them, ask them to pray for you, and get away with it.

Many people are eager to have someone to talk to them about Christ.

Humility is not a degrading word for meek but describes a disarming, debonair lifestyle.

You can pray everywhere.
Letters are for answering anytime, anywhere, and promptly.
Friends are for loving and affirming.
The church is God's greatest gift to God's children.
Happiness is having a good secretary.
Your headquarters is wherever you are.
Clothes do not make the man.
There are no little churches.
You don't need a desk.
You don't need a watch either.
One shirt is better than two.
People who live in retirement homes can be cranky.
The closing altar service is the best time to run for your
　　plane.
A funeral service is a coronation.

—Howard W. Ellis

To me Harry Denman set the mold for being a Christian. He
never put a tag on anyone. He was much like Paul. He didn't
want people following the man or the building; he wanted
them serving God.

—Gerald Frye

In the early 1960s, Dr. Denman conducted a revival at my
church in Greenville, Texas. I was among a group that met
with him following a service, and each received a gold cross.
For almost thirty years, I have carried that cross in the coin
purse of my billfolds, and I am reminded of his message each
time I reach for money. Though it has rubbed against many a
coin in those years, its finish is still bright and shiny—just like
my memory of that very extraordinary man in his familiar,
well-worn suit.

—Fawn Summers

Harry Denman visited in our home on a few occasions. I remember one night we noticed that his suit coat was a little ragged; the pockets had holes in them. We *finally* persuaded him to let me sew up the holes. After he went to bed, I removed an item or two from his side pocket so I could repair the lining. His New Testament was there. I opened its cover to see written inside the cover: "Today I asked God for forgiveness. He forgave." Every time I think of this message, I am touched. It is inspiring to think that one who was so committed to Jesus Christ and so faithful in his walk for so long was still humble to the point of needing forgiveness daily.

—*Mary Jo Harrison*

One time when Harry Denman was preaching in a small church near Asheville, we tried to get him to stay with us. But he preferred a motel outside of town. My husband later found out the main reason for this choice—Harry was leaving the motel each morning around six o'clock so he could walk the road to the church, knocking on doors along the way and inviting persons to the service.

—*Mary Jo Harrison*

I remember Dr. Denman as a unique personality and as a layperson who loved the Lord and His church. The whole world was a great concern upon his heart. We will not see the likes of him again. No person can replace him!

—*W.E. Moore*

On a cold, wintry January afternoon in 1947, we walked along the sidewalks in Sterling, Colorado, as they were being cleared of snow. We came to a popcorn stand.

Harry bought some, and then asked the proprietor, "What church do you go to?"

The proprietor answered, "I am a Roman Catholic."

Harry replied, "Fine, you pray for me the next time you go to Mass."

On down the street, a fellow was shoveling snow, and Harry asked him the same question. When the man indicated that he didn't go to any church much anymore, Harry briefly mentioned the meeting being held that evening at the church.
—*Glenn H. Barney*

The first time I saw Dr. Denman was at an event that changed my life in 1959. I was sixteen years old. I was a member of First Methodist Church, Birmingham, Michigan, and our youth group attended a district youth rally at Metropolitan Methodist in Detroit. Dr. Denman was the speaker. His talk so moved me that evening that I gave my life to Christ. I remember distinctly that he had us write in our Bibles, "Jesus Christ is Lord." I still have that Bible, and I remember that experience as if it were yesterday. That was the beginning of a new understanding about Christianity for me—that one can have a personal relationship with Christ and God. That was the beginning of a faith journey that has been, and continues to be, exciting and uplifting.

I never saw or heard Dr. Denman speak again, but he touched my life again a few years ago. One of my closest friends, who was part of my faith journey, was presented the Harry Denman Award for evangelism at our annual conference in Lakeside, Ohio.
—*Celesta L. Warner*

In 1948 Dr. Harry Denman came to our house in South Carolina with the local Methodist minister to visit my family.

He had just led a revival that week, which we attended. I was only twelve years old, but I remember the event well, for it was a major happening in the life of our family.

My father was only thirty-two when he met Harry Denman, and being caught up in the clutches of alcoholism, he was on a collision course with disaster.

One of his fellow workers told him, "John, there is a man preaching at the Methodist church that you should go hear."

My father, amazed that he was so out of touch, responded, "How much does it cost?"

After hearing and meeting Dr. Denman, he decided to make a commitment to the Methodist Church. This was a big decision for him because all his family were Baptist, and they never really supported his choice. His father and sisters never understood his reasons, but he went on to become an outstanding church worker and servant of God.

I've always wished that I knew what his private conversations with Dr. Denman were like. I do know that Dr. Denman told him, "Any man who would send his child to church and not go himself would be better off if he tied an anvil around his neck and jumped from the nearest bridge." That certainly got my father's attention, and after talking to Dr. Denman he never took another drink. He credited Harry Denman with turning his life around.

—*H. John Cribb, Jr.*

I have a special story to tell and have never had an opportunity to tell it until now. Dr. Denman was one of three evangelists preaching at the Hollow Rock Camp Meeting (oldest Holiness Camp meeting still going on). I was about nine years old. My family had been going to Hollow Rock for several years. Dr. Denman was preaching in the afternoon service. I was sitting in the front row. During the song service, I wandered around and ended up in one of the preachers' chairs on the platform. I sat there through Dr. Denman's sermon. He came over to me after the service, talked with me, and took my name and address. He gave me a missionary world bank. He promised to write to me every month, to pray for me, and to send me a silver dollar to put in the missionary bank. And he did that. Next year at Hollow Rock, my mission offering was twelve silver dollars.

Oh, how I wish I had kept his letters. But his sacrifice, spirit, and words of encouragement have been a great testimony and inspiration to me. Never have I known a man more committed to Christ. He took time to talk to a nine-year-old boy, wrote letters, prayed, and sent twelve silver dollars. What an example of Christlikeness!

—*William J. Moran*

My most vivid memory of Dr. Denman was when I was in Singapore. Here was a man of God, traveling light—only one suitcase (I gather two drip-dry shirts). He shunned hotels and would stay with Christian friends. I was pastor in Paya Leban Church, and he spoke to us. He touched especially my wife (now deceased) and gave her a Christian name, Esther, in place of her Chinese name, Sieu Lang. He even gave her a peck on her forehead. I am sure they are both in heaven having tête-à-tête as I pen these lines. To me he was an example of deep devotion and a man of prayer. He loved everyone.

—*Hoon Hee Wong*

I especially remember one of the sermons Harry Denman delivered in the chapel, in which he so beautifully talked of Christ's love for each one of us. He talked with such fervor that to this day I can still see him as he preached. I often think back on that day because I was going through some personal difficulties at that time, and I felt he was talking just to me! He helped lift my spirits!

—*Kitty Mann*

I remember one of the greatest stories about Harry Denman. He was in one of his great city crusades. Someone needed to get in touch with him. The person went to his hotel room. He was not there. While walking down the corridor of the hotel, the person seeking Denman stopped to ask a woman on her knees cleaning the floor if she had seen Harry Denman. The woman looked up with big tears in her eyes and said, "I don't know whether it was Harry Denman or not, but a man just told me about Jesus." Of course, that man was Harry Denman.

—*Harry Snyder*

I have many happy recollections of Harry Denman. One is that in the course of several taxi rides with me, he never failed to witness to the taxi driver in an attempt to bring him to a decision for Christ. I also remember that when some of us came to Nashville to speak at some occasion related to the Board of Evangelism, we were presented with a basket of fruit or a bouquet of flowers from Harry Denman. I was personally the recipient of several such gifts, for which I am grateful.

—*Bishop James K. Mathews*

Jim, a young man living at the "Y" across the street from the church, had been attending services. He was present every night to hear Harry preach.

Harry asked Jim, "What do you do?"
Jim answered, "I am a hood."
"A what?" exclaimed Harry.

"A hood," the fellow repeated. "You know, a hoodlum."

"No, young man, you are not a hoodlum; you are a lawbreaker." Then Harry spoke with Jim about his need to give himself to Jesus Christ. Eventually Jim drifted on. We did not see him again. But he had encountered Harry Denman, and surely his life was never the same.

—*FayDel Sewell*

I have so many memories of Harry Denman. I remember there was a woman with whom I really had trouble, and I could *not* get it straightened out. Harry came to our church for a wonderful week of services. He knew nothing about my problem, and I never mentioned it to him, but his sermons went so deep into my heart that I gained the strength to deal with the problem, and the woman and I became good friends.

—*Mary Gatewood Banks Kelley*

As a child growing up in the mountains of northeastern West Virginia in the 1940s and 1950s, I heard my ministers tell stories about Harry Denman. But he was only a name to me until one wonderful day in 1973. I had married in 1964, and my wife and I moved to Virginia. I answered the call to the ministry in 1971. After completing work at Duke Divinity School in the Lay Pastors' School in order to receive my deacon's ordination, I attended a twenty-four-hour evangelism retreat our Bishop Kenneth Goodson sponsored.

Bishop Goodson held a fall ordination service for the eight of us who were eligible to take that step. It was a very special time. However, my favorite memory is of Mr. Denman, who served as preacher for that service. That may be the only time a layperson ever preached an ordination sermon!

The service was held at a Presbyterian Campground near Harrisonburg, Virginia—Massanetta Springs. The temperature was very hot, and the humidity was oppressive. Dr. Denman mopped sweat with his handkerchief and delivered a wonderfully heartfelt message. What a saint he was! I shall always cherish getting to meet him.

—*Ronald R. Jones*

My most memorable experience was a conversation with Harry Denman at a restaurant in Huntington, West Virginia. As he shared with a waitress, I commented that he never missed a person. His response was that during a series of services in Hattiesburg, Mississippi, the Lord impressed him to speak to the morning clerk in the local hotel. He put it off for several mornings. At length, before the week ended, he approached the hotel desk but was informed by the night clerk that the morning clerk had taken his life. Harry said to me, "I went to my room, fell on my knees, and promised God that I would never miss another person."

—*Wallace Chappell*

On Tuesday, Christmas Eve, Mr. Denman and several friends came to visit us. My husband, Roy, was there and his mother, Effie, who lived with us. I had heard that Mr. Denman liked turnip greens very much. My mother-in-law was a great cook, and she fixed a regular Southern dinner, turnip greens and all—even fried cornpones. After the blessing, which Roy voiced, Dr. Harry got up and walked toward the kitchen. Thinking he was looking for the bathroom, I followed. He was talking to Betty, our helper. Serious talk! I returned to the table, and he followed soon. In his hand I noticed a bottle of pepper sauce.

He said, "Sister Polly, you can't eat turnip greens without pepper sauce." Everyone agreed.

However, before he left the kitchen he had asked Betty

about her faith and her soul. He never missed a chance to witness.

—*Polly Garris*

My story goes back fifty years. I was active in youth work but had every intention of being a farmer all my life. Three years out of high school, I was asked by my pastor to attend a meeting at Emporia, Kansas. That evening I came home and wrote in the cover of the little Bible my mother had given me in 1926 when I was six years old: "Feb. 19, 1941. After hearing Dr. Denman, I resolve to give my best to the Lord and to say, 'What will thou have me to do ?'" On the first Sunday of June 1941, I preached my first sermon at my appointment in Olpe, Kansas. On the first Sunday of June 1991, I preached my last sermon under appointment. For fifty years I tried to keep that promise I made on a cold February in Kansas, when my heart had been strangely warmed by the powerful witness of Harry Denman.

—*Neil Heidrick*

On one occasion, Dr. Denman was seated on an airplane by a person who ordered an alcoholic drink. As usual, Dr. Denman engaged the man in conversation and got to talking about work. The man expressed surprise that Dr. Denman had had a drink. Dr. Denman explained that he was drinking ginger ale. The man said, "It looked just like mine." From that time on, Dr. Denman always ordered Coke so it was evident that it was not alcohol.

Soon after tourists could visit Russia, Dr. Denman and Dr. Potts began planning a trip to Russia. They had problems with the passports and visas. In order to speed up the process, I was sent to Washington, D.C., to personally deliver some documents. The big iron gates at the Russian Embassy were closed. I reached for the door and heard the electric locks being opened. I entered, stated my purpose, and asked for help. A staff person led me into a large, ornate area. A completely bare desk was in the center. After stating my purpose again and showing my documents, the staffer opened a drawer and brought out a telephone. I then talked to someone on the telephone, repeating my request. Whether I was talking to someone upstairs, in New York, or in Russia, I do not know. I made it very clear to everyone with whom I talked that Dr. Denman and Dr. Potts were going as tourists, not as evangelists. Finally I secured the visas.

They made the trip, staying two or three weeks. When they returned to America and had to pass through customs, Dr. Potts's baggage—his usual two bags plus camera bags—passed routinely. But customs would not believe Dr. Denman had been gone so long and only had one bag with not much in it. He must be smuggling something. They literally turned his briefcase inside out, almost tore it apart, but found nothing.

—*Brooks B. Little*

One of the unforgettable things about Harry was his love for children. When I was still pastor in Louisville, I went with him to the West Coast. We had to change trains in Omaha. He went up to the ticket counter and bought an insurance policy.

I said to him, "Why are you doing that? Have you no faith?"

He said, "I do this lots of times. I take out the policy in the name of some child I know and if the train wrecks some night, some child will have a better chance to go to school."

I was sitting at the table of a missionary in Fiji. They had a little eight-year-old girl. She asked me, "Do you know Uncle Harry?" He had been in their home a year or so ago and had been writing to her regularly.

—*Bishop Roy H. Short*

During my husband's stay in the hospital, Harry called Sam every week from wherever he was, and it meant a lot to Sam. Then when Sam died, he would call me every week and check on things—like the kind of locks I had on my doors, how my outdoor lighting was, and so on. This went on for four years until Kel and I married. When we became engaged, I called Harry to tell him about it, and we kept in touch with Harry.

—*Mary Gatewood Banks Kelley*

In the summer of 1968, I was a college student who spent the summer working at Lake Junaluska, North Carolina. My employment was at Lambuth Inn, where I served as a desk clerk, reservations clerk, and part-time bellboy. Dr. Denman arrived, and I was at the desk when he checked in. He requested room 203. I explained that we did have other nicer rooms in the hotel available. He quietly stated that room 203 would suit him just fine. I rang the bell to summon a bellboy to carry his luggage, but he promptly informed me that he had no luggage other than the briefcase he was carrying. Dr. Denman stayed with us at the hotel for two or three weeks, and he was probably the least demanding guest that I encountered that summer. In the years that have elapsed since 1968, I have done some lay speaking in The United Methodist Church, and I often use the story of Dr. Denman as an example of the humility for which we strive.

—*John J. Scott*

That night Dr. Denman's voice rang out from the tabernacle across the forest, echoing back to a hushed congregation. The spirit of God moved mightily. We knew we were in the presence of a man of God. The mussed hair, unpressed trousers—and at times spitting delivery—were unimportant! Here was one who had left all to follow Christ.

I had come to the camp with several suits, several pairs of shoes, many shirts. When the week ended, I wanted to give them all away; and from that time, things have never had the importance they had assumed in my young life.

—Joe Hale

I first met Harry Denman in 1948 when he came to Weatherford, Texas, for two days of meetings with pastors and laity. The superintendent went to meet him at the train. Harry got off on the opposite side of the train.

That night, as the superintendent explained to a packed audience that Harry, as he is called, did not arrive, Harry stood and said, "Here I am."

"Where have you been?" he was asked.

"Well, I just walked to the church and visited in homes along the way, asking people to pray for me. How many are here tonight that I visited this afternoon?"

"More than three dozen persons held up their hands. On the closing night, while people were praying at the altar, Harry quietly slipped out and took a train to Little Rock.

—Charles D. Whittle

A church conference was being held in Taejon, but Dr. Denman was more interested in visiting in Pusan, where he was to speak. I remained in Taejon, where I was attending the meeting while Dr. Denman was put on the train to Pusan. Mrs. Harper was to meet him at the station. Pusan station is the end of the line, so all the passengers alighted from the train there—all except Dr. Denman, who didn't get off with them. Thinking that he was still walking toward the front, Mrs. Harper walked along the side toward the back, looking in the windows as she made her way toward the end of the train. Still no Dr. Denman. So she boarded the train and started walking through the empty coaches toward the front of the train. She found all the coaches empty. The only thing she could do was to get off and try to learn what had happened to the foreigner who had boarded the train in Taejon. As soon as she alighted, she saw a tall man looking a bit bewildered. He was surrounded by a host of curious Koreans. Dr. Denman didn't know one word of the Korean language: no wonder he had a bewildered expression. That expression disappeared the moment he saw Elva. With a glad smile he said, "Daughter, am I glad to see you!"

—*Charles H. Harper*

Part Two

WRITINGS

INTRODUCTION

In the following pages, we have edited a representative sampling of the writings of Harry Denman, quite different from the collection of meditations that Dr. Thomas F. Chilcote, Jr., has put together in the final section of this anniversary tribute.

The ten articles, which Brother Harry wrote, appeared in various publications. These are followed by salient portions of ten annual reports or promotional letters that Harry Denman prepared. And then ten sermons illustrate in a number of ways the evangelistic zeal that this prophet of Christ so completely exemplified.

When all is said and done, Harry Denman really was a man with only one message, and that was the validity and vitality of evangelism as the sharing of the good news of the new life in Jesus Christ and a call to all persons to follow Christ as Lord and Savior.

This is true of reports and articles as much as it is of the sermons.

These thirty presentations contain nothing profound or earth-shattering. They are biblically based and easy to understand. But they contain in one form or another the essential truths of the Christian evangel, and they communicate accurately the passion of this twentieth-century prophet for the souls and hearts and minds of people.

—Robert F. Lundy

ARTICLES

The first article appeared in the *Alabama Christian Advocate*, Harry Denman's home annual conference periodical. It defines what an evangelistic church is.

The second and third articles appeared in *Together* magazine. They are explications of John Wesley's experience at Aldersgate Street in London and the centrality of prayer for the Christian life.

Then follows a series of articles, all of which appeared in *Shepherds*, a journal published from 1944 to 1956 by the General Board of Evangelism for pastors of The Methodist Church. It was discontinued by decision of the 1956 General Conference of the denomination, which established one magazine, *Together*, with the understanding that the news and concerns of all the boards and agencies would be carried in this single publication.

These seven articles are presented in the chronological order in which they were published.

What Is an Evangelistic Church?
by Harry Denman

At the annual meeting of the council on World Service and Finance last September, I was making a report for the Board of Evangelism. When I finished, a member asked, "Why are some Methodist churches evangelistic and others not?"

My reply to the questioner was that it was a theological problem. Some churches believe that every person needs Christ as a Savior, and they go out to tell the good news of the gospel. With our lips we say we believe. We profess that our main business is to help Christ seek and save the lost. But we do not perform.

Some Methodist churches believe that the "good tidings of great joy shall be to all people." Some believe that "God so loved the world." They believe that God loves the inner city as much as suburbia. They believe that God loves the people who live in houses with three and four bedrooms and two baths as much as he does those who live in low-price rooming houses and use a public bath.

It is easy to place a beautiful cross on the altar, but when we do we are saying that we believe Christ lived and died for every person. Our behavior must represent a belief of that kind. We must go to seek the lost.

You say, "Persons are lost today?" Yes, they are lost in themselves. They are lost in pleasure. They are lost in business. They are lost in racial prejudice. They are lost in nationalism and provincialism. They are lost in the business of making money.

Men, women, and youth are lost today. They are lost in their wealth, in poverty, in keeping up with the Joneses.

Others are lost in scholarship and literacy. They are lost in commercial organizations, civic and social clubs, fraternities, sororities, unions—and many other organizations.

They are so busy with many legitimate causes that they do not have time for God and for the enrichment of their own souls.

Our government has a propaganda movement called the "Voice of America." We are so busy telling the world about the wonder of the United States that we do not hear the voice of God.

The United States needs an Ear of America. We need to hear the voice of God in our public and private sanctuaries. We need to hear about the wonders of other nations of the world. We need to hear the cry of those who desire freedom from colonialism.

Jesus put it rather bluntly: "And why call ye me, Lord, Lord, and do not the things which I say?" What did he say? "The Son of man is come to seek and to save that which was lost." "Go ye therefore, and teach all nations, baptizing them in the name of the Father, and of the Son, and of the Holy Ghost: Teaching them to observe all things whatsoever I have commanded you: and, lo, I am with you alway, even unto the end of the world." He said, "Come—Tarry—Go."

The evangelistic church will have a concern for persons. Some churches have spent large sums of money to make their property beautiful and commodious, while near them are persons who do not have churches or a church building.

Other churches have made their buildings beautiful, commodious, and comfortable for themselves but have also had a concern for other persons and therefore have furnished members and money for the purpose of starting new churches in unchurched communities.

Those churches having concern for other persons and communities will help to make this nation a Christian nation, for today our great need is for more units of operation. I believe that all Methodist churches should be evangelistic. Some have said that there are no unchurched or unconverted persons in their communities; but when we have gone out to visit from house to house, we have found many who did not belong to Christ and the church.

What they meant was that there were not any persons of the kind they wanted for their churches. Jesus never saw caste—he saw persons. He never saw color—he saw persons. He never saw property—he saw persons. He never saw an institution—he saw persons.

The evangelistic church will serve as Christ served. It will love as he loved. It will lose its life as he lost his life. It will worship and witness to all persons as he worshiped and witnessed to all persons.

An evangelistic church is one that believes in God and believes that every person needs to be reconciled to God through Jesus Christ.

—Alabama Christian Advocate

What Aldersgate Means to Me
by Harry Denman

Several years ago, when a man asked me, "What happened to John Wesley at Aldersgate?" I prayed for help before answering. The Lord did help me. I quoted Wesley's own words from his *Journal*:

"I felt my heart strangely warmed. I felt I did trust in Christ, Christ alone for salvation, and an assurance was given me that he had taken away *my* sins, even *mine*, and saved *me* from the law of sin and death."

Now the editor of *Together* has asked me: "What does Aldersgate mean to you?" I have prayed, and I know the Lord is helping me to answer.

At Aldersgate, John Wesley received the assurance of salvation. He knew Christ as his *personal* Savior, and he knew that he knew it. For thirteen years he had searched for this assurance. He was a good churchman. He had daily, disciplined devotional habits. He was a scholar. He had a concern for persons because we read of his humanitarian ministry. He was a missionary to the Indians in Georgia. He knew Christ was the Savior of the world.

When A.G. Spangenberg, the Moravian preacher in Georgia, asked Wesley, "Do you know Jesus Christ?" he replied, "I know he is the Savior of the world." But the questioner persisted, "True, but do you know he has saved you?" Wesley replied, "I hope he has died to save me." The Aldersgate experience was yet to come.

Back in London, he tried to find salvation in Christ by reasoning with Peter Böhler. (Susanna Wesley had testified how her son John liked to reason.) However, at Aldersgate he finally found salvation in Christ by a simple faith which he felt. This came from the heart and not from the mind.

He became an "in Christ" person rather than an "in scholarship" person. Christ thereafter used the mind and the knowledge of John Wesley as never before.

He became an "in Christ" person rather than an "in church" person. Christ used him to try to bring a new birth to the church of which he was a priest, but when he was resisted by this fellowship, a new movement, which was to become a new church, was born.

He became an "in Christ" person rather than an "in social reform" person, but Christ used him as never before to reform the nation and the new continent on which it was loosed.

We, as Methodists, need to be "in Christ" persons instead of "in church" persons. The church is more than a club for the payment of dues, for faithful attendance at worship service, and for faithful committee work. The church is more than this. It is the living Christ incarnated in persons who are his body and his voice in the sin-sick world—a world which needs reformation but cannot be reformed except by persons regenerated through the grace of God.

After Aldersgate, John Wesley began making Christ known to others. Previously, he held to the attitude expressed in these words: "I should have thought the saving of souls almost a sin, if it had not been done in a church." But after hearing Whitefield[1] preach in the fields his attitude quickly changed. As he says, "I submitted to be more vile." Wesley preached Christ to people wherever he found them. As he wrote many times, "I gave them Christ. I gave them Christ."

Prior to Aldersgate, Wesley had gone to Georgia as a missionary. Full of concern for persons, he went to them. After Aldersgate, Christ in John Wesley went to the unwanted, the unloved, and the neglected of the eighteenth century. He was the voice of Christ with a love message for *all* persons. He was the body of Christ with his concern and compassion for *all* persons.

His lay preachers came to the new continent to make Christ known on the American frontier. They did it with their lives and their lips.

Today America is a frontier nation of cities and suburbs needing Christ. We have the inner city with its high-priced apartment dweller and tenement-house resident, with its minority groups of different races, languages, and nationalities. Suburbia is a frontier whose inhabitants are saturated with things. It is hard for them to be dominated by the spiritual when material things are in such abundance. We need "in Christ" persons to make the Savior known in both frontier places.

Methodism needs an Aldersgate. Methodism needs to know Christ as Savior. We know him as a man, we know him as a prophet, we know him as a teacher; but we must know him as the Savior of *all* persons.

Wesley had something to give to persons, something more than an institution, more than money, more than prestige or knowledge. He had a person—the Christ as a loving Savior—to give. He could say what Simon Peter said to the lame beggar at the gate of the Temple: "I give you what I have."

If all we have is a pulpiteer, then that is all we can give. If all we have is a building, then that is all we can give. If we have a Savior and we know that our sins are forgiven, then we can give other persons a Savior who forgives, who redeems, and who reconciles.

Wesley, after Aldersgate, made Christ known to the social order of his day. He had a concern for the children of the streets who needed to know about Christ. He was against the evils that destroyed or harmed personality.

Methodism's founder preached and lived not a slanted gospel but the gospel of redemption. He knew that a new person in Christ becomes a new person in all relationships. A changed person changes society. The social order is not changed by resolutions but by "in Christ" persons who live revolutionary lives.

People of the twentieth century need Christ as much as the people of the eighteenth century needed him. All areas of life—economic, financial, educational, ecclesiastical, political, recreational, and family—need to know Christ as Savior. This is easy to write or say, but it is difficult to do.

Christ is made known by the performance, by the behavior, and by the deeds of his disciples.

We are thankful for the men, women, and youth who have become or will become "in Christ" persons by having the assurance of Christ as their personal Savior.

Let us pray that the followers of John Wesley will experience a "heart-warming" conversion and will come to know Christ as their Savior as Wesley did at Aldersgate.

—*Together*, May 1963

[1]For the story of this early Methodist preacher and his influence on English and American Methodism, see "Eloquent George Whitefield," *Together*, March, page 28.—EDITORS.

WHAT PRAYER MEANS TO ME
BY HARRY DENMAN

Prayer is my way of thanking God for his goodness, his mercy, and his love. What a blessed experience it is to praise him for creating me, for redeeming me, for filling me with himself!

That, in simplest terms, is what prayer means to me. But I also have more particular reasons for, and satisfactions from, prayer.

I pray because I need the strength of faith to forgive those who have sinned against me. Only after I have forgiven them can I pray for forgiveness of my own sins. And only when I have sincerely repented do I feel that I am no longer separated from God but in fellowship with him.

Prayer enables me to have fellowship with others. It changes my attitude toward them. I used to criticize bishops, superintendents, and other officers of the church. Now that I pray for them daily, I love and defend them.

Some have laughed because I pray by name. I like to think that this method identifies persons whom God knows and I know. I pray daily for each bishop of The Methodist Church. I pray, too, for members of the many prayer groups which have extended to me the privilege of membership. I cannot meet face to face with them daily, so I take lists of their names and remember them in my prayers.

I pray also for many who are not aware that I do. Some live next door; others are thousands of miles away in remote parts of the world. My prayer is that God will give them my love and will care for them.

Through prayer I am able to have fellowship with scores of the world's rulers every day. Often I cannot agree with them, but I desire that they listen to the voice of God rather than the voices of political parties and of people. I have fellowship, too, with those who no longer live in the flesh. I ask God to care for them until Resurrection morning.

I pray for those who labor for God. The Methodist Church needs preachers, missionaries, other full-time workers. God will call them if I ask. But most of all—more than financial, numerical, and organizational influence—my church needs spiritual power. I pray for this.

My greatest joy in prayer comes when I intercede for those who request prayer for themselves or for others who are sick of soul, body, and mind. What a joy to know that our loving Father hears and answers every prayer with a yes, a no, or a wait!

Prayer is an agonizing experience, for it involves a willingness and a commitment to do God's will. It is not easy to give all of one's self to Christ. But I am ambitious for Christ to be on the throne of my life.

I ask you to pray for Harry Denman, a sinner who wants to be filled with the Holy Spirit, to be God's man and a servant of the Lord Jesus Christ.

—*Together*, April 1959

TO BELIEVE IS TO BEGIN
BY HARRY DENMAN

Jesus was a believer. When Jesus was dying on the cross, the chief priests, the elders, and scribes who were instrumental in having him crucified, said, "He trusted in God." What a great tribute to come from one's enemies!

Jesus did not trust in self-righteousness as did the Pharisees. Jesus, when called "Good Master" by the rich young ruler, replied "None is good, save one, that is God." Jesus spoke a parable "unto certain which trusted in themselves that they were righteous, and despised others." He told about a Pharisee who commended himself to God in comparison to a publican. When you trust your righteousness you exalt yourself, and Jesus said everyone who does that will be abased. Jesus did not trust in his righteousness; he trusted in God. When he was dying on the cross the centurion, who was in charge of putting Jesus to death, glorified God and said, "Certainly this was a righteous man."

Jesus trusted in God to the extent that God could give him the words to speak and could do his works through him. This is what Jesus said to his disciples in John 14:10-11: "Believest thou not that I am in the Father, and the Father in me? the words that I speak unto you I speak not of myself: but the Father that dwelleth in me, he doeth the works. Believe me that I am in the Father, and the Father in me: or else believe me for the very works' sake." Because Jesus trusted in God, "he began both to do and to teach." What did He begin to do?

The Time Is Fulfilled

He "came into Galilee, preaching the gospel of the king-dom of God, and saying, The time is fulfilled, and the king-dom of God is at hand: repent ye, and believe the gospel. . . . He saw Simon and Andrew his brother casting a net into the sea: for they were fishers. And Jesus said unto them, Come ye after me, and I will make you to become fishers of men."

Jesus came preaching the gospel to the poor. He se-cured disciples from Galilee, out of which no prophet came, according to the Sanhedrin. He healed those who had suffi-cient faith. He healed the brokenhearted. He went about doing good. He thought more of persons than he did of property. He was more interested in the inner life of people than he was in institutions. He believed his Father's house was a place of prayer rather than a place of profits. Prayer meant more to him than the making of profits from the poor. He loved all persons—the publicans, the Pharisees, the poor, the rich, the holy, the harlots, the sinners, the Sanhedrin, the thieves and the tax collectors, the centurion and the children, the lepers and the licentious, the blind and the beggars, the selfish and the sick, the Sadducees and the Samaritans. He loved his enemies and his betrayers, his persecutors and his providers. He trusted in God. He loved all the children of God regardless of their class or caste.

He Taught with His Life

Because of what "he began to do," he could teach with authority and not as the scribes and elders. The sinners and publicans drew near to hear him. He taught with his life before he taught with his lips.

When death faced him, he could pray to his Father whom he trusted, "Not my will, but thine." On the cross he prayed, "Father, I trust my spirit to thy hands" (Luke 23:46, MOFFATT). In the upper room Jesus said to his disciples, "He that believeth on me, the works that I do shall he do also; and greater works than these shall he do; because I go to my Father. . . . If a man love me, he will keep my words: and my

Father will love him, and we will come unto him, and make our abode with him." "I am the vine, ye are the branches. He that abideth in me, and I in him, the same bringeth forth much fruit: for without me ye can do nothing."

After the ascension of Jesus, the disciples believed in Jesus and began to do what he commanded them. They went to the upper room and prayed with one accord for ten days. On the day of Pentecost, they were sitting in a house, and they all were filled with the Holy Ghost and began to speak. They preached this Jesus "whom ye crucified, . . . whom God hath raised up, having loosed the pains of death." He is the Christ. He is alive. We are his witnesses. "Repent, and be baptized."

They began to heal in the name of Jesus. They began to secure disciples. They began to teach with their lives and lips. They began to be obedient to God rather than the Sanhedrin. They began to be stoned, imprisoned, beaten, and crucified. They began to preach everywhere to all persons, the Sanhedrin and the Samaritans, those in Jerusalem and those in the uttermost parts of the world.

They believed in a living Christ, and they began to proclaim that he was alive. They abided in Christ, and He abided in them. Their enemies perceived that they had been with Jesus. In Antioch they were called Christians, followers of Christ.

The living Christ did greater works through them than God had done through him in the flesh. Thousands were baptized. Persons were healed, even as Peter passed by. The living Christ lived in them as they went everywhere telling that he was alive and calling all to repentance.

Bear Fruit Today

Karl Marx is dead. Christ is living today. Many give their all to the philosophy of Karl Marx. We must believe more in our living Christ than they do in their faith. We must love the living Christ and obey his words; and he will abide in us, and we will abide in him; and there will be much fruit. The living Christ needs branches in every community. Will you be a branch? Believe in him, and begin today to bear fruit.

The disciples of secularism are dedicated to more profits and more pleasure. Let the disciples of the living Christ dedicate themselves wholly to him. He will fill them with the Holy Spirit, and they can begin to do what he did. The living Christ needs flesh. Paul said, "Christ liveth in me." Today we need men and women to be crucified with Christ and let the living Christ live in them.

We Can Begin

When this is done, the twentieth century will have a greater evangelistic movement than the first and second centuries. We can have it. First, let us go to the upper room and stay until we know that Jesus is the Christ and that he is living; and then begin to tell it with our lives and lips, regardless of any suffering that will have to be endured. If we are crucified with Christ, nothing can hurt our bodies. We will be filled with the Holy Spirit, and we can *begin*.

Dr. Paul Hutchinson, editor of *The Christian Century*, speaking at the Methodist Ecumenical Conference held in Springfield, Massachusetts, said that [humanity] has lost faith in science, self, and the state; and that we must have a Savior. Thank God we have one; we have a Savior, and He is alive.

Let us so live that persons will say of us, "They trust in Christ." Then we can say Christ doeth the works.

—*Shepherds*, October 1949

The Home—The School of Christ
by Harry Denman

We heard a speaker say to an audience, "Many of you say you do not believe in mass evangelism because you think there may be some emotionalism. You are entitled to that belief. But do you believe and practice parental evangelism?" You can win your child for Christ and the church easier than anyone because your child believes in you. The parent is the child's first teacher. Why should you not be the child's first evangelist?

Your child is getting some kind of religion from you. It may be secularism. It may be communism. It may be atheism. It may be Christianity. Why not have your child make a definite commitment to the religion that you are teaching by precept and example?

If you are a follower of the living Christ and belong to the church, why not have the child, at the proper time as the result of your teaching, make a definite commitment for Christ? You as the parent can guide his or her emotions to act as you think best.

Some persons ridiculed Decision Day in the Sunday school because they said there was too much mob psychology: the children were following a crowd and did not know what they were doing.

When a mother and father, after years of praying, teaching with lips, and life, come to the time when they think their child should make a commitment to Christ, all they have to do is to have a talk with the child, without undue emotion, without a mob, but just a family gathering. The person of the living Christ can be presented to the child, and he or she can make his or her decision for Christ in the most sacred group in the world, the family.

If you need the help of the minister, invite him or her to aid and to make suggestions.

Parents can win their children for Christ and the church easier than the church school teacher or the pastor. The child knows of his parents' great care and concern for him or her in regard to body, mind, and social life. The child knows all the time and training that has been bestowed upon him or her. Naturally a child would expect parental concern about his or her spiritual life. The child would expect them to give as much time and thought to the development of his or her spiritual life as they do to the physical, mental, and social life.

The Supreme Court of the United States has ruled that religion cannot be taught in the public school system of this nation. Therefore, it must be taught in the home and the church. In this secular age, the church has very little of the child's time. Therefore, whatever the child knows of Christ must be taught by the parents and caught from them because they know, love, and obey Christ.

Fathers and mothers teach children to eat, to walk, to talk, to obey, to read, to spell, to write, to play, to dress themselves, to be polite, to be honest; why not teach them faith in God through Christ? Why not teach them to pray, to read the Bible, to do good, to love, to give, to worship God at home and at church? Why not guide them in living as Christ would have them live and listen and obey his voice?

If the living Christ is to advance, he must do it through the flesh of parents. There are 32 million children under 12 years of age in this nation. Will they be Christians or communists, secularists or pagans? It depends on their parents who are teaching them daily with their lives and lips. Will they be alcoholics and slaves to tobacco? To a large extent, it depends on their parents.

We are concerned that the children in our homes have the right kind of food diet. Also, we are trying to eliminate from our schools any who would teach anything that pertains to communism. We do not want the church-school literature to hint of socialism. But what are we doing as parents to feed the children in the home a spiritual diet? Physical bodies must have bread if they are to grow. Spiritual lives must have the manna of God if they are to develop. The bodies and minds of our children are well-fed, but how about their souls? Are they getting spiritual food or chaff? They learn at the motion picture house; they learn from the radio and from television. They are taught by the comics. They learn on the playground. What do they get from their parents besides food for their bodies, clothes for their bodies, shelter for their bodies?

We need parents who will become evangelists for the living Christ. The parents of America, not the preachers, can make this nation a Christian one.

The teachers in the homes, the teachers in the school, can save the nation for God and democracy.

We used to say that the hand that rocks the cradle rules the world. We may not have a cradle, but we still have the child.

The other day on a train the writer heard a little boy talking to his mother. She was pointing out to him some extraordinary sight, and quick as a flash, the little fellow said, "I bet my daddy could do it." Of course, his daddy could. His daddy can do anything that needs to be done. We believe his daddy can teach him about Christ.

Let us make the homes of America schools for Christ. If we do, our public schools will be better, and our church schools will do greater spiritual work. We need teachers for the school of Christ. We have them. We believe the mothers and fathers of this nation will consecrate themselves to be teachers in the school of Christ.

—*Shepherds*, February 1950

The Challenge of a New Half-Century
by Harry Denman

December 31 is the last day and the last Sunday in the current year. It is also the last day and the last Sunday of the first fifty years of this century. With January 1 the last fifty years of the century will begin.

December 31 can and should be a day of thanksgiving and dedication. We can thank our heavenly Father for all the material and spiritual blessings of the last half-century and dedicate ourselves to the task of seeing that as individual members of this nation we grow richer in spiritual resources than in material resources.

If we compare 1900 with 1950, we will see that we have accomplished more in the field of science than we have in the field of the spirit. In 1900 our theology was better than our technology. In 1950 the reverse is true.

Increasingly in the past fifty years we have given time to gadgets that would relieve us from drudgery only to release ourselves from the discipline of the spirit. Today we have the gadgets. We work only half the time that we did in 1900, but our leisure has been given to the dissipation of the flesh rather than to the discipline of the spirit. As we enter the last half of this century, let us determine that our time will be given to the cultivation of the mind and the soul. We are rich in the material; let us become rich in the spiritual. Let us determine to know God better than we know how to accumulate gold. Let us determine to know Christ as our Redeemer and Savior and to know him better than we know the art of recreation. Let us determine to make December 31 a day for the Holy Spirit to empower us rather than a day when we will be

137

possessed of unholy spirits. What can we do to make Sunday, December 31, 1950, a holy day?

1. All Christian families and individuals can have a worship service in their homes early Sunday morning. Not all worship services have to be held in the church sanctuary. We need more worship services in the sanctuary of the home. We believe in the priesthood of believers. Families or individuals can use their regular devotional book; or they can use special devotions prepared for this purpose; or they can sing a hymn, read from God's book, and pray.

Every family and individual should be praying for peace and spiritual power in order that this civilization will be worth saving.

2. Some churches will desire to have a Communion breakfast for men and boys. College and university students will be home for the holidays. Many young people from the military camps will be home. Some will be leaving for military camps. Why not have a Communion breakfast for men and boys? Let fathers and sons have the fellowship of kneeling at the altar of the church for the purpose of dedicating themselves to Christ and his church.

3. Special emphasis should be given to this day in the Sunday school. The young people home from college and military camps should be recognized. Someone should tell about the Sunday school of 1900, which consisted mainly of a primary class and a boys' and girls' class. The youth and adult movements have been born in these last fifty years. Also, relate the progress that has been made in making the Sunday school an educational institution by the increase in curricula and training for teachers. Then the members of the Sunday school should dedicate themselves to making it a great evangelistic agency of the church during the next fifty years by each one's reaching one each week for Christ and the church.

4. The Sunday morning worship service can be a time for thanksgiving and dedication. The sacrament of the Lord's Supper can be observed. Some churches will use this Sunday as a time for the members of the church to make a covenant

with God to try to win at least one person for Christ and the church between that day and Easter Sunday, March 25, 1951.

What would happen to this nation and to the kingdom, if 10,000,000 Protestants would go out from this service on December 31 determined to win some by being winsome for Christ!

Millions in America are waiting for some consecrated Christian to tell the good news that Christ is alive and will save to the uttermost if persons will repent and believe. The Sunday morning worship service should be a memorable day in all our churches.

Because it is the last day of the year and of the first half of the century, Sunday afternoon will be a good time to visit the unchurched. Many persons will be thinking of changing their way of life. The Holy Spirit is working on America. This will be a good time, psychologically, to secure commitments. If we can get 100,000 churches to make evangelistic visits, we will win 1,000,000 persons for Christ and his church on the last day of the year.

In what better way can church members spend the afternoon or evening than by making evangelistic visits? There are young couples in every community who would be glad for the ambassadors of Christ and the church to visit them.

Early Sunday evening can be used for great evangelistic services in every church. Why should churches be closed while taverns and night clubs are open to celebrate the closing of the year? Every church in America should be open.

There can be a time for fellowship for young and old, either before or immediately following the evening evangelistic service. Sunday night should be a time when we proclaim the living Christ and his power to save this civilization from destruction. We need to preach that Christ and his kingdom are more powerful than communism. Closed churches on Sunday night mean that communism and secularism have a better chance to capture this nation.

Late Sunday night, from 10:30 or 11:00 until midnight, there should be in every church a large group of members on their knees praying for our world and our churches. This can be called a New Life Service. As we come to the new 50 years of this century we need to find new life in Christ in order that this nation will become a Christian nation. We need to be praying that we will have a world revival instead of a world war. Let us pray that youth will become soldiers of the cross and overcome atheistic communism. Let us pray that our wealth and incomes will be dedicated to Christ's cause rather than to military causes.

Let us make December 31 a holy day with many spiritual activities. The church can be kept open all day for prayer and communion with our living Christ. Spiritual visits can be made to jails, institutions, hospitals. Services can be held over the radio and on the streets.

Let us determine that American Protestantism shall take the gospel of Christ in absolute earnestness to every person in America. We believe that a great revival of Christianity can begin on December 31 and that it will sweep on for the next fifty years.

Let us believe;
Let us witness;
Let us pray;
Let us work;
Let us give;
Let us praise.

—*Shepherds*, December 1950

Prayer... and the Power That Redeems
by Harry Denman

Since Christmas the newspapers have been telling us how some Americans commemorated the birth of Jesus Christ our Savior.

Mr. Westbrook Pegler says, "That night (Christmas), in New York, in the 50s and along Park, Madison and 5th avenues, and Lexington and 3rd as well, young men and women were reeling drunk, squawking and vomiting in a horrifying spectacle while the pictures were still trickling into our papers of American corpses rolled aside on a Korean road and of American soldiers, with their little carbines at the ready, warily treading their way of sorrow with ghastly expressions on their tired faces."

Listen to George E. Sokolsky:

"I had a very difficult time getting a taxi, and upon inquiry I discovered that on the eve of Christmas many taxi drivers take to the garages when the Christmas office parties break up. They don't like the drunks, particularly drunken women, who dirty their cabs and sometimes leave without paying. They also dislike quarrelsome men who forget where they live.

"Now, that is in New York and I suppose other large cities, but it is not Christmas. The office party has become a pollution of Christmas, a pagan revival of the feast to Bacchus. It may bore you to be reminded of high purposes, but the madness of the 1920s will surely die in the 1950s.

"You say, let's have fun while we can! It is not a question of fun; it is a question of a lost horizon, of a nation that is suffering its first great military defeat and does not recognize it or its consequences.

"Those sons of ours who lie in the Korean snows have as much right as we have to fun and life, to homes and little children. Think of them sometimes. Each one of them might have been you or your son or your youngest daughter's husband.

"They are entitled to be mourned, if not in deep sorrow, surely in the resolve that they shall not have thrown their young lives into the Korean snow for nothing.

"Christmas is a religious holiday with overtones of feeling even for those who are not Christians. It is a joyous but not a raucous holiday. It is a festival but not a debauch. It is a gift-giving time but not a gargantuan madness. It is a glorification of the ideals of love and peace, not of license and lewdness. It is the holiday of children in families."

The newspapers told us of the large number of persons in America who were killed on Christmas Day, not by an atom bomb, but by persons who thought that gasoline in the car and alcohol in the driver made a good combination—but they found to their sorrow that they do not.

Some newspapermen called it "our Black Christmas." We can thank our heavenly Father that not all Americans made Christmas a drunken debauch. Some went to church to pray. Some worshiped Christ at home in family services.

The bishops of our church have called us to prayer.

It is time for us to pray. We need to pray in our homes, in our offices, in our manufacturing plants, in our stores, and in our churches. We need to pray for forgiveness for trusting in gold instead of God, for having more faith in self than in our Savior, and for indulging in the unholy things of life more than obeying the Holy Spirit in our daily living.

We need to leave the far country of living as swine and come back to the fellowship of our Father's house. We need to confess to him that we have sinned and are not worthy to be his child. We need forgiveness. We need faith, and we need to become a force for righteousness.

We need to be cleansed. We need to consecrate ourselves to Christ, and we need to be concerned about every person.

All of this will happen if we become a praying nation. Those who pray have forgiveness, faith, and force. Those who pray are cleansed, consecrated, concerned, and courageous.

The person whose trust is not stayed in God is full of fear. Today we are full of fear. Why? We have quit praying.

The early church could defy the Sanhedrin because its faith was in God, and it was a praying church.

Luther could defy a decadent church because his faith was in God, and he prayed many hours each day.

The army of American colonies could defy the armies of England because we had a praying general.

A praying nation is a nation of faith. A praying family is a family of faith. A praying church is a church of faith and action. A praying individual is a person of faith and force.

Let us become men and women of prayer.

Jesus had great faith because he prayed. Jesus was a person of action because of his faith. Let us be like our Christ.

—*Shepherds*, March 1951

The Hour Is Come
by Harry Denman

Philip and Andrew came to Jesus in Jerusalem and told him that certain Greeks desired to see him. This took place after the triumphal entry and the cleansing of the temple. Jesus replied, "The hour is come, that the Son of man should be glorified." The long-expected hour had arrived.

The Hour of Opposition

That was his hour of opposition. His opponents were becoming vocal. The shadow of the cross had disappeared, and he was facing the prospect of actual death.

This is our hour of opposition. On every side, the church is being attacked. Liquor dealers and beer barons are trying to make this nation—including our soldiers—a drunken nation. Gambling syndicates are trying to prostitute this nation for their own interests. Pseudo-statesmen are creating racial prejudice. Some of our members who wish to live according to Christ and the Sermon on the Mount are being vilified by those who wish to make the church the agent of the "ism" to which they subscribe. All over the world atheistic communism is trying to build a new order by attacking Christ and his church, while secularism with its belief in pleasure and profits strikes at the heart of our faith in a living God.

There are those who sincerely believe that might, rather than the meekness of the Prince of Peace, will prevent war.

This is our hour of opposition. The church of the twentieth century will face it as did our Christ and his church of the first century.

The church of the first century was opposed by the

Sanhedrin and by the Roman Empire. Christians were imprisoned, beaten, stoned, persecuted, and put to death; but the gates of hell did not prevail. The church of the living Christ conquered the Sanhedrin and the Roman Empire. The church of the living Christ was at its best during those 300 years of persecution. Today, the church of the living Christ is going to face its opposition with high courage. We do not have a dead Christ but a living Christ. His church is not the agent of any "ism."

The Hour of Obligation

That was the hour of obligation for Jesus. He said, "Now is my soul troubled; and what shall I say? Father, save me from this hour: but for this cause came I unto this hour." He had come for such an hour. And he was going to be true to that obligation. He was going to obey his Father because of his great faith in him. He commissioned his church to go as he had gone. "As my Father hath sent me, even so send I you."

This is the hour of obligation for the church of the twentieth century to live as he lived. We must be Christlike. This is our hour of obligation to serve and to have mercy on all those who are needy; regardless of their creed, their color, or their nationality.

What a great hour for the church to show its obligation to all persons of the world by being a neighbor and a servant! We are obligated to be concerned about the spiritual, the physical, the political, the economic, and the mental welfare of every person in the world.

What an obligation—what an hour!

The Hour of Opportunity

That was the hour of opportunity for Christ. He had wept over the city. He had seen the multitudes and had compassion on them. He had fed them. He had taught them. His compassion had led him to do this. But would he die for them? Yes. He was going to make the supreme sacrifice for the body-hungry and soul-hungry multitude.

This is the hour of opportunity for his church. Today, multitudes throughout the world are hungry for bread for their bodies. But also, multitudes throughout the world are hungry for the heavenly manna for their souls. Today in America, we face hundreds of communities that need churches. We have thousands of communities that need additional churches. Will we be true to this hour? Will we make the necessary sacrifices?

Thirty-two million children under twelve years of age in America will either grow to youth believing in Christ and his church or will become devotees of secularism or communism.

We salute the Board of Education for its program of evangelism in the local church school and on the campus. What a force for evangelism if every teacher in our local church schools and colleges would become a personal worker for Christ! We praise God for those teachers and members of adult classes who are evangelistic visitors.

Millions of young adults should be won for Christ and his church. There are sufficient laypersons who can be trained to win these for Christ. Will we make the sacrifice?

Dr. Arthur Compton, in an article published in *The American Magazine* for October, says, "There was never a time in the history of the world when religion was more necessary than it is today." He points out that because of our scientific and urban life, we need practical Christianity.

Because of migration in America we are losing thousands of our Negro members. The Roman Catholic Church has a great program to win the Negro and those who live in rural areas. Our church must go into evangelistic action to win the Negro and rural America. We have a program of evangelism that will take us to every person in America. This is our visitation program. With this program new churches can be organized with a hundred charter members within one week. They can become self-supporting in one or two years. We have the know-how. Let us go into action in every city, county seat, town, and village in America. Let us proclaim Christ to every person.

Another great opportunity is to win the family for Christ and his church. We know that Family Visitation Evangelism can win entire families for Christ and the church. Not only must the family be won for Christ, but the family must be taught the importance of daily family worship. We believe that it is more important for our soldiers to have a copy of *The Upper Room* than to have a can of beer. The family must become a Christian unit, or this nation will go the way of all the nations that have forgotten God.

We have the greatest evangelistic opportunity that we have ever had. America is yearning for a mass movement. Wherever certain evangelists hold services, thousands attend their meetings. The Holy Spirit is working on this nation. We believe that God is giving America another chance. Evangelistic visitors who go into homes are usually met with these words: "We have been thinking about this matter. We are glad you came."

This is the hour of opportunity to win children, youth, young adults, and families for Christ by all methods of evangelism.

The Hour of Operations

This is the hour of great evangelistic operations. Jesus had a worldwide program of evangelism: "Go ye therefore, and teach all nations." John Wesley had a worldwide program of evangelism: "The world is my parish."

Under the leadership of Bishop Fred P. Corson and the district superintendents of the Philadelphia and New Jersey Conferences, we held a great United Evangelistic Mission. A movement was born. Since then United Evangelistic Missions have been held in the Peninsula Conference, the Kansas-Nebraska Area, the Syracuse Area, the Des Moines Area, the Wyoming Conference, the state of Arizona, and Metropolitan Baltimore. All of these enterprises were held under the auspices of the presiding bishops and the district superintendents. Fifty-nine districts and 2,965 charges were involved.

A United Evangelistic Mission uses all methods of

evangelism. All the churches of an area, conference, or district participate in it. It is a combination of Pulpit, Visitation, Public, and Educational Evangelism. The purpose of a United Evangelistic Mission is to get each new convert to be an active member of the church school, the MYF, the Women's Society of Christian Service, or the Men's Club and to worship regularly in the home and in the church. We thank our heavenly Father that The Methodist Church is in action for Christ and his church.

Also we asked every church to have a week of visitation evangelism at the beginning of the Advent Season. We wanted thousands of new converts to give themselves to Christ and unite with the church on Christmas Sunday. We wanted Christmas to be a Christian festival rather than a commercial fair. We want every church to participate in the National Week of Visitation Evangelism under the leadership of the superintendent and hope that every district will have a week of simultaneous visitation. During that week we hope to secure 500,000 persons for Christ and the church. We want the Lenten Season to be the greatest in the history of The Methodist Church.

The opportunity grows greater all the time. This is a great hour.

The Hour of Optimism

For this hour we need the optimism of Jesus. He asked his Father to "glorify thy name." A voice from heaven said, "I have both glorified it, and will glorify it again." Jesus said, "And I, if I be lifted up from the earth, will draw all men unto me."

This is not bragging. This is holy optimism. We cannot face the hour of opposition, the hour of obligation, the hour of opportunity, and the hour of operation without the holy optimism of Christ. We need to lift him up with our lives and lips.

Many of us have lived the first fifty years of this century. The last fifty are going to be best in the realm of the spiritual. Our generation went to the far country of humanism; but today we are back in our Father's house. We are not worthy to be sons; but he had compassion on us and made us sons.

We went out into the far country of the sinking sands of liberalism; but today we are back in our Father's house, which is built on the fundamental rock of an everlasting faith in a loving God, who is our Creator, Redeemer, and Judge.

We went out to eat the food at the swine pen of secularism; but thank God, we are back in our Father's house, eating the fatted calf of the sacred and the spiritual that only He can give us.

We have learned to lift up Christ and his church in our Crusades and Advances. We know that, once he is lifted up, he will draw all unto him. If he is to be lifted up, he must live in us.

We need to make our entire consecration to the living Christ. He will baptize us with the Holy Spirit for the facing of this hour.

This can be Methodism's finest hour. It will be. The next fifty years are to be golden years for Christ and his church. Every fifty years The Methodist Church doubles its membership. We will do it the next half-century. Let us advance into this hour with prayer, faith, and complete sacrifice. For if we do, we will see a mighty spiritual awakening throughout the world.

> God of grace and God of glory,
> On thy people pour thy power;
> Crown thine ancient church's story;
> Bring her bud to glorious flower.
> Grant us wisdom, grant us courage,
> For the facing of this hour.
> For the facing of this hour.*

—*Shepherds*, January 1952

*From the hymn "God of Grace and God of Glory" by Harry Emerson Fosdick. Used by permission of Elinor Fosdick Downs.

Majoring in Evangelism
by Harry Denman

Many church bulletins are mailed to me. Not long ago I found one that has an interesting program for a downtown church:

Sunday
8:30 A.M. The Church in Worship
9:30 A.M. The Church in Study
10:45 A.M. The Church in Worship
6:15 P.M. The Church in Training
7:30 P.M. The Church in Evangelism

Wednesday
7:30 P.M. The Church in Prayer

Thursday
6:30 P.M. The Church in Visitation

This church believes in worship, study, evangelism, training, prayer, visitation, and fellowship. What I have listed is not the entire program of the church, but it is the regular weekly schedule.

Some churches limit their worship to one service per week. Some have two services. This church has two worship services on Sunday morning and a great evangelistic service on Sunday night. It does not neglect prayer, training, study, and visitation.

The following appeared on the back of a recent bulletin:

Why Should I Visit?

Visitation strengthens the home in which you visit. It brings into our church services new people who have the opportunity to hear the Word of God taught and preached.

Visitation is the most effective way of letting people know you are concerned about them.

Visitation brings a joy and fellowship that cannot be secured any other way.

Whom Should I Visit?

Visit that neighbor who recently moved into your neighborhood.

Visit that friend who is not attending any church or Sunday school.

Visit those you know who are sick.

Visit that absentee in your class.

When Should I Visit?

Visit this week, next week, and every week.

Visit Now!!!

Nearly all churches organize for study by having a church school. But only a few organize for weekly visitation in order to increase the attendance at the church school.

We believe that it is just as important to visit as it is to pray, to worship, to give, and to study. Suppose Jesus had given his ministry only to worship, study, and prayer. He would never have found Levi, Zacchaeus, James and John, Mary of Magdala, the man at the pool of Bethesda, or the man in Gadara. Jesus visited the neglected people of his day. Nicodemus came to see him. The nobleman came to see him. The Roman centurion came to see him. The rich ruler came to see him. But Jesus went to see the publicans, the Galileans, the Samaritans, and others.

Why do we major in worship or in study when Jesus majored in prayer and visitation? He sent the twelve out visiting. He sent the seventy out visiting.

The church that is concerned about persons will spend as much time in visiting as it does in praying or in studying.

Some churches spend more time in fellowship at supper than they do in fellowship with Christ at prayer. The church is a fellowship; and we need to make it a sacred, wholesome, creative fellowship. If the church is just a club, then it is not necessary to visit. Yet luncheon clubs visit their sick and absent members.

The following study on salesmanship shows the importance of visiting:

> 80 percent of all sales are made after the fifth call
> 48 percent of salesmen make one call and quit
> 25 percent make two calls and quit
> 12 percent make three calls and quit
> Only 10 percent keep on calling. These make 80 percent of the sales.

What is true for salesmanship is very true for evangelical Christianity. The Christian church is to reproduce Christ in the community. Let us reproduce *all* the activities of Christ.

—*Shepherds*, April 1955

What Is a Christian?

by Harry Denman

Almost any person will tell you that to be a Christian is to be like Jesus, our Christ. What did he do? *Jesus sought persons.* He left the synagogue to seek those who were unsought by the worshipers in the synagogue. He sought Levi, a publican, who collected taxes. Finding him at the tax table, Jesus said to him, "Follow me." And Levi did.

Jesus sought Zacchaeus. He found him up a tree. They went home together. The religious people murmured that Jesus had gone home with a sinner. Jesus said, "I am come to seek. . . ."

A Christian's Business

My business as a follower of Jesus is to seek the unsought, as he did. The unsought heard him gladly. They will hear us gladly as we seek them out and tell them about the love of Christ for every person.

In a small community a pastor's wife said to me, "The president of the Women's Society of Christian Service and I did something this afternoon that we have never done before." Immediately I asked, "What did you do?" She said, "We went to see the town prostitute. We told her that Christ loved her and that we loved her. As we talked to her, she sobbed her penitence and said she was tired of living as she did." These two women were seeking persons as Christ did. A Christian will seek persons to tell them the good news of the gospel of Christ.

A Christian will live so attractively that he will attract persons to Christ. She will be so winsome that she will win some for Christ. He will be so gracious to all persons that they will want the grace of God which enables him to live gracefully.

The self-righteous sought Jesus. Nicodemus, a ruler, visited Jesus at night and said, "Rabbi, we know that thou art a teacher come from God: for no man can do these miracles that thou doest, except God be with him." The rich ruler came to Jesus and said, "What shall I do to inherit eternal life?" A lawyer came to Jesus with the same question. Simon, the Pharisee, invited Jesus to have dinner in his house. The "sought" sought Jesus because he had life. Christians possess life. Others will seek them if they live differently from the world.

One night a lawyer and I visited a young man in his home to invite him to be a follower of Christ.

He said, "I have been thinking of visiting Mr. McNutt" (my teammate).

I said, "Why were you going to see Mr. McNutt? He is a lawyer."

The young man replied, "I want to be a Christian."

But I asked again, "Why were you going to see Mr. McNutt?"

He replied, "I want to be a Christian." Then he explained, "I lived next door to Mr. McNutt for three years. I know how he lives." This lawyer was saving a man for Christ by his daily, neighborly living.

A Christian lives as Christ lived. Persons come to Christians to find out what they have. A Christian is salt to save the individual and society. A Christian is light to persons in the darkness of sin and self. Jesus said, "I am come to seek and to save."

A Christian's Service

A Christian is a servant. Jesus took a towel to wash the feet of those who wanted place and position, of him who took a sword, and of him who took silver. The non-Christian thinks of self. The Christian thinks of others. A Christian would rather serve others than self.

The lawyer sought Jesus to find life. Jesus told him about the Samaritan who loved God with all his heart and whose heart was filled with compassion for a beaten and robbed man. This Samaritan loved God with all his mind, and his mind was on a neglected man. The Samaritan loved God with all his soul, was full of mercy for a friendless man. The

Samaritan loved God with all his strength, and his body was given to a man neglected by representatives of religion. The Samaritan *had* life because he *gave* life. A Christian is living because he or she is serving those who need mercy.

A Christian will seek the unsought. A Christian will be saving others by daily living. A Christian will serve by being a neighbor to those who need mercy. A Christian will live as Christ lived. A Christian will live as Christ wants him or her to live.

A Christian's Concern

Jesus sought persons and gave them an invitation to discipleship. If they accepted, he taught them until they decided to follow or to turn away. If they accepted, he continued the living and the leading in order that they might develop. He said to them on one occasion, "I have given you an example."

The time has come for us to sharpen our work. All our concerns and activities should have these three objectives:

To seek persons for Christ
To win persons for Christ
To develop persons for Christ

Are we seeking persons for Christ? Are we winning persons for Christ? Are we developing disciples for Christ? If not, what *are* we doing? And why are we doing what we are?

The local church is the agency for doing this work. It is comprised of persons. The local church that is not seeking, winning, and developing disciples for Christ is not functioning. That church is dead. There are millions of children, young people, and adults to seek, to win, and to develop.

The liquor industry is making every effort to seek, to win, and to develop drinkers. The tobacco people are using all means of communication to seek, to win, and to develop smokers. The merchant is using all possible legitimate means to seek, to win, and to develop customers.

Christ gave his ministry to seeking, winning, and developing disciples. A Christian is one who does the same.

—*Shepherds*, June-July 1955

REPORTS

Again, the first three of these reports appeared in *Shepherds* in 1945, 1946, and 1949. Selected passages from annual reports in 1950 and 1951 follow.

The World Methodist Convocation of Evangelism in Philadelphia in 1953 was the setting for the next report.

Dr. Denman presented "A Vision of the Need" at the annual meeting of the Board of Evangelism, under the theme of "Outreach" in 1954.

The yearbook *Rejoice* featured in 1956 the report that contains the segment "We Have a New America."

Dr. Denman presented the statement titled "Double Affirmatives and Double Negatives" to the General Council on World Service and Finance in 1957.

The final report was a noteworthy paper, later printed in brochure form, presented at the World Methodist Conference in Oslo, Norway, in 1961.

CRUSADING EVANGELS
BY HARRY DENMAN

The 1944 *Discipline* of The Methodist Church defines the work of the General Board of Evangelism this way:

"Its objects are religious, evangelistic, designed to diffuse the blessings of the Gospel of the Lord Jesus Christ, by the promotion and support of all forms and phases of evangelism; to promote evangelistic intelligence, interest, and zeal throughout the membership of The Methodist Church; to promote the practice of intercession and of individual and family worship; and to stimulate the entire membership of the Church in worship and in Christian service."

Such a definition of labors humbles all the persons identified with the Board of Evangelism. Reading the *Discipline*, they know the church has entrusted the guiding and leading of the church in its most vital mission to them.

The rather specific procedures included in this manual represent the Board's effort to be of the greatest possible assistance to the local churches as they engage in the Year of Evangelism. But behind all the helps and suggestions lies an insistent conviction. That conviction is this—*we must have a spiritual rebirth within the church itself.* This rebirth must come from God; it cannot come otherwise. Pertinent to that fact is another—the rebirth can come only to a willing people. We must desire it, prepare ourselves for it, expect it, and work for it.

An attractive evangelism that goes out to revitalize the church and to reap a Christian harvest among the unchurched will be no mere appendage to the total program of the church or no trifling effort to meet the world's total spiritual need.

What a high calling is ours—we are evangels crusading for Christ!

—Shepherds 1945

A Great Time to Do Evangelistic Work
by Harry Denman

What a great time this is to live and do evangelistic work!

We are at the beginning of the Atomic Era. We must have the power of the living Christ in our lives or this era will destroy our civilization.

We are in the midst of a social revolution. The industrial era has passed. We are interested in the rights of all. We are trying to give financial security by providing jobs for every one. Persons may only work thirty or forty hours a week. We need Christ, or the other hours will become hell for us.

The drinking of intoxicating beverages is destroying our nation. We must get individuals to be converted from drunkenness and social drinking to sobriety and abstinence. Christ will inspire them for great and noble living.

The church has measured its success by financial giving and not by the winning of men and women to the Christ-way, the Christ-truth, and the Christ-life. The church must have the indwelling Christ or become a dead formal institution rather than a living organism.

Today is the day. What a glorious day to live with and for Christ! Our crusade is for Christ; not for the church, not for the clergy, not for the acquiring of more members, but for Christ.

We will have a new world when, and only when, we have new citizens. These new citizens are born into the kingdom when they become Christ-men and Christ-women.

—*Shepherds*, February 1946

FIFTY GOLDEN DAYS OF EVANGELISM

Dear Friend:

This letter is to ask every pastor not to *observe* Pentecost on June 5, *but to meet the conditions* so that every church will have a Pentecost on that day. It can be done if we will organize our church to witness to the fact that Jesus is Christ, and that he is alive and can save persons from sin and death.

Easter to Pentecost
Fifty Golden Days of Evangelism

EASTER—We celebrate the resurrection of our Lord and Redeemer. We have a living Christ. This is the beginning of evangelism. Why shouldn't every church organize visitation teams to visit one night each week during this period and secure thousands of first commitments for Christ and his church, to be received on Pentecost Sunday, June 5?

FAMILY WEEK, MAY 1–8—This is a splendid time to visit young families and secure their first commitment for Christ and his church and establish a Christian home. What holy days there are—Easter to Pentecost—including Family Week!

There were one-hundred-twenty in the upper room. They were all filled with the Holy Ghost. Three thousand were baptized that first Pentecost. How many will be baptized in our churches on Pentecost Sunday, 1949?

Let us pray and work daily that every church will have a Pentecost.

Your friend,

HARRY DENMAN
—*Shepherds*, May 1949

The Kingdom Is Coming

Fifty years ago we were approaching December 31, 1899. Some of us can remember how the whistles blew and the bells rang as we closed that year and came into the year 1900. There was a thrill about it. In the beginning of this twentieth century, we lived a rather simple life. We were not bothered with television, radio, automobiles, picture shows, airplanes, electric refrigerators, electric stoves, and sweepers. We were not the richest nation in the world, and we did not have the atom bomb. We were not bothered with gadgets, and we had a very simple faith in God. Some of these inventions began to intrude on us during the first decade of this century.

We came to December 31, 1919, feeling full of pride. We had won a world war and had made it safe for democracy. Monarchs were gone. The saloon was voted out, and the sale and manufacture of intoxicating beverages was prohibited by law. We would never have another bank failure because of the Federal Reserve Act. Woman had been given her political freedom, and from then on American politics would be pure.

As we approached December 31, 1929, we were gambling on Wall Street. Henry Ford was paying laborers five dollars a day, and so-called free enterprise was not free enough to keep from criticizing him. Everyone was wearing a silk shirt. Poverty was abolished. These were the golden twenties. Of course, Wall Street had just crashed in October, but we hadn't really felt it by December 31.

During the thirties we had many horrible experiences: the banks failed; the bread lines formed, the Ph.D.s sold apples.

Something worse than the saloon and prohibition came back. Unemployment was everywhere, and in America the

Paternal State was born. In Europe the Totalitarian State came into existence, which was worse than the monarchy.

The forties brought war on a worldwide scale. We won on the battlefields but were not successful at the peace table.

During the twenties we put our faith in self; during the thirties we put our faith in the state; in the forties we put our faith in science and gold.

What is going to happen in the fifties? We are approaching December 31, 1949. We will soon be in the fifties. *This is going to be the ten years of a great spiritual awakening.*

Paul Hutchinson, speaking at the Ecumenical Conference in Boston in September 1947, said, "Man has lost faith in self, in the state, and in science. He must have a savior." Thank God, we have one.

I believe that *during the fifties* we are going to put our *faith* in God. At the present time, five of the six bestsellers are about faith. Persons are searching for something to believe. The newspapers are increasing their circulation by printing columns about faith in God and how to live on their front pages. We know that gadgets can never replace God, who gave us the gadgets that we might have more time to worship him. Persons are seeking *life*. We have Jesus, who is the Christ, and who is alive, and who brings life to all. We are going forth to tell a dying nation that we have a living Christ, and that he will give it life if it will only repent and believe.

Thank God that the leaders of The Methodist Church are following him and are sensitive to his Spirit. It is no mere coincidence that we are studying "Our Faith" at this time. Our bishops planned this three years ago.

Persons must have a faith.

During the fifties we will have a great faith in God.

Also during the fifties we will see *the family won for Christ*. Only a Christian home will save our nation and Western democracy. Today in America there are 32,000,000 children under twelve years of age. During the next ten years they will be won either by the living Christ or by the philosophies of communism, secularism, humanism, and paganism. They will be converted to some *ism*. Some psychologist said that every child in America is being taught some kind of religion, and this is true. The next ten years will determine the spiritual destiny of America, democracy, Christianity, and Protestantism.

During the fifties, the *family of nations* will become a fact. Today we are saturated with fear. When faith in God takes the place of fear, we will work for the family of nations as we have worked for war. Faith in God will cause us to advocate freedom for all minorities and to eliminate all injustices for all races and nations. When we become Christian, we will recognize the rights of all nations, and we will cherish their freedom more than we do their oil.

During the fifties we will *talk more about our faith* than our fear. Neighborhoods do not thrive when they are fearful of one another. But when each neighborhood puts its faith in God, then brotherhood and sisterhood begin. This is going to happen in the fifties, and the family of nations will become a fact.

What a glorious time to live! I ask God to let me live the next ten years if he desires. I wish to help in a small way to see the fifties and to see this nation have a simple faith in God, to see the family become Christian, and the family of nations become a fact. Let us go from this historic place of faith [St. George's Church, Philadelphia] to this glorious task.

The last fifty years were unusual in the realm of the secular—the next fifty years will be unusual in the realm of the spiritual.

Bishop G. Bromley Oxnam in his book, *Personalities in Social Reform*, says of Sidney and Beatrice Webb that with the tools of measurement, publicity, principle, permeation, program they fashioned the social reform that is contemporary Britain.

> If two persons can change the social thinking of a nation, can we not as a Board, by using the above tools saturated with prayer, change the social

thinking of this nation from secularism to evangel-icalism?

In the future, with your help, we are determined to use the science of measurement until we have the evangelistic facts about our church and nation, and then we are determined to publicize the facts until this church knows them. Certain principles will evolve, and by permeation we hope this church of ours will become a great evangelistic church with an ever enlarging program of evangelism.

Jesus measured the ecclesiasticism and secularism of his day and gave the facts about them to his disciples. The principles of his kingdom were taught until his disciples were permeated with them. After the ascension of the risen Lord, his disciples gathered in an upper room and prayed with one accord. On the day of Pentecost they were all filled with the Holy Spirit and received power for a great program of evangelistic witnessing, of living and of preaching.

What was that program?

1. That this Jesus is the Christ;
2. That God raised Him from the dead and He is alive;
3. That He can bring life to all persons if they will repent and believe;
4. That we are going to live and tell his message if we die.

They gave themselves completely to the living Christ; and in a few centuries, the living Christ captured the Roman Empire.

To do this we must work through the present expanding circles. In the first circle are the leaders of the church, which is composed of bishops, board members, superintendents, secretaries, editors, conference and district secretaries, conference and district lay leaders, conference and district leaders of the Women's Society of Christian Service, conference and district leaders of Methodist Youth Fellowship, administrators and teachers of our colleges and seminaries.

In the second circle are pastors, local church trustees, stewards, teachers, and leaders of all local church organizations.

In the third circle are the faithful members of the congregation.

In the fourth circle are the great masses in America who have not been reached for Christ and his church.

Today a warm, intelligent evangelistic zeal is beginning in the first circle. Soon it will spread to the second circle and to the third and to the fourth, and we will see a mighty spiritual awakening in the church and nation.

We want this first circle to have the evangelism of Jesus, which was as we see it as follows:

1. Evangelism is a great conviction. "He trusted in God."
2. Evangelism is a life true to that conviction.
3. Evangelism of lips—teaching that conviction.
4. Evangelism of a complete sacrifice for that conviction—death.

We praise God that everywhere persons are beginning to have a great conviction.

1. Complete trust in a living Christ.
2. Living that conviction.
3. Teaching that conviction.
4. If need be, dying for that conviction.

This redemptive living will stop the totalitarian state, atheism, communism, secularism, humanism, alcoholism, war and will bring peace, sobriety, godliness, life of the spirit, theism, and Christian democracy.

Bishop Oxnam in this same book has a chapter on Walter Rauschenbusch and says about him, "He prayed 'for a share in the work of redemption' and his prayer was granted." This should be our prayer as we begin the last fifty years of this twentieth century, which has seen already much material progress and will see a great spiritual growth. Rauschenbusch said, "Spiritual regeneration is the most important fact in any life history." He had his experience, which he said "influenced my soul down to its depths." He resolved to become a preacher and said, "I wanted to do hard work for God. Indeed one of the great thoughts that came upon me was that I ought to follow Jesus Christ in my personal life and die over again His Death. I felt that every Christian ought to participate in the dying of the Lord Jesus Christ, and in that way to redeem humanity. And it was that thought that gave my life its fundamental direction in the doing of Christian work."

Rauschenbusch wrote, "The main thing is to have God; and to live in Him; and to have Him live in us; to think His thoughts; to love what He loves and hate what He hates; to realize His presence; to feel His holiness and be holy because He is holy; to feel his goodness in every blessing of our life, and even in its tribulations; to be happy and trustful; to join in the great purpose of God and to be lifted to greatness of vision and faith and hope with Him—that is the blessed life."

The theme for the Methodist Evangelistic Advance at Philadelphia was *United Praying, United Believing, United Witnessing.*

During the next half-century, this is what we will be doing. When this century was born, the great method of evangelism was revivalism or mass evangelism. This church of ours was committed completely to this method. Revivalism led to a renewed interest in the Sunday school movement, especially among adults and youth. Christian education and great visitation campaigns came into being. Revivalism waned and died in some sections of the church.

The last fifty years we have found all three of these methods successful in themselves, but in the next fifty years we are going to use the best in revivalism, the best in Christian education, and the best in personal and visitation evangelism and work *unitedly* in *United methods to Advance for Christ and His Church.*

Arnold Toynbee said in his book *Civilization on Trial,*

"This may be the generation of which God hath chosen to evangelize the world." The first fifty years of this century saw a great advance in the realm of science. The next fifty years will see a great advance in the realm of the spiritual. We have television by which we can see persons from a distance. We need a vision of the living Lord high and lifted up in order to see those near us. We have speed in the realm of the physical but there are no shortcuts to the growing of a saint. It takes the daily discipline of practicing his presence. We have effected labor-saving devices until we believe we can eliminate spiritual disciplines.

A writer in *Time* magazine said that one word characterized the spirit of this century and that word was *more*. It is a good word, but it was used by the American people to get *more* wages, dividends, profits, sales, houses, automobiles, radios, and gadgets of all kinds. While the rest of the world has less, we have more of the material. In fifty years we did get more.

The next fifty years will see us get more of Christ and his Spirit and share the more we have of the material with those who have less. Our Christ said, "What shall it profit a man, if he shall gain the whole world, and lose his soul?"

The kingdom is coming. We shall be saved from a godless state to a Christian democracy, from the disintegration of the family to the importance of the Christian family, from worthlessness of the individual to the Christian worth of the individual, because

> Faith in God is stronger than the force of humanity;
> The Christian family is the foundation of the nation;
> The fraternity of nations is an absolute.

The kingdom is coming. Instead of fear we will have faith, instead of war we will have peace, instead of discord we will have accord, instead of hate we will have love.

The kingdom is coming. Today young men and young women are presenting their bodies as living sacrifices to our living King as soldiers of the cross for the ministry of healing, of preaching the word, of Christian education, and of witnessing in every land.

The kingdom is coming. Men and women are giving themselves and their money for the purpose of evangelizing the world.

The kingdom is coming. Men and women are sensitive to the Holy Spirit and are yielding themselves to him, and they are being filled. The spiritual awakening is beginning in many places.

The kingdom is coming. God is alive. Christ is alive. The Holy Spirit is alive. We are alive. "May Jesus Christ be praised."

The kingdom is coming. The King needs you. The King needs me. The King needs others. We kneel and yield our will to Him. He is our King today, tomorrow, and forever.

The kingdom is coming.

> *For the darkness shall turn to dawning,*
> *And the dawning to noon-day bright;*
> *And Christ's great kingdom shall come on earth,*
> *The kingdom of love and light.**

And the twentieth century shall be greater than the first century for our King and his kingdom.

In your daily prayers remember

Harry Denman
Annual Report
Cincinnati, Ohio, 1950

*From the hymn "We've a Story to Tell to the Nations" by H. Ernest Nichol.

Looking Forward
by Harry Denman

We must do more than reach persons for Christ and the church. We must see that they become active, growing Christians in the church, the community, the nation, and the world. It is wonderful to get a commitment to Christ and the church, but it is more wonderful to see committed Christians begin family worship, tithing, participating in church organization and regular church worship, as well as taking their places as Christians in the political, economic, educational, and social life of the community and world.

An article in *Pageant* magazine for July 1951, stated that to escape from prison one needed three things: patience, courage, and a new idea. This is what we need in evangelism—patience, courage, and a new idea.

During the quadrennium 1944-48, we were successful with the idea of visitation evangelism. However, not all churches have accepted it. Two thousand one hundred charges did not report a single person received on profession of faith during 1950. We believe that if one team of two persons in each of these charges had used the method of visitation evangelism, every charge could have won at least one person for Christ and his church. We need patience and courage.

During this quadrennium we have given, and are trying to give to the church, the idea of the United Evangelistic Mission. We want you to study the brochure "To Save the Present Age." We want every church to have a United Evangelistic Mission in 1952.

Looking Forward

During the next quadrennium we want The Methodist Church to believe that it is the duty and privilege of every member to witness for Christ and the church. Methodists of yesteryear called it "personal work," "burden for souls," "one win one." Perhaps we should call the idea "Each one reach one." Suppose we make this the habit of a Methodist—"Each one reach one for Christ and the church." What great things would happen! Methodism began as a lay evangelistic movement, and it must continue to be one.

Not only must we win families for Christ and the church, but we need to bring the idea of parental evangelism to our church and constituency. There are 51 million persons under 18 years of age in America. This is one-third of our population. They will be Christians or communists. They will be the servants either of the Messiah or of the military-minded. They will be spiritual or secular. They will be merciful or materialistic. They will belong to the flesh or to the faith.

Also, we need to stress the matter of family worship. Families that worship together at home will most likely worship together at church. I heard Dr. J. Manning Potts, editor of *The Upper Room*, speaking at Lake Junaluska, use the phrase "an Upper Room Service." Why not have an Upper Room Service at the supper table following the meal? The first Upper Room service conducted by our Lord was a supper. We need to get the families of Methodism to have an Upper Room Service each day at the supper table.

If Methodism is to be an evangelistic movement and reach the masses, we must instill in the minds, hearts, and wills of our laity the necessity of organizing new churches. As new communities come into existence, new Methodist churches should come into being. Many communities need a second and third Methodist church in order to reach the people who are being neglected.

There is a great mass movement on in America. I want our Methodism to be in the vanguard of that movement. The masses are going to have something. Can we say the words of the founder of The Methodist Church, "I gave them Christ"? Let us lift up Christ, and he will draw them to him.

It was my privilege to attend the National Sunday School Convention of the Assembly of God at Springfield, Missouri, which had for its theme:

Reach all you can
Teach all you reach
Win all you teach } for Christ and his Church.
Train all you win
To reach all they can

We must help our churches in their great program of church school evangelism, which is being done so effectively under the leadership of the Board of Education. Today the youth of our homes, churches, and campuses are waiting to be challenged by the daring cause of evangelism. They will give their all to personal witnessing, to organized visitation evangelism, to United Evangelistic Missions, to work camps of evangelism, to the ministry, and to the mission field.

I have listed the following major objectives in evangelism for your consideration for the next quadrennium:

1. Personal evangelism
2. Parental evangelism
3. Family evangelism
4. United Evangelistic Missions
5. Organization of new churches
6. Provision of leadership in mass evangelism
7. Upper room service in every home
8. Organization of lay visitation evangelism
9. Cooperation in church school evangelism
10. Film and radio evangelism
11. Youth evangelism
12. United Spiritual Life Missions

Our bishops, superintendents, pastors, and laity are leading us in a great evangelistic movement.

We wish to thank you, as the annual conference and district leaders of evangelism, for what you have wrought, for what you are doing, and for what you are going to do. You are the leaven. You are those who are helping to make this church of ours a great evangelistic movement.

You have courage, patience, and ideas. Let us rededicate ourselves to the cause of evangelism. As the staff of the General Board, we salute you.

—*Annual Report*, "Altar and Action," 1951

The Mind, Message, Mission, and Method of Jesus
by Harry Denman

The purpose of the World Mission of Evangelism is the same purpose that Jesus had when he lived in the flesh.

I. The Mind of Jesus

The World Mission of Evangelism must have the mind of Jesus. Jesus was God-minded. He was a one-God person, and he made God *his* Father. The chief priests asked Pilate to put Jesus to death. The charge they brought against Him was that "He made himself the Son of God." When Jesus was dying on the cross, the chief priests said, "He trusted in God." "When the centurion, and they that were with him, watching Jesus, saw the earthquake, and those things that were done, they feared greatly, saying, Truly this was the Son of God." Those who maneuvered the death of Jesus, and those who crucified Him, testified to the great faith that Jesus had in God.

Jesus witnessed to the fact that he abided in God and that God abided in him. The last night Jesus lived in the flesh, many questions were asked him by his disciples and by the members of the Sanhedrin. I think the one that hurt his heart most was Philip's. Philip said, "Lord, shew us the Father, and it sufficeth us." Jesus said to Philip, "Have I been so long time with you, and yet hast thou not known me, Philip? he that hath seen me hath seen the Father; and how sayest thou then, Shew us the Father? Believest thou not that I am in the Father, and the Father in me? the words that I speak unto you I speak not of myself; but the Father that dwelleth in me, he doeth the works. Believe me that I am in the Father, and the Father in me: or else believe me for the very works' sake" (John 14:9–11).

When one loves God with all one's mind, then one's mind is filled with God. Jesus came to reveal to us God the Father. He abided in God, and God abided in him because, as the chief priests said, "He trusted in God." He believed in the reality of the living God. He lived this faith. He taught this faith and died for it.

Must Reveal God

The World Mission of Evangelism must reveal God to every person in the world. God is alive today. He is willing to live in us as he lived in Jesus if we will trust and live in Him as Jesus did. The world must see God. The best way for persons to see God is in men and women who are willing for the living Christ to live in their flesh. When one sees Christ, one sees God. Christ can only be seen in flesh. One can see God, the Creator, in nature; but God, the Son, our Redeemer, must be seen in the flesh of men and women.

Today men and women are tired of worshiping the material, pleasure, self, bombs, military might, plans for a new world. They want reality. We have reality. We have God, the Father, our Creator. We have God, the Son, our Redeemer. We have God, the Holy Spirit, our Reprover, our Comforter, and our Teacher.

The purpose of the World Mission is to reveal God, Creator, Redeemer, and Sanctifier, to every person in the world.

II. The Message of Jesus

The World Mission of Evangelism must have the message of Jesus. "Jesus came into Galilee, preaching the gospel of the kingdom of God, and saying, The time is fulfilled, and the kingdom of God is at hand: repent ye, and believe the gospel."

In this year, 1953, we repeat the words of our Lord, "The time is fulfilled, and the kingdom of God is at hand." What is the kingdom of God? What did Jesus say about it?

One night a learned rabbi came to see him. He was a

member of the Sanhedrin. He knew the law. But Jesus possessed something that the learned rabbi wanted. He knew that the movement of which Jesus was the leader came from God. Study what he said to Jesus: "Rabbi, we know that thou art a teacher come from God: for no man can do these miracles that thou doest, except God be with him."

Jesus said, "Except a man be born again, he cannot see the kingdom of God." Remember, this was said to a Pharisee who kept the law, who was a ruler of the nation. He was not a sot from the gutter. Nicodemus raised the questions that we raise, "How can a man be born when he is old? can he enter the second time into his mother's womb, and be born?"

Jesus said, "Except a man be born of water and of the Spirit, he cannot enter the kingdom of God. That which is born of the flesh is flesh; and that which is born of the Spirit is spirit. Marvel not that I said unto thee, Ye must be born again. The wind bloweth where it listeth, and thou hearest the sound thereof, but canst not tell whence it cometh, and whither it goeth: so is every one that is born of the Spirit."

You can hear the wind blow. From whence did it come? You do not know. Where does it go? You do not know. But you can see the results of the blowing wind. Even so, you can know when a person has been born of the Spirit by the fruits of his or her life. God is with him or her. There are miracles.

Before God can use flesh for miracles, the flesh must be dominated by the Spirit. Birth in the flesh is a great miracle. The new birth in the spirit of God is a greater miracle.

At his baptismal service, Jesus saw the spirit of God descending like a dove and lighting upon him. He heard "a voice from heaven, saying, This is my beloved Son, in whom I am well pleased. Then was Jesus led up of the spirit into the wilderness to be tempted of the devil." The wilderness is the battlefield of the soul. God and the devil are the contenders.

"And when he had fasted forty days and forty nights, he was afterward an hungered. And when the tempter came to him, he said, If thou be the Son of God, command that these stones be made bread. But he answered and said, It is written,

Man shall not live by bread alone, but by every word that proceedeth out of the mouth of God" (Matthew 4:2-4). This is the temptation of secularism, which comes to each of us. We are born of the flesh. We must have bread for the body. But bread for the body cannot feed the spirit. The spirit hungers for the manna of heaven, the Word of God. Persons born of the Spirit live according to the Word of God. When you are born of the Spirit, you take the Word of God by which to live.

Preach, Teach, Live the Word of God

The World Mission of Evangelism believes that we must preach and teach the Word of God from the pulpit and in the classroom. The World Mission of Evangelism believes that those who have taken God will read God's Word and live according to God's Word, as revealed in his Book and revealed today. Believers, because they have direct access to God himself, can hear the Word of God for themselves, if they are willing to listen. The World Mission of Evangelism has for its purpose the urging of all persons to read and live according to the Word of God.

"Then the devil taketh him up into the holy city, and setteth him on a pinnacle of the temple, and saith unto him, If thou be the Son of God, cast thyself down: for it is written, He shall give his angels charge concerning thee: and in their hands they shall bear thee up, lest at any time thou dash thy foot against a stone. Jesus said unto him, It is written again, Thou shalt not tempt the Lord thy God" (Matthew 4:5-7).

This temptation comes to every person. Persons born of the flesh will live for the glory of self. After a person is born of the Spirit, he or she lives for the glory of God by doing the will of God. Jesus is not going to tempt God to set aside his laws in order that he himself might be glorified by doing something sensational. Jesus is going to keep the laws of God, "My meat is to do the will of him that sent me, and to finish his work." When you are born of the Spirit, you take God and his will.

The purpose of the World Mission is to get persons to

do the will of God. "Not every one that saith unto me, Lord, Lord, shall enter into the kingdom of heaven; but he that doeth the will of my Father, which is in heaven." The message of the kingdom of God is to do the will of God. Someone said recently that we want to establish the kingdom of God but leave God out. We cannot do that. It is God's kingdom, and we must do his will in our individual lives. Then the kingdom will come.

The World Mission of Evangelism has for its purpose the worship of God. "Again, the devil taketh him up into an exceeding high mountain, and sheweth him all the kingdoms of the world, and the glory of them; and saith unto him, All these things will I give thee, if thou wilt fall down and worship me. Then saith Jesus unto him, Get thee hence, Satan: for it is written, Thou shalt worship the Lord thy God, and him only shalt thou serve" (Matthew 4:8-10).

Jesus is going to worship God and serve him only instead of the kingdoms of the world. This temptation comes to each of us. All of us worship and serve some kingdom. Either we are slaves of the kingdoms of gold, pleasure, power, lust; or we are the servants of the kingdom of God. The flesh worships the material. The spirit worships God.

Worship in Church and Home

The Council of Bishops of The Methodist Church has called this nation to a Church Attendance Crusade, New Year's Day to Easter, 1954, in order that the indifferent church members and nonchurch members may be urged to attend churches and learn to worship God. In many countries today the percentage of the population attending worship services in the churches is very small.

The World Mission of Evangelism has for its purpose the urging of every home to have worship at a definite time each day. We must worship and serve God at home. On the day of Pentecost, the Holy Spirit came upon a group in an upper room in a home. The Holy Spirit came on a group in the home of Cornelius. The Holy Spirit came on a group in

Ephesus. There were only twelve, and I believe they were in a home. The Holy Spirit came on a group in Samaria. I believe this happened in a home. Our homes must not become taverns and theaters, but temples of worship and culture. The World Mission of Evangelism has for its purpose the establishing of family and individual worship in every home.

The kingdom of God is a movement that was born in the wilderness. John the Baptist came preaching that the kingdom of heaven was at hand. Jesus also came preaching that the kingdom of God was at hand. The time was fulfilled.

In the wilderness, Jesus took God. When you take God, you take his Word, by which you live. When you take God, you take his will. This is your life of action for the kingdom. When you take God, you worship him and serve him only. This is the expression of your spiritual life. You worship him instead of the kingdoms of this earth. When you take God, he takes you; and you become his witness. You are filled with the spirit of God. God uses your flesh for his works.

The purpose of the World Mission of Evangelism is to urge persons to be born of the Spirit and to enter the kingdom of God.

Nicodemus asked, "How can these things be?" We raise the same question: "How can these things be?" Jesus said to Nicodemus, "Art thou a master of Israel, and knowest not these things? . . . We speak that we do know, and testify that we have seen; and ye receive not our witness."

Nicodemus knew that Jesus came from God and that God was with him. Nicodemus was supposed to come from God, and God was supposed to be with him, but Nicodemus had not been born again. Jesus had had a great experience of God in the wilderness after the baptism of water and righteousness by John the Baptist. He came out of the wilderness to be God's witness. He was going to live according to the Word of God, the will of God, and he was going to worship and serve God only. He was not going to yield to secularism but yield to the spiritual. He was going to live not for the glory of self but for the glory of God. He was not going to worship the wealth of the kingdoms of this world but worship God and Him only.

We love the world as God loves the world and not as flesh loves the world. The birth of the Spirit means that we are new persons. We love the world as Jesus loved the world and not as flesh loves the world. "For God so loved the world." The new birth means that you love as God loves, and you see the kingdom of God.

The kingdom of God is entirely different from the philosophy of the American way of life, or the philosophy of Karl Marx, or the philosophy of Fascism, or the philosophy of any human system of political or economic theory.

The Kingdom of God

The kingdom of God is very important to Jesus. He said, "But seek ye first the kingdom of God, and his righteousness; and all these things [food, drink, clothes] shall be added unto you" (Matthew 6:33).

"He went throughout every city and village, preaching and shewing the glad tidings of the kingdom of God" (Luke 8:1).

"And he sent them [the twelve] to preach the kingdom of God, and to heal the sick" (Luke 9:2).

"Jesus said unto him, Let the dead bury their dead: but go thou and preach the kingdom of God" (Luke 9:60).

"And Jesus said unto him, No man, having put his hand to the plough, and looking back, is fit for the kingdom of God" (Luke 9:62).

"And the people, when they knew it, followed him: and he received them, and spake unto them of the kingdom of God, and healed them that had need of healing" (Luke 9:11).

"And when he was demanded of the Pharisees, when the kingdom of God should come, he answered them and said, The kingdom of God cometh not with observation: Neither shall they say, Lo here! or, lo there! for, behold, the kingdom of God is within you" (Luke 17:20-21).

Pilate asked Jesus, "What hast thou done?" "Jesus answered, My kingdom is not of this world: if my kingdom were of this world, then would my servants fight, that I should not be delivered to the Jews: but now is my kingdom not from hence" (John 18:36).

The new birth is the door to the kingdom of God. You become a new creature. You love as God loves. Christ loves as God loves. Christ believed in the kingdom of God. He lived it. He taught it. He died for it.

After Jesus' resurrection, Luke, in the Book of Acts, said, "To whom also he shewed himself alive after his passion by many infallible proofs . . . and speaking of the things pertaining to the kingdom of God" (Acts 1:3).

The disciples asked him, "Lord, wilt thou at this time restore again the kingdom of Israel?" (Acts 1:6).

Even after all his suffering and death, they were thinking of the kingdom of this world. When we think of our kingdom, Jesus gives us the same answer he gave to the disciples: "It is not for you to know the times or the seasons, which the Father hath put in his own power. But ye shall receive power, after that the Holy Ghost is come upon you: and ye shall be witnesses unto me both in Jerusalem, and in all Judaea, and in Samaria, and unto the uttermost part of the earth" (Acts 1:7-8).

The message of the World Mission of Evangelism is the Kingdom of God. The Kingdom of God is the answer to secularism. The Kingdom of God is the answer to a world that is pleasure mad and gold crazy. The Kingdom of God is the answer to an atheistic civilization. The Kingdom of God is the answer to those who make the state their God. The Kingdom of God is the answer to a generation that is full of fear and confusion. The Kingdom of God is the answer to those who are enslaved of sin. The Kingdom of God is the answer to those who are afraid of death.

The message for today is the message of Jesus—repent and believe the gospel of the Kingdom of God. Repent, believe, experience the new birth. Do not live in the flesh.

Live in the Spirit. Be a new creature. Be born of God. Enter his kingdom.

> We've a message to give to the nations,
> That the Lord who reigneth above
> Hath sent us his Son to save us,
> And show us that God is love,
> And show us that God is love.*

III. The Mission of Jesus

The World Mission of Evangelism must have for its purpose the mission of Jesus. He told us about his mission. "I am come that they might have life, and that they might have it more abundantly" (John 10:10).

"Think not that I am come to destroy the law, or the prophets: I am not come to destroy, but to fulfill" (Matthew 5:17).

"For the Son of man is not come to destroy men's lives, but to save them" (Luke 9:56).

"For God sent not his Son into the world to condemn the world; but that the world through him might be saved" (John 3:17).

"For the Son of man is come to seek and to save that which was lost" (Luke 19:10).

"For even the Son of man came not to be ministered unto, but to minister, and to give his life a ransom for many" (Mark 10:45).

The kingdom of God is for every person, regardless of color, nationality, age, sex, talents, training, wealth, or political party. The new birth is for every person. The only requirement is to be born of the Spirit. The new birth enables you to love every person as God loves him. Jesus did this, and it took him to a cross. And it will do the same for us.

Who are the greatest in the kingdom of God?

"And they brought young children to him, that he should touch them: and his disciples rebuked those that brought them. But when Jesus saw it, he was much dis-

---

*From the hymn "We've a Story to Tell to the Nations" by H. Ernest Nichol.

pleased, and said unto them, Suffer the little children to come unto me, and forbid them not: for of such is the kingdom of God. Verily I say unto you, Whosoever shall not receive the kingdom of God as a little child, he shall not enter therein. And he took them up in his arms, put his hands upon them, and blessed them" (Mark 10:13-16).

For the greatest, Jesus did not take the general of the army of occupation; who, Jesus said, had more faith than any in Israel. He took a child. He did not take the rich young ruler, whom he loved. He took a child. He did not take Nicodemus, a ruler of the Sanhedrin. He took a child. He did not take Simon Peter, the leader of the disciples. He took a child.

In the kingdom of God, children are the greatest. The least are the greatest. Persons born of the Spirit believe that children are the greatest.

"At the same time came the disciples unto Jesus, saying, Who is the greatest in the kingdom of heaven? And Jesus called a little child unto him, and set him in the midst of them, and said, Verily I say unto you, Except ye be converted, and become as little children, ye shall not enter into the kingdom of heaven. Whosoever therefore shall humble himself as this little child, the same is greatest in the kingdom of heaven. And whoso shall receive one such little child in my name receiveth me. But whoso shall offend one of these little ones which believe in me, it were better for him that a millstone were hanged about his neck, and that he were drowned in the depth of the sea" (Matthew 18:1-6).

This World Mission of Evangelism has for its purpose the reaching of the entire family for Christ and the church.

Children and Youth

In the United States, more than 22 million babies have been born during the last six years. In 1952 there were more than 3,850,000 babies born. This is the largest number of babies ever born in one year in the history of this nation. Our population is increasing at the rate of two million persons per year. Yet the number of children in the nursery division of our church school decreased in 1952. When Dr. Mary Alice Jones, the director of our children's division of the Board of Education, told of this decrease, I could not believe it until I read the figures in the 1952 yearbook. This World Mission of Evangelism must stimulate every church to become child-centered. We need to become conscious of the children who are here to be reached for Christ.

For five years we have had a decrease in the youth division of our church. There are some reasons for this, such as youth going to war. However, they should not be dropped from our church school rolls. We must forget the reasons and follow the leadership of our Board of Education in the great youth movement for this quadrennium as directed by the General Conference. According to Mr. Harold W. Ewing, director of Youth Work of the Board of Education, there are 20 million youth in the United States who are not being reached by any church—Roman Catholic, Protestant, or Jewish. Mr. Ewing states that by 1960 we should have, according to population growth, 4,600,000 in our youth department, as now we only have 1,125,000. One-third of our population today is under eighteen years of age.

We hope that this World Mission of Evangelism will stir every church to give dynamic leadership to youth. We must quit trying to entertain our youth with recreation and entertain them with the idea of giving themselves to the kingdom of God. We must ask every youth to be born again, to love the world as Christ loved the world, and to give himself or herself as Christ gave himself. Youth want recreation, but they want to be new creatures and to do something worthwhile. Youth will respond to the greatest challenge we can make. They will organize new churches, if we will let them. They will give their testimony on the streets. They will go from tavern to tavern to talk about Christ, if we encourage them. Youth is not defeated. Youth is daring. They will go from house to house, giving their witness about Christ. They have demonstrated it. Our camps, institutes, and summer assemblies must more and more become training camps for youth who will become evangelists for the kingdom of God, which is a youth movement.

This World Mission of Evangelism must challenge the adult classes of our church school, our official boards, our men's clubs, and the Woman's Society of Christian Service to invest their lives in great children's evangelistic crusades and youth evangelistic movements.

Love Every Person

The mission of Jesus was to love every person. He loved the world so much that he gave himself for and to every person. He gave himself to publicans. The Pharisees did not like it. He ate with sinners, and the religious leaders criticized him. He healed a man on the Sabbath, and those who should have healed the man at the pool of Bethesda plotted to kill Jesus for doing it. He touched a leper. He forgave the sins of a penitent and believing woman who anointed him; and Simon, the Pharisee, who was entertaining Jesus at dinner, accused him of not being a prophet. Jesus spoke to the woman at the well in Samaria, and his disciples marveled. Jesus had to leave Gadara because he thought more of one demon-possessed man than he did of two thousand hogs.

Jesus was colorblind, for he never distinguished among races. He loved Samaritans. He helped the woman at the well to forget that she was a Samaritan. One who thinks he is superior never forgets he is superior. It is hard for him to enter the kingdom. Jesus never heard of the caste system. He helped Zacchaeus and Levi forget that they were publicans. A Pharisee always remembers that he is a Pharisee. That is the reason it is hard for him to come into the kingdom.

Jesus could waste two thousand hogs in order to help a demon-possessed man. One who trusts in riches finds it hard to enter the kingdom of God. "It is easier for a camel to go through the eye of a needle, than for a rich man to enter into the kingdom of God." We ask, as they did then, who then can be saved? "With men, this is impossible; but with God all things are possible."

Jesus could help a man walk who had been a paralytic for thirty-eight years, even if it was the Sabbath. He forgot institutions and traditions in order to minister to one who needed him. Dr. Halford E. Luccock reminds us that some of us worship and revere ivy. Some of us are like the Pharisees. We are ivy-minded—tradition gets in the way of compassion.

Jesus was willing to die because of his love for one person—anyone. He did not worship property, race, caste, institutions, and traditions. Persons were in desperate need. If they had faith, Jesus ministered to their bodies, minds, and souls.

The World Mission of Evangelism must go to all persons, be they members of the manufacturers' association or the labor union. We must go to those who live on boulevards and to those who live on back streets. We must go to the taverns and the theaters. We must go to the sidewalks and the country crossroads. We must go to the beaches and the park benches. We must go to political halls and pubs.

Norman Cousins, writing in the *Saturday Review of Literature*, said, "Christianity has not truly involved itself in the human situation. It has become strangely adjacent to the crises of man.... In order to get inside man, the Church must get outside itself." The kingdom of God never is concerned with itself but with others. Stringfellow Barr wrote a book, *Let's Join the Human Race*. The kingdom of God is the human race born again.

We thank God that our Evangelistic Missions are reaching all persons. Those who sit in this audience can testify to it better than I, because you have seen the miracle of the new birth happen in thousands of lives.

In December 1949, a movement was born in this city of Philadelphia. We named it the United Evangelistic Mission. Under the leadership of the Council of Bishops, it has spread to nearly every Annual Conference. Through this one evangelistic method there have been 209,037 persons to make a first commitment to Christ and 142,193 persons have transferred their church letters, which means that thousands have become active instead of indifferent church members.

Our mission is the world, but we reach individuals. Jesus said, "Go...to every creature." "Go ye into all the world." Jesus said, "Ye shall be witnesses unto me both in Jerusalem, and in all Judaea, and in Samaria, and unto the uttermost part of the earth.'

IV. The Methods of Jesus

The World Mission of Evangelism must have the methods of Jesus. He came preaching the gospel of the kingdom of God. He sent out the twelve, two by two, to preach the gospel of the kingdom of God. He sent out the seventy, two by two, and told them to say unto those they visited, "The kingdom of God is come nigh unto you."

The twelve and the seventy were sent to houses. The message of the kingdom of God is to be taken by disciples to the homes of the people. The Bible says, "And into whatsoever house ye enter, first say, Peace be to this house." The twelve and the seventy were appointed to go to people in their homes. This is the method that Jesus used for the kingdom of God, and this is the method that we must use. Disciples must go two by two to tell all persons that the kingdom of God is nigh unto them.

Dr. W.E. Hocking, in one of his great addresses on evangelism, said, first, "The obligation to preach rests, not on any part of the Church, but on the whole Church." Second, "The parish of all preaching is the world." Third, "The preaching of Christ is also a learning of Christ—the two go together."

Dr. John Pitts, in an article, "Conversion: Its Nature and Necessity," published in the Spring, 1953, issue of *Religion in Life*, says, "As Bishop Mandall Creighton used to say, 'Religion is continually decaying in the hands of the multitude; it has to be revived in the hearts of individuals.'"

Jesus came teaching the kingdom of God. He taught everywhere—in synagogues, in the Temple, in houses, by the seaside, on the mountainside, by a well, and at the marketplace. Anywhere, Jesus could teach one person or five thousand persons. Behold how the assembled multitudes followed him, and he used every opportunity to instruct them in the things pertaining to the kingdom of God.

The Old Testament says, "Now for a long season Israel hath been without the true God, and without a teaching priest, and without law. But when they in their trouble did turn unto the LORD God of Israel, and sought him, he was found of them. And in those times there was no peace to him that went out, nor to him that came in, but great vexations were upon all the inhabitants of the countries. And nation was destroyed of nation, and city of city: for God did vex them with all adversity" (2 Chronicles 15:3-6). Israel had been without a teaching priest.

The new Greek disciples in Antioch, Syria, were called Christians after Barnabas and Saul of Tarsus had spent a year teaching the people.

We must teach about the kingdom of God in the pulpit, in the church school, in the church college, in all of our assemblies and institutions, and in the home.

Parents are teachers. The World Mission of Evangelism is to get parents to become teachers for the kingdom of God.

We must teach the kingdom of God by such instruments as the radio, television, the printed page, books, billboards, tracts, and newspapers. We must use all media of mass communication to tell the unreached millions about the kingdom of God.

Our laity, two by two, must go from house to house, teaching that "the kingdom of God is come nigh unto you." The World Mission of Evangelism must become a great lay movement. Laypersons will testify by their lives and with their lips in all the relationships of life.

The World Mission of Evangelism must have some great prophets who will go across the world calling all to repentance, for the kingdom of God is at hand. The Methodist pulpit is a free pulpit. When we preach the kingdom of God and his righteousness, we will be called all kinds of names by those who are opposed to the kingdom of God. Jesus was called a devil, a Samaritan, a blasphemer, a glutton, and a wine bibber. It was said that he was beside himself. What do we care for names, so long as we believe in the worth of the individual because God loves him or her? Congressional committees can call us names, but we go on preaching and living the kingdom of God.

We will use all methods—preaching, printing, teaching, healing, counseling, visiting, social righteousness, worship, airways, and highways—to help our living Lord to bring in the kingdom of God.

V. Modern Miracles Needed

The World Mission of Evangelism must be willing for Christ to work miracles today. Jesus said that God did the works. The last night Jesus lived in the flesh, he said, "He that believeth on me, the works that I do shall he do also; and greater works than these shall he do; because I go unto my Father."

Jesus had an unlimited faith in his Father; therefore, God could do unlimited works through him. Today we limit God and his Kingdom by our lack of faith. God keeps his promises. We can have a limited God or an unlimited God, according to our faith. His Kingdom will come today if we will let it. His Kingdom is coming. He will not be defeated. God is alive.

Miracles can happen today. There can be the miracle of a new person. There can be the miracle of a new home. There can be the miracle of a new church. There can be the miracle of a new community. There can be the miracle of a new nation. There can be the miracle of a new economy. There can be the miracle of a new political party. There can be the miracle of a new labor party. There can be the miracle of a new world. There can be the kingdom of God on earth, a miracle through faith.

We need the faith of a mustard seed to see the mountains of atheism, secularism, nationalism, sin, death, and pleasure disappear. Faith is the victory. All God needs today is faith lived in flesh. Individuals can be saved from sin and death. We have seen it happen. Persons can be healed from alcoholism, selfishness, and fear. Through faith we have seen it happen. Homes can be saved through faith. We have seen it happen. Communities can be changed. Civilization can change its trend. We have seen it happen.

"Christ can change the world—through you." The kingdom of God is at hand. The miracle is taking place. Before the end of this decade, we are going to see a great worldwide evangelistic movement.

The World Mission will become a movement if we have a new birth. The kingdom of God is a movement. It cannot be static and become institutionalized. It is always breaking out in new places. The miracle of a new experience broke out in the mind, heart, soul, and body of a little man in England. The miracle that happened on May 24, 1738, began an evangelistic movement that is going on in the world today. That miracle of the warm heart gave the Methodists a fire that burns on every continent.

World Methodists must have the mind of Christ. Methodists must have the message of Christ. Methodists must have the mission of Christ. Methodists must have the method of Christ. Methodists must have the miracle of Christ.

This movement will take us to city slums, rural areas, neglected peoples of the world. Multitudes are waiting to hear that, through faith in God, persons can know their sins are forgiven, that they are free from the law of sin and death, and that they can trust Christ for salvation.

The Kingdom Is Coming

The Methodist Movement must go to all neglected places in this world and establish societies. The miracle of the new birth that took place on May 24, 1738, in the life of John Wesley changed the world. The miracle of the new birth that took place on May 21, 1738, in the life of Charles Wesley changed the world. The wind is still blowing. The kingdom is coming.

We believe that men and women are being born of the

Spirit now. We believe that June 28, 1953, will be a day long remembered, because the new birth is taking place. Persons are seeing and entering the kingdom of God.

We believe that World Methodism is going to believe in the kingdom of God and make children the greatest. We believe that World Methodism is going to have a great youth movement. We are going to challenge the youth of every nation to enter the kingdom of God movement and let God's kingdom come. With the dynamic faith of youth and with their sacrificial living and dying, the kingdom will come.

We believe that our official boards, our adult classes, our men's clubs, and our Women's Societies of Christian Service are going to engage in a great movement of establishing churches in all the neglected areas of the world—in our neighborhood and on all continents and islands of the sea.

We believe that thousands of young men and women are going to give their lives to the Kingdom of God movement and be ministers and missionaries in different parts of God's world to let him establish his kingdom.

We believe that millions of Methodists are going to experience the new birth and see the kingdom of God come through the instrumentality of their paying of the tithe and their sacrificial giving. We believe that their property, income, and wealth are to be dedicated to the kingdom.

We believe that our homes are to become the kingdom of God on earth. We believe that miracles of the new birth will take place. We believe in the kingdom of God. We will live the kingdom of God. We will teach the kingdom of God. We will die for the kingdom of God. We give our all to the kingdom of God. We believe and know the kingdom of God is coming. The time is fulfilled. The kingdom of God is *here*.

—*For the World Methodist Convocation of Evangelism*
June 26–28, 1953

A Vision of the Need

We believe we must sharpen the work of evangelism. Many persons are talking about evangelism and including many activities under the name of evangelism. In a sense all the activities of the local church should look toward the finding, winning, and developing of disciples for our Lord Jesus Christ. Jesus gave the invitation to two men to "come and see." That was the beginning of evangelism.

Recently in leading a discussion with preachers on evangelism, I asked, "What is the business of the church?" and they replied, "Saving souls and helping them to grow." I agreed with this statement. I tried to illustrate this by relating the interview of Jesus and Zacchaeus. When I quoted the words Jesus said to the Pharisees after the conversion of Zacchaeus, I discovered that Jesus said, "The Son of man is come to *seek* and to save that which was lost." We must get our church seeking persons. We visit those who make some contact with our church, but we must seek and make the contacts.

Prayer life must be developed among our church members. Prayer cells need to be formed. Simon Peter became a man of prayer, and then he had a vision of the Gentiles who needed the gospel. We hope prayer cells can be formed in every home and in every local church Commission on Membership and Evangelism.

We must try to create a Christian mission to the home. Missionaries tell us that communists destroy institutions when they take over a nation. There will always be homes in the United States even if we live in caves. We may not have churches, but there will be family units. We need to take the message of the gospel to the family.

This has been a wonderful year for me. You have enlarged my vision and enabled me to know some of the great Christians of today and to see some of the great places of the earth. I have ridden in a jeep over the dirt roads of Brazil with a young Negro of Georgia, who with his wife is giving his life to Christ and the church by teaching in our school at Juis de Fora; with a young missionary from a Georgia parsonage home whom I knew as a boy, who with his family is serving the small towns of the interior of Brazil as a pastor-evangelist; with a young Brazilian accepted supply pastor who has twenty-nine churches and preaches every night in the week and five times on Sunday and has to ride a horse over a parish three hundred miles long and who wants to go to seminary, but his salary is only $50 per month, and he has a family to support; and with J. Manning Potts, the redactor of the *No Cenaculo*.

I have seen the faithful teachers, missionaries, and administrators of our school in Latin America. I am thankful for the educational thrust that has been made by the Women's Division and the World Division of our Board of Missions in the several Latin American countries, where we evangelize and educate; namely, Cuba, Mexico, Costa Rica, Panama, Brazil, Uruguay, Bolivia, Chile, Peru, and Argentina.

I have prayed with Charles Butler, a young man of Alabama, in our mission station that he is reviving in the downtown section of Panama City, where it seemed to me there were 500 children in the block where this dilapidated building is located. This young evangelist is trying to raise $40,000 for a building to minister to all these children.

We have been with Bishop John Branscomb in the dedication of a small thatched rural church in the interior of Cuba. This church was practically built by the Cubans. Miss Eulalia Cook is the pastor-evangelist of this church, as well as many more on her circuit. We saw the bishop baptize eight children of one family.

We have been with the superintendent of the Nord-Vestre District of Norway. In the winter he leaves Bergen and

A PORTRAIT OF DR. HARRY DENMAN, painted by Warner Sallman, has been hung in the lobby of the Methodist General Board of Evangelism building, located in Nashville, Tennessee. Shown with the portrait are Dr. Denman (left), general secretary of the board, and Bishop W. Angie Smith, Oklahoma City, board president. The portrait was commissioned by the executive committee of the board and presented to the board at an annual meeting in Fort Monroe, Va.

Sallman is the artist who painted the *Head of Christ*, which is said to be the most popular art work in the world.

DR. HARRY DENMAN

DR. HARRY DENMAN (left) shown with Dr. Dawson Bryan, a member of his staff.

DR. HARRY DENMAN delivering one of his meaningful messages.

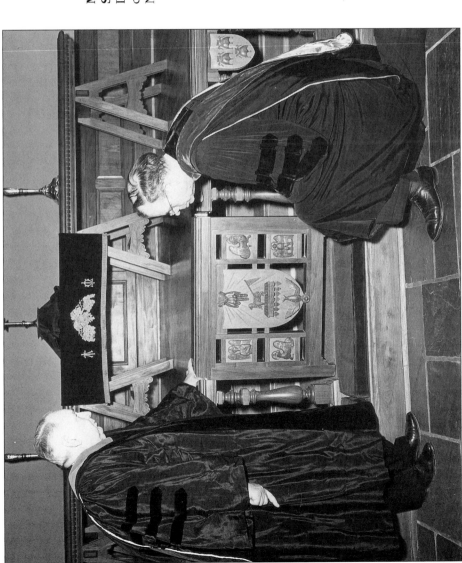

METHODIST BISHOP W. ANGIE SMITH (left) and Dr. Harry Denman at the railing of the chapel of The Upper Room in Nashville, Tennessee.

DR. HARRY DENMAN

Dr. J. W. Golden (left), Bishop Charles F. Golden (center), and Dr. Harry Denman (right), in the new office provided for Bishop Golden in the Denman Building after efforts to place him in other buildings in Nashville had failed. Dr. Golden, the bishop's father, was a member of Dr. Denman's staff.

IN 1953, DR. HARRY DENMAN, preaching from the lectern in the chapel of the Upper Room, in Nashville, Tennessee.

DR. HARRY DENMAN (right) WAS PRESENTED THE **1965** UPPER ROOM CITATION FOR WORLD CHRISTIAN FELLOWSHIP at a dinner September 22, in Dayton, Ohio. Giving him a peek at the citation before the dinner is the Rev. Dr. J. Manning Potts (left), Nashville, who later made the presentation. The president of the National Council of Churches, Bishop Reuben H. Miller (center), Indianapolis, a leader of the Evangelical United Brethren Church, was the principal speaker for the occasion.

DR. HARRY DENMAN in a photograph taken in 1961.

BISHOP GERALD KENNEDY (left) from Los Angeles, sometime president of the General Board of Evangelism, with Dr. Harry Denman (right) from Nashville.

HARRY DENMAN,
the speaker.

HARRY DENMAN,
the listener.

METROPOLITAN NICODIN OF THE ORTHODOX CHURCH OF BULGARIA with Dr. Denman in 1961.

AT ONE POINT IN HARRY'S LIFE, HE DECIDED TO SHAVE HIS HEAD so that he might avoid the daily routine of combing it.

THE INTERNATIONAL MOVEMENT FOR PEACE occurred over the Thanksgiving Holiday at Lake Junaluska, N.C. In attendance were (left to right, front row) Miss Isobel Young, Chathan, Ontario, Canada, a school teacher; John Munjoma, Umtali, Rhodesia, President of the IPF; Dr. Helen Kim, Southern Korea's Ambassador-at-Large; (back row) Won Yong Na, Wonju, Korea; Kil Sang Yoon, Seoul, Korea; Dr. Harry Denman, Secretary of the IPF; and Tai-Hsiang Yang, Captain of the Republic of China's Air Force.

DR. HARRY DENMAN WITH BISHOP ANGIE SMITH, once president of the General Board of Evangelism, standing at the base of the lectern in the chapel of The Upper Room in Nashville, Tennessee.

travels his district in a boat all the way to Narvik and Hammerfest and is gone three months from his family.

We have stood where Moses stood on Mt. Nebo and looked over Jordan to Jericho and Jerusalem. We have, in our imagination, seen the house of Zaccheus at Jericho. We have prayed for Christ to be born in us at Bethlehem. We have walked with him at Bethany. We heard him say, "Wilt thou be made whole?" to the man at the pool of Bethesda. We have prayed with him at Gethsemane. We have walked with Jesus to Calvary and suffered with him. We have stood at Mt. Olivet with the living Christ and heard him say, "But ye shall receive power, after that the Holy Ghost is come upon you: and ye shall be witnesses unto me both in Jerusalem, and in all Judaea, and in Samaria, and unto the uttermost part of the earth."

We have walked the street called Straight in Damascus. We have seen the window in the wall where Paul was let down when his life was threatened. We have stood on Mars Hill and heard Paul preach. We have prayed with Christians in Athens. We have prayed with children in one of our churches in East Berlin, Germany. We have stood and prayed under the broken reproduction of Thorvaldsen's *Christ* in one of our churches in West Berlin, Germany. We have prayed in Thorvaldsen's church in Copenhagen as we looked up in the face of his Christ. We have seen the living Christ in the faces of the radiant Christians of Germany as they rebuild their homes and churches.

We have seen the hatred of those in Jordan and Jerusalem who have been dispossessed. We have visited the tombs and the temples of the pharaohs at Luxor. We have crossed the Nile. We have seen the ruins where Joseph lived as Pharaoh's son.

We have seen hunger for food in the faces of children whose bodies were naked and full of parasites in different places of the world. We have seen the tragedy of war in the bodies of men and women. We have seen the ruins of churches and homes where 42,000 persons were destroyed by bombs in one hour one afternoon.

We have heard the joyous singing of the Methodist Christians in Scandinavia. We have heard the testimony of consecrated laypersons in Narvik, Norway, and Borlange, Sweden. We have seen young men and women give their lives to Christ and the church to be ministers and missionaries in Copenhagen and Skein. We have heard our great evangelistic leader, Bishop W. Angie Smith, agree to send all of them to seminary. We have found Christians in every country. We belong to a great Christian fellowship. We said to a preacher in Chile, "What kind of evangelism do you have?" Very quickly he replied, "The same as you have in North America. We read *Shepherds* magazine every month and follow the program." We have found readers of *The Upper Room* in every city and community we visited regardless of denomination, color, or nationality. Many doors have been opened to us because of *The Upper Room* fellowship.

We have heard the testimony of Christian businessmen in Beirut, Lebanon, and other places. We have seen the victorious living Christ in men and women who have come through war, death, life, suffering, and sacrifice.

We have had a vision of the need of our living Christ for the world. Every time we come back to the United States, we determine to give ourselves completely to the task of trying to make this country a great Christian nation dedicated to living for Christ and helping the other nations of the world to know Christ. You have made all this possible for me. You have been so gracious as to provide the opportunity for visiting many countries for Christ and your Board of Evangelism of our great church. I am indebted to you for an enlarged vision of our Father's world and the spiritual needs of all his children.

I have had the great privilege of traveling with Bishop and Mrs. W. Angie Smith, Bishop Roy H. Short, Bishop John Branscomb, and Dr. J. Manning Potts. These friends have been very patient and understanding of my frailties and weaknesses as we have gone together in a traveling fellowship. How rich I am in being permitted to be associated with you in this great enterprise of seeking, winning, and developing disciples for Christ! I am thankful for your daily prayers, your dynamic faith, and your love for Christ, which includes me. Christ is the hope of the world.

As Julia Ward Howe expresses it, we too have seen!

Mine eyes have seen the glory
   Of the coming of the Lord;
He is trampling out the vintage
   Where the grapes of wrath are stored;
He hath loosed the fateful lightning
   Of his terrible swift sword;
   His truth is marching on.

He has sounded forth the trumpet
   That shall never call retreat;
He is sifting out the hearts of men
   Before his judgment seat;
O be swift, my soul, to answer him;
   Be jubilant, my feet!
   Our God is marching on.

In the beauty of the lilies
   Christ was born across the sea,
   With a glory in his bosom
   That transfigures you and me;
As he died to make men holy,
   Let us die to make men free,
   While God is marching on.*

One day the local church of Jerusalem had a congregational meeting with their leader at Mt. Olivet. He had been crucified because of his faith. God had raised him from the dead. They knew he was alive. They had seen him and heard him talk several times. He is meeting them for final instructions, for he is going back to his Father.

*"The Battle Hymn of the Republic."

Today we take a look at this local church in Jerusalem.

First, let us look at the personnel of this church. They were Galileans. Later in the day, after Christ had ascended, two men in white apparel addressed them, "Ye men of Galilee." On the day of Pentecost the multitude came together and said, "Behold, are not all these which speak Galileans?" The Sanhedrin, comprised of scholars, philosophers, and theologians, were sure that "no prophet came out of Galilee." According to the Sanhedrin, the Galileans were unlearned and ignorant people.

There were some converted harlots and publicans among them. It was a rather weak church as far as personnel was concerned. They were not wealthy: "Silver and gold have I none." It was a small group. Only 120 were present on the day of Pentecost. They did not belong to the Jerusalem Rotary Club, or the Mount Olivet Country Club, or the Bethany Garden Club. Later they started the Upper Room Club.

I wonder if some of our churches would like to have Simon Peter as chair of the official board, or the Woman of Sychar as president of the Women's Society of Christian Service, or Zacchaeus as treasurer, or Levi as charge lay leader, or the man of Gadara as church school superintendent.

Second, this local church was provincial. Listen to the question that they put to Jesus: "Lord, wilt thou at this time restore again the kingdom to Israel?" They wanted Israel to rule. They were tired of the occupation of their country by Rome. I wonder how it would feel to live in a country that was prostrated by bombing and then for nine years occupied by four victorious conquerors?

These Galileans knew the insults of Roman soldiers to them and to their families. They wanted Israel restored in order to eliminate the Romans. They, no doubt, were nationalists and wanted a national religion. Today we think of America and an American church. Recently a man asked me how many members are in our church, and I replied, "Nine million." He said, "Does that include your overseas members?" I said, "No, there are a million overseas." I was ashamed that I had not included those who are overseas. We have a world church. I wish we had a world headquarters in some nation besides the United States.

This first church of Jerusalem could only see the community in which they lived.

Third, that day before he went away, Jesus gave these men a program of work. "Ye shall be witnesses unto me both in Jerusalem, and in all Judaea, and in Samaria, and unto the uttermost part of the earth."

This program was not just for Jerusalem but for all Judaea. It was not just for the Pharisees but for the publicans, not just for the rich but for the poor, not just for one caste but for the outcast, not just for the brown but for the white, not just for the Jew but for the Gentile, not just for the wise but for the unwise, not just for the Greek but for the barbarian, not just for adults but for youth and children, not just for the good but for the bad, not just for the urbanites but for the ruralites, not just for those on the boulevard but for those in the slums and alleys.

"For God so loved the world," not just a few persons but all persons. Wesley said, "The world is my parish," not one class of people but all people.

We strengthen the local church by giving it a world program. A local church will die with a local program. It must have a task bigger than itself. A local church grows when it is straining at a spiritual task. There cannot be a local church. It must be a part of a world church if it is to be the church that Christ is building.

This program became flesh on Pentecost, and the disciples were empowered of the Spirit. They began to witness in Jerusalem and in all Judaea. They witnessed in Samaria to entire cities. They went to the desert place to witness to one man. They went to the Gentiles. They went to the Greeks. They went to Athens. They went to Rome, to Corinth. They went to the world. Persecution came, but they witnessed. They were stoned, but they witnessed. They were beaten, but they witnessed. They were imprisoned, but they witnessed.

This Jerusalem church obeyed its living Lord. It waited

in Jerusalem. It engaged in prayer for ten days until all of them entered into the fellowship of one accord. They had a fellowship—the fellowship of one accord. They had one common faith.

They believed that Jesus is the Christ, the Son of God. They believed that God raised him from the dead and that he is alive. They believed that he could bring life to those who would repent and be baptized. They determined to be witnesses to their faith.

The local church in Jerusalem sent representatives to the church in Antioch in Syria. That local church sent missionaries to Perga, Iconium, Antioch in Pisidia, Lystra, Derbe, and on to Ephesus, Thessalonica and to the known world.

Today the atheistic philosophers are witnessing to the world. Dr. James S. Bonnell said recently, "The next fifty years will determine whether the world will be ruled by the atheistic communists or by the kingdom of our living Christ."

God through Christ redeemed a world, not a part of it. The Methodist Church must tell the world of this Redeemer. We must live a Christianity that the nations of the world want. They want our gold stream; but we pray that they will want our Christ, because of the way we live.

Christ is the hope of the world. I pray that the World Council of Churches, at Evanston, will launch a program of evangelism. The World Council has a world relief program. Why not have a world program of regeneration? We have a Redeemer. We can have regeneration.

A few days ago, in a very small rural church of fifty members, I saw on the altar a globe of the world and two small flags—one our Christian flag and one our national flag. This church has a worldview.

Let us pray that our General Conference will adopt a quadrennial program or a ten- or fifty-year program by asking every church to take the world for its parish. This is no time for provincialism, nationalism, or churchism. We must be born again and see and love the world as God and Christ do.

Why do we talk about strengthening the local church? There is no local church in Methodism. No one ever joined a local Methodist church. One joins The Methodist Church, which is a world church. One becomes a member of the body of Christ, which has a world message and a world mission.

This is no time for classes. There is only one class—persons. This is no time for different races. There is only one race—the human race.

We hope that this Board will authorize its chairman and secretary to send a communication to the official delegates of The Methodist Church to the World Council of Churches urging the adoption of a world program of evangelism for the next ten years.

Let us pray daily that this Board of Evangelism will be willing to be used of God to tell all persons about a living Christ who can bring salvation to a person and transform a society. The new world order must have new people. We become new creatures when we have been reconciled to God through Christ. We have one God. We have one Savior. We have one world. Let us become one fellowship in Christ. Then we will have a new world order!

Dr. T. A. Kantonen closes his book, *Theology of Evangelism*, with these words:

> The whole church, from local parishes and general church bodies to the highest levels of interdenominational co-operation, must emerge as a world-wide evangelizing fellowship, with a realistic strategy and a rededicated will to carry out its central purpose to win every area of life for Christ. To this end every man and woman in our pews must be enlightened to the true meaning of the Christian fellowship and consecrated to the tasks of the universal priesthood. They must become the means by which men in every stratum of society, from the ranks of unskilled labor to the sophisticated intelligentsia of the universities, are confronted with the living Christ.

If this goal is to be achieved, the theology of evangelism must not remain an exclusive preoccupation of ministers and men preparing for the ministry. If every Christian is to be an evangelist, every Christian must also be a theologian. [Laity] must be taught the vital truths of the Gospel in language which they can understand and in thought-patterns which they can apply. This calls for a theology that is clearly and frankly kerygmatic instead of merely academic. While theologians manipulate Christian truth for the purpose of their erudite analyses and esoteric debates, vague sentimentalities take the place of positive Christian convictions among the rank and file of church members. The "I believe" of many of them has no more definite content than the popular song bearing the title and saying, "I believe that somewhere in the darkest night a candle glows...I believe for every one that goes astray someone will come to show the way...I believe that someone in the great somewhere hears every word" of prayer. Such sentiments are an improvement over the usual content of the "hit parade," but they are a sorry substitute for the Christian faith. A Christian does not believe in "someone in the great somewhere" but in God the Father Almighty, in Jesus Christ, his only Son, our Lord, and in the Holy Spirit, who in the one holy Christian church through the Word and the sacraments forgives our sins, gives us eternal life, and commissions us to witness.

The present study of the theology of evangelism has sought to show that faith in God the Creator establishes evangelism as God's work, that faith in God the Redeemer establishes the basis on which sinful men can do God's work, and that faith in God the Sanctifier consecrates us to the doing of this work. When Christian people learn to live by and to live out that faith, the Church will once more be clothed with power from on high to accomplish its God-given mission.

The late Archbishop Temple said:

Christ needs men of zeal and courage who are willing to move forward and make adventures in His name. Never mind if methods prove later to be wrong and results not as anticipated, we must be willing to *do* something. He could not use Gamaliel—so wise, so pious, so afraid; but He could and did use Saul, whose crusading zeal against the early Christians He could transform and redirect into a great missionary passion.

Today we dedicate ourselves to follow our living Christ in this world enterprise.

Respectfully submitted,

HARRY DENMAN, *Executive Secretary*
—*Annual Report*, Outreach, 1954

We Have a New America

Let us look at the evangelistic opportunity in America today:

69,000,000 persons have no church affiliation.
19,000,000 of these are youth 12–23 years of age.
31,000,000 persons move each year.
Crime is growing four times as fast as population.
37,000,000 babies were born 1945–1955.
42,000,000 estimated to be born 1955–1965.
Population increasing at the rate of 2,500,000 per year.
Estimated population by 1965—190,000,000.
833,000 new family units established 1950–55.
2,000,000 more new units will be established 1955–1965.

Mr. Henry Ford, Jr., has announced that the Ford Motor Company will spend five hundred million dollars in 1956. Mr. Ford states, "Just to keep from losing ground, we've got to move ahead." He observes that 1960 is "only four short years off," and there is not much time to plan and to prepare, to build the plants and machines to meet the expanded market of that period. Other manufacturing corporations are spending billions of dollars in preparation for the New America.

The estimated population for 1965 is 190,000,000. In ten short years we will have a net increase in our population of 25 million persons. This is the New America.

In 1784, when The Methodist Church was organized in Baltimore, did we have 25,000,000 persons in America? We had a New America in 1784. We have a New America now.

It is estimated that there will be forty million babies born in the next ten years. This is the New America. We are to have new stores, new plants, new homes, new communities, new cars, new highways, new jet planes, new gadgets. We are dedicated to the new.

We are desperately in need of something new, more than machines and plants and highways. We need new persons with a new philosophy.

What makes a nation great? What makes a university great? What makes a corporation great? What makes a home great? What makes a church great? What makes a city great? It is a *person*.

We must have a new nation. Congress gave us a new philosophy, this "nation under God." The New America must be under God. When we salute the flag or pledge our allegiance, we say, "One nation under God." I want this nation to be under God.

1. The New America must have a dynamic faith in the reality of the living God.
2. The New America must live by the righteousness of God.
3. The New America will find new life in God through Christ.
4. The New America must give itself to the world as God gave himself to the world.
5. The New America must give its time and talent to making the family Christian.

This New America must be reached for Christ. The Methodist Church must have a large share in this evangelism of reaching the New America. It can be done.

Our supreme task will be to "Evangelize the Evangelist." I borrow these words from Bishop G. Bromley Oxnam. We must give ourselves to evangelizing the membership of the local church. Our church members need an experience of Christ until they have a *concern* for every unchurched person in the community. Evangelism must not be a special effort in the local church, but it must become the main business of each church member. In order to reach these new families, these new children, these youth and adults, every Christian must become a witness for Christ. The local church Commission on Membership and Evangelism must pray and promote an evangelism that will reach those who need to know Christ.

The Methodist Church has about 15 percent of the Protestant church membership in the United States. This means that we should have a net gain of 400,000 persons per year for the next ten years.

We need to organize new churches for this New America. Church extension needs millions of dollars for this great enterprise. Our local churches must have two great missionary enterprises—Advance Specials to win the world for Christ and Advance Specials to win the local community for Christ. The Methodist Church has the lay-power and the financial-power and the knowledge-power. We must give all this to Christ to win the New America and the new world. Other religions besides Christianity have great evangelistic endeavors, and we must accelerate our labors and giving in the local church. New Sunday schools must be started wherever there is a need.

We must have more preachers. This is the greatest need of The Methodist Church. The Board of Education gives us valuable information about this need. In 1954 The Methodist Church had 17,070 effective ministers (annual conference members appointed to pastorates). This is 559 fewer than we had in 1940. In 1940 we had 3,341 supply pastors, and in 1954 we had 5,918. The magazine *Church and Campus* for November-December, said:

> The Methodist Church needs more ministers and needs them now! In 1954 there were 1,129 ministers removed from annual conference membership by retirement, death, withdrawal and location. In the same year 927 men were received into full connection. The number received on trial in the same year shows an even more serious drop. Only 910 were admitted into the "on trial" classes in the total church. There were fewer ministers appointed to charges and special appointments in 1954 than in 1940 at the time of

unification. A comparison of these figures shows that we are not meeting our manpower needs for replacement.

We believe that a great evangelistic movement in the local church will help to secure the manpower we need for these new churches.

The Methodist Church must think seriously about training laymen for certain work in our Boards and annual conferences and local churches. There are 2,105 effective members of annual conferences serving in special appointments.

We believe that in the near future, automation in industry will bring a 30-hour week and then a 24-hour week. Laymen who work only three days per week will have four days that can be used to secure college and seminary education and become pastors and give full time to one church. These lay preachers will secure their income by another vocation but will give two and three days per week to one church.

Every church needs a pastor all day on Sunday and other days for visiting. Under our circuit system—which made the Methodist churches—some churches have a pastor for only one hour on Sunday and what time he can spare during the week. He never meets with the Sunday school and the young people unless the MYF meets during the week. We do not plead for an uneducated lay ministry. We want the laymen to be college trained and seminary trained so that they can serve effectively for Christ.

We talk about urban, rural, and suburban churches. Our people are all the same today. The farm people have all the machinery for the farm and gadgets for the home—the same as the urbanite. Our young couples in rural life are high school and college trained. We have one people today, and all of them need to be told about sin and salvation. If you do not care for those words, then they need to know about the disintegration of self and integration in Christ.

In 1900 The Methodist Church was the largest church of any Protestant denomination in the United States. This was true in 1950. It may not be true in 1960. In 1900 The Methodist Church was a great evangelistic movement. During the first forty years of this century, we gave more emphasis to education than we did to evangelism. We should have given emphasis to education, and perhaps more than we did; but we should not have neglected evangelism.

At 1950 we find ourselves emphasizing both Christian education and evangelism. We believe that the next fifty years are going to be the glorious years of Methodism. We believe that when we reach the year 2000, the United States will have a population of more than 275,000,000 persons and The Methodist Church will have more than 20,000,000 members.

This can be done if our Christian education continues to become more and more evangelistic and our evangelism becomes more and more educational. Piety plus knowledge makes for the kingdom of God. I want The Methodist Church to become a great evangelistic movement because of its social passion concerning the welfare of every individual.

The Methodist Church has a philosophy, a program, and a passion. Today we dedicate ourselves to reach the New America for Christ until this New America becomes, not the American way of life, but the Christian way of life—the kingdom of God.

Sincerely your friend,

HARRY DENMAN
—*Rejoice*, 1956

DOUBLE AFFIRMATIVES AND DOUBLE NEGATIVES
by Harry Denman

To Members of the Council on World Service and Finance:

Last spring we sent you a copy of the printed annual report of the Board of Evangelism. Also we have prepared for you the statements that you suggested pertaining to budget expenditures and to activity of work.

Dr. Dow Kirkpatrick states that there are three groups of persons in every community:

1. The double affirmatives, who have said *yes* to Christ and *yes* to the church
2. The double negatives, who have said *no* to Christ and *no* to the church
3. The single affirmatives and the single negatives, those who have said *yes* to Christ and *no* to the church and those who have said *no* to Christ and *yes* to the church.

Our task of evangelism is to persuade and help the double affirmatives to live the redemptive life personally and socially and thereby witness to the double negatives.

Evangelism is stressing the attendance of the double affirmatives at worship services so that they may disperse to work and witness to society and to the double negatives.

Evangelism is urging the single affirmative who has said *yes* to the church but *no* to Christ to say *yes* to Christ and become a double affirmative.

The Methodist Church, under the leadership of our bishops, is going forward with its evangelistic work. Each year we add more new persons to our church rolls than the previous year. The church school is doing splendid evangelism by winning the boys and girls for Christ. The Methodist Youth Fellowship, with the Christian Witness Evangelism, is securing the youth for Christ and the church.

Methodist Men are trying to win 50,000 men for Christ and the church. The Women's Society of Christian Service has a great objective for evangelism, and this objective is becoming a reality.

The Methodist Church is working at evangelism. We are securing new persons, but we are not increasing our church membership percentage as fast as the population increase. This is due to the large number of members removed from our rolls by action of the quarterly conferences of our churches.

As long as The Methodist Church apportions amounts of money to be raised by the local church on the basis of so many dollars per member, then the local church will continue to remove from its roll those members who do not pay. Many churches do not see the spiritual enrichment in giving. They only see that if they can discontinue 200 members from the church roll they will decrease the amount of their apportionments.

We know that through the method of visitation evangelism a new church can be organized in one month with more than one hundred charter members. We know that an evangelistic church can be self-supporting in one year or two years. They do need money for capital investments.

Our greatest evangelistic opportunity is to increase our number of churches and church schools. We must have men and women to be the pastors of these new churches.

We are sponsoring evangelistic missions to members. We are urging the churches to have Spiritual Life Missions. We are trying to do as did our founder, John Wesley. He wrote many times, "I give them Christ."

During the 1940s we discovered humanity. During the 1950s we discovered our faith in God. During the 1960s the church will discover Christ and live as he lived.

Our evangelistic task is to reach the double negatives, and there are millions of them. We must take Christ to them. They do not attend our churches, our organizations, or the great mass evangelistic crusades. The only way is to do as Jesus did—go to them.

A great bank in Dallas, Texas, has this slogan, "Give us the opportunity to say *yes*." I wonder if the double negatives are not waiting for us to come in order that they can say *yes*. Zacchaeus said Yes. Levi said Yes. Simon Peter said Yes. Philip said Yes. Andrew said Yes. James and John said Yes. The woman at Sychar said Yes. They were not in synagogues, but they were at the place where Jesus found them.

Mr. Kiplinger, in his letter of September 15, gave us some valuable information about the increase in our population. We will give you a copy of his statement. This a great evangelistic challenge. The Methodist Church must gird itself for this task. Business is doing it. The General Conference of 1960 should be known as the General Conference of the Twentieth Century for Church Extension.

The Methodist Church should be organizing two new churches a day instead of one. From 1960 to 1964 the war babies will be getting married. We must have churches for them.

Our task in evangelism is to see that the double affirmative members who have truly said *yes* to Christ and the single affirmations who have said *yes* to the church and *no* to Christ will have Christ in their hearts and will so live the gospel that no quarterly conference will be able to remove them from the church roll.

Our great field of evangelism is the church itself. We must labor and pray until the church becomes a force for Christ.

In the last few days, a young woman has come to Scarritt College as a Crusade Scholar. She is the first missionary to be sent out by our church in the Philippines. She has served in Okinawa for three years. She is quoted as saying, "If you have Christ in your heart, you are a missionary. If you do not have Christ in your heart then you are a field for the missionary enterprise."

One can say, "If you have Christ in your heart, you are an evangelist; if you do not have Christ in your heart, then you are a field for evangelism."

One can cay, "If you have Christ in your heart, you are a redeemer; and you live the redemptive life. If you do not have Christ in your heart, then you are a field for redemption."

—*For the General Council on World Service and Finance*
September 23, 1957

THE UNIVERSAL GOSPEL OF CHRIST
BY HARRY DENMAN

The Christian gospel is universal because it concerns and identifies itself with all persons. Jesus himself, in the days of his flesh, gave proof of his concern for all persons and his complete identification with them.

Jesus was the self-invited guest in the home of Zacchaeus, who was chief among the publicans and designated a sinner by the self-righteous. Jesus was at ease in this home. No doubt Zacchaeus was ill at ease until he declared his faith by making material things second in his life. The self-righteous were uneasy in their minds because their institutional religion was under attack by what Jesus was saying and doing.

Legalism sees caste, but the gospel of universal redemptive love sees a person created in the image of God and redeemed by redemptive love on a cross. Jesus Christ is a Savior for all persons, or he is not a Savior for any. The night he was born, the angel said to the shepherds, "I bring you good tidings of great joy, which shall be to all people." The good tidings is that a Savior is born not only for Pharisees but also for publicans.

At the time that Zacchaeus found salvation in his house, Jesus said, "The Son of man is come to seek and to save that which was lost." The followers of institutional religion did not seek to redeem the lost because the attitude of the religious authorities was that their religion was for a few and for only one class of persons.

Jesus identified himself with the Pharisees. Simon the Pharisee invited Jesus to his home for dinner. Jesus proved to the self-righteous Pharisees at the table that he was not a prophet, for he was willing for a woman known to be a sinner to touch him as she bathed his feet with her tears and dried them with the hair of her head. This woman received forgiveness, salvation, and peace because of her faith. The Pharisees were not willing even to acknowledge Jesus as a prophet, much less as a Savior. They believed in law, but Jesus believed in the universal love of God for all persons.

Jesus identified himself with the Samaritans. One day at high noon he sat at a well and counseled with a woman who had had five husbands and was living with a man who was not her husband. She was surprised that Jesus, a Jew, would have dealings with her, a Samaritan. His nationalistic and race-conscious disciples marveled that he talked with this Samaritan woman. Christ's gospel for all humankind does not see a Samaritan or a woman but sees a person who is trying to satisfy the things of the spirit with the things of the flesh.

By speaking with her, Jesus revealed to her that he was the Messiah. Universal love speaks to every person, regardless of race and color. Jesus could have bypassed Samaria in going from Judea to Galilee, but he had no prejudice toward the Samaritan people.

Those who know Christ as Savior are willing to go to the largest metropolitan city or to the smallest barrio and village of the world. Today, we thank God for those who are identifying themselves with the refugees in Hong Kong, in Calcutta, and in other parts of the world.

A layman in Bangalore, India, reminded us of what can happen in one day. He said, "At high noon this Samaritan woman found a Savior, and before dark she had brought the men to Jesus." That day the disciples went to Sychar. They did not bring men to Jesus as the woman did, but they brought meat for the body.

Jesus identified himself with the Galileans. He came into Galilee preaching the gospel of the kingdom of God. From among them Jesus secured many of his disciples, although members of the Sanhedrin said that no prophet came out of Galilee. Jesus never saw Galileans; he saw persons.

There is no place for the caste system in the kingdom of God. The gospel of the kingdom of God teaches abolition of caste and class. The kingdom of God is classless.

Members of the Sanhedrin marveled when they perceived that the Galileans were unlearned and ignorant men. Saul of Tarsus, the intellectual giant of his day, became a part of this great kingdom of God movement after his experience of the living Christ on the road to Damascus.

The universal gospel is for the learned and the unlearned; for the rich and the poor; for the Pharisee and the publican; for the Galileans, Samaritans, and Judeans; for the lepers and the demon-possessed.

Jesus identified himself with the children. The disciples sent them away, but Jesus took young children in his arms and blessed them, and said, "Suffer the little children to come unto me, and forbid them not: for of such is the kingdom of God."

The non-Christian religions of the world are growing faster today than the Christian religion because of the population explosion. It is estimated that the world population will be five billion by 1990. What a challenge this is to the Christian gospel!

Jesus is most attractive to children. Today we must give our major attention to the youth and the children. By 1970 half of the population in some parts of the world will be under twenty-one years of age.

At the World Methodist Conference in Oslo, much was said about missions, missionary cooperation, and who should do it. I sincerely hope that we can avoid duplication and overlapping. I am more interested that we have a great missionary movement than I am in who does it. I can see the children of the villages and barrios of Korea, Malaya, India, South and North America, and the Philippines, who need to have Christian nurture. Children and youth do not wait for world organizations to make plans. They become adults while we plan and discuss. World Methodism should dedicate itself to reaching the children and the youth for Christ and his kingdom.

Jesus identified himself with the multitude. The disciples urged him to send them away. He had compassion on them and taught them. The gospel of Jesus Christ is not for the few but for the masses.

We hear much about universal relief. We believe every child should have food for his or her body; but as a world organization, do we spend as much money for the culture of the souls of children and youth as we do for the feeding and healing of their bodies and for the secular training of their minds? We have world health organizations. We have world relief organizations. We have world literary movements. We need a Universal Gospel Movement for the children, youth, and multitudes.

There must be an Oxford Club for depth, but there must also be an evangelistic movement to the multitudes. There must be an upper room in which a small group of persons will continue in prayer until they have one mind and a new life in the Spirit. There must be a small group that believes in "justification by faith," in order to have a reformation that will take the gospel to the neglected multitudes.

The gospel of Jesus Christ calls for motivation by a divine quality that demands all of a person. This kind of quality believes in quantity. Paul had a quality gospel that took him to many cities on the Mediterranean and in Macedonia. Paul identified himself with the outcasts of Corinth, the philosophers of Athens, the young fortuneteller in Philippi. He told the Roman guards about the gospel, and they became saints in Caesar's household. John Wesley told the multitude about the gospel of Jesus Christ. He became "more vile," as he described it, in order to make known to them the gospel. He also encouraged the formation of small groups in order that there would be spiritual depth and participation.

In Samaria Jesus said, "Lift up your eyes, and look on the fields; for they are white already to harvest." The fields in Samaria are always white unto the harvest.

The gospel of Jesus Christ must never be identified with any *ism* or movement. Today there are certain sincere laypersons who believe that God has called them to save the church from the influence of atheistic communism. On the other hand, they are willing for the church to be influenced by some who make capitalism their god. The gospel of Christ is for the atheistic communist and for the godless capitalist; it is for those who are non-Christian in labor, social, and political movements.

Jesus identified himself with those who were sick of mind, heart, soul, and body. He gave himself to the demon-possessed man of Gadara. In the Decapolis, this man became a publisher of the universal gospel. Jesus put his hand on lepers, and they became whole. A woman who had been sick of body for twelve years found comfort, peace, faith, and wholeness when she had faith in him and touched the border of his garment. He preached the gospel to the poor. He healed the brokenhearted. He fed the multitude. He brought sight to the blind. He preached deliverance to the captives. He set at liberty those who were bruised. He brought life to the dead. He went about doing good. He healed persons on the Sabbath day, though he knew that the religious leaders who believed in oxen and sheep more than in persons would kill him. Jesus had a passion for all to be made whole. Of some he would ask, "Wilt thou be made whole?" To others he said, "Thy faith hath made thee whole." Blind beggars found sight in him. Some lame beggars were made to walk because of obedience to his word.

It is estimated that 100,000 babies are born every day. If they live to be seventy years old, more than half of them will be hungry all the days of their lives. Today men and women are hungry for bread. They are lonely. They are unwanted. They are neglected. They are sick in body, heart, mind, and soul.

We who believe in the gospel of Christ must have Christ's social passion for all persons. We believe in individual and social redemption. We believe in the conversion of the individual and society. The gospel of Christ directs the *haves* to share with the *have-nots*. The people of China starve for food, while in some countries food is stored because of surpluses. People in a Christian nation may not agree with the political philosophy of another nation, but can it be called a Christian nation when its people will not share a surplus of food with those who are without food?

The Christian gospel teaches, "Love your enemies, bless them that curse you, do good to them that hate you." Which is Christian—spending billions of dollars to go to the moon, or sharing billions of dollars with our Father's children who are sick and hungry?

Meets Spiritual Needs of All

The gospel of Christ is universal because it offers the grace of God for all our spiritual needs. We see this grace of God in the person of our Lord Jesus Christ.

"The Word became flesh and dwelt among us, full of grace and truth." Jesus was and is full of grace for all conditions of humanity.

Persons are selfish and desire to have their way. Our tendency is to obey self and disobey God. This separates us from God. This is sin and gives us a guilt consciousness.

Jesus was full of forgiving grace. He said to men and women, "Thy sins are forgiven." The legalists said that he was a blasphemer. Law does not show mercy. Administration of the law may show mercy. Redeeming love always shows forgiving grace.

Law, in the mind of the self-righteous, said to Jesus about a woman taken in the act of sin: "Moses in the law commanded us, that such should be stoned: but what sayest thou?" Forgiving grace in the heart of Jesus did not condemn her but said, "Go, and sin no more."

Sometimes we cannot find forgiveness at the hands of friends, family, society, or the church; but always, when we come to Christ in penitence, we find forgiving grace.

The gospel of forgiving grace not only brings the assurance of forgiveness but helps us to forgive ourselves. John Wesley said about Aldersgate: "I felt I did trust in Christ,

Christ alone for salvation, and an assurance was given me that he had taken away *my* sins, even *mine*, and saved *me* from the law of sin and death." What a blessed assurance to know that the grace of God abounds more than all our sin! Furthermore, the followers of the gospel of Christ are full of forgiving grace. They seek to forgive all who have committed sin against them.

Jesus was full of redeeming grace. When a person knows that he or she is a sinner and separated from God, he or she then becomes conscious of the need for redeeming grace. The woman in the home of Simon the Pharisee needed redeeming grace. She had performed the works of penitence, humility, sorrow, love, and gifts. But it was her faith that brought redeeming grace to her. Jesus said to her, "Thy faith hath saved thee."

Jesus was born a Savior. He said, "For the Son of man is not come to destroy men's lives, but to save them." "For the Son of man is come to seek and to save that which was lost." As he was dying on the cross, his enemies said, "He saved others; himself he cannot save."

Redeeming grace never thinks of itself but always of others. Redeeming grace, living in the flesh, will help all to desire this way of love. Redeeming grace will always give itself to others. Redeeming grace in the flesh of a person at the steering wheel of an automobile will help one to drive safely and carefully, not to save his or her own life but to save the lives of neighbors. Redeeming grace loses its own life in order that the lives of others can be saved.

In the town of Laur in the mountains of the Philippines, the bones of a Methodist preacher are buried beneath the pulpit of a small Methodist church. Loving hands of the members of that church brought his bones from the mouth of a cave where he had taken some of the people during the war in order to save them. The people were found by the enemy. The Methodist pastor and the Roman Catholic priest were slain, but they saved their people. Redeeming grace never thinks of self.

Jesus was full of witnessing grace. He had a concern for the unconcerned. He sought the unsought. He loved the unlovely. He desired the undesirable. He was gracious to the ungracious. He wanted the unwanted.

Witnessing grace sends us to the Samaritans, the Galileans, the harlots, the outcasts, the publicans, the lepers, the demon-possessed, the children, and the multitude. Nominal church members say, as did the disciples who were not yet Spirit-filled, "Send [the multitude] away." Witnessing grace sends us forth to all persons.

The universal gospel gives us grace to witness to a Samaritan woman at a well, to a publican in his home, to a demon-possessed woman on the street, to a thief on a cross.

Universal means *all* persons. A church that witnesses only to those who come to its sanctuary will soon be a museum or a mausoleum. The church that believes in the gospel of Christ will go to the community in which the church is located, as well as send its sons and daughters to witness to others who are far removed from its community.

Many who claim the experience of redeeming grace say that they are unable to witness concerning their experience. All persons are witnesses. There are two kinds of witnesses: those who are for, and those who are against. We either witness for Christ or against Christ. We either live for the glory of God or for the glory of self.

We obey either the will of God or the will of self. We cannot serve God and self. Jesus said, "I came down from heaven, not to do mine own will, but the will of him that sent me." Jesus said, "Not every one that saith unto me, Lord, Lord, shall enter into the kingdom of heaven; but he that doeth the will of my Father which is in heaven."

The believers in Christ will be full of redeeming grace, and they will live so attractively that others will be attracted to Christ. They will be so gracious that others will desire the grace of the Lord Jesus Christ. They will be so winsome that their living will win some. We witness wherever we are—in the home, in the factory, in the school, in the social room, in society, in the political hall, in the business house, in the church.

Our witnessing will bring persons to Christ or send them away. The church must be the body of Christ. If Christ is the body, then the members of the body will be Christ-living. Today we need Christ-living evangelism.

Social salvation comes when the individual members of society believe in Christ, behave as they believe, and perform as they profess. The universal gospel is impotent unless lived. It is not what we say but what we do. Why have a creed unless it becomes a fact in our lives?

The Christ of the gospel is anxious for all to be whole. He is full of plenteous grace; but as Charles Wesley sang,

> I am all unrighteousness;
> False and full of sin I am.*

The gospel of Christ is our hope of salvation. The Christ of the gospel redeems the penitent who believes in him. Jesus said to the woman who emerged from the throng and admitted that she had touched him: "Daughter, thy faith hath made thee whole; go in peace." Jesus said to blind Bartimaeus, "Thy faith hath made thee whole." This gospel of Christ offers hope for everyone, for it is concerned that all persons be made whole.

Humankind has conquered land, sea, air, and outer space; but not self. We can never conquer self by self-will, for in self-will lies our weakness. Therefore, in order to be strong, we must let Christ have our weakness. As the Lord spoke to Paul, so he speaks to us, "My strength is made perfect in weakness." We are made strong when we are willing to become weak. Self is controlled by Christ when we become his bond slaves. We need our lives to be Christ-controlled.

Paul had a thorn in the flesh. Thrice he asked for its removal, but the Lord said, "My grace is sufficient for thee." It may have been a physical disability. It could have been jealousy, temper, desire to have his way, prejudice, anger—but

*From the hymn "Jesus, Lover of My Soul."

the grace of Christ was sufficient for his need. Whatever spiritual need we have, whatever physical disability we have, whatever our afflictions, Jesus has sufficient and plenteous grace for us.

We are afraid of the haunting hound of death—death of the body. But Jesus has conquered this haunting fear. He gives us grace to overcome this hound. The Gospels reveal to us that Christ conquered the grave. We are untroubled and unafraid about the death of the body because our faith is in the living Christ. Long before Jesus came to earth, the psalmist sang, "The Lord is my light and my salvation; whom shall I fear? The Lord is the strength of my life; of whom shall I be afraid?" In the light of Christ's victory over death, the words of Christ take on added meaning: "Because I live, ye shall live also."

Paul said, "O death, where is thy sting? O grave, where is thy victory?... Thanks be to God, which giveth us the victory through our Lord Jesus Christ." John Wesley looked death in the face and said, "The best of all is, God is with us."

The grace of the universal gospel gives us strength for living in the flesh day by day. It also gives us a joyful experience now and an expectancy beyond the mortal life, of life in the spirit with our Savior.

The universal gospel meets all the universal needs—forgiveness, salvation, wholeness, witnessing, living in the flesh, and living in the spirit. All persons must hear about this wonderful and amazing universal gospel.

Uses All Methods of Communication

Believers in this universal gospel must use all methods of communication. Jesus came preaching, teaching, praying, visiting, healing, calling persons and training them to communicate the gospel.

In the pulpit and in the classroom, it is our privilege to proclaim Christ to persons. In our visitation evangelism, we must tell persons about Christ the Savior. On the radio, the gospel must be proclaimed. In our audiovisual ministry such as television, the filmstrip, and the motion picture, Christ must be lifted up. He is the gospel. He is the Savior.

We hope that the day will come when, by words, every Methodist will be an evangelist in personal living or testimony. In many places there is a movement among the laity to take this gospel to every house by knocking on every door. The telephone is being used to ascertain information about the spiritual condition of the occupants of each home.

John Wesley, after Aldersgate, took the gospel to those who were assembled outdoors. In 1963, when we commemorate the 225th anniversary of the Aldersgate experience of John Wesley, I hope every Methodist will have a heartwarming experience.

During 1963, we should, as Methodists, take this universal gospel to all persons where we find them—the pubs, the cinemas, the drive-in theaters, the parks, the seashores, the vacation resorts, the prisons, the industrial plants, the remote places, the inner city, and suburbia. We should go to every barrio and village. Many persons are waiting to hear the gospel. All means of communication must be used to make this gospel known.

If we believe that this gospel is universal, we will make it universal by taking it to all persons. I hope that Methodism in 1963 will major in:

1. Depth evangelism for small groups.
2. Mass evangelism for the multitudes.
3. Reaching families and individuals by knocking on the door of every home.
4. Pulpit and classroom evangelism for the church members until the church becomes a *force* instead of a *field* for evangelism.
5. Pew evangelism—every member of the priesthood of believers witnessing to the gospel of Christ.
6. Social evangelism—penetrate every part of society and condemn all evils that are destroying individual and family life.

7. Audiovisual evangelism—use all the means of communication to reach the unreached for Christ.

The Methodist Church must have something to give.

Simon Peter said to the lame beggar at the Beautiful Gate of the temple at Jerusalem, "I have no silver and gold, but I give you what I have." Peter gave him Christ.

We have more means of communication than Peter had, but he had something to give. On the day of Pentecost, something happened to Simon Peter. He could say to the people in Jerusalem, "This Jesus hath God raised up, whereof we all are witnesses." Later, before the Sanhedrin, he said, "We are his witnesses." The Methodist Church must be willing to tarry until we are endued with power from on high. We need to be filled with the Holy Spirit and then use all the means of communication for making the gospel of Christ known to all persons.

The Methodist Church is accused of being an activist movement. Thank God that it is. I desire that it be more active in communicating the gospel. My prayer is that every Methodist will be an *active* evangelist. This demands much activity. Let us be called activists, but let us be as active as Christ was in witnessing to all persons. Let us be as active in the living room for Christ as we are in the committee room.

Solves Social Problems

The gospel of Christ is universal because it has the truth for all problems of the social order and the spiritual power to change them.

War and Peace. The gospel of Christ says, "Blessed are the meek: for they shall inherit the earth. . . . Blessed are the peacemakers: for they shall be called the children of God." "Put up again thy sword into his place: for all they that take the sword shall perish with the sword." "Love your enemies, bless them that curse you, do good to them that hate you, and pray for them which despitefully use you, and persecute you."

We can accept the teachings of our Savior and have peace, or we can let our love for materialism bring about the end of civilization. We do not want Marxism to rule the world, but we want the followers of Christ to accept him as Lord and let him rule and reign over their lives.

Hatred and Brotherhood. Jesus said, "A new commandment I give unto you, That ye love one another; as I have loved you, that ye also love one another. By this shall all men know that ye are my disciples, if ye have love one to another." "If ye love me, keep my commandments." "This is my commandment, That ye love one another, as I have loved you."

The universal gospel is a gospel of love for all persons. "For God so loved the world, that he gave his only begotten Son, that whosoever believeth in him should not perish, but have everlasting life." Paul expressed his gratitude, saying, "I live by the faith of the Son of God, who loved me, and gave himself for me."

The love of God is redemptive love and gives self. If we live by this truth we will have brotherhood.

Integration and Segregation. When we say "integration" and "segregation," we think of color, but I am interested both in color and class integration. Is a church Christian if a person is unwanted because of class, color, or caste? The Christian church becomes non-Christian when it identifies itself exclusively with any culture, class, or color. Methodism must never be known as an Eastern or Western church. Our founder said, "The world is my parish." It is easy for an autonomous church to become nationalistic and of a certain culture. We speak of British Methodism, American Methodism, Korean Methodism, and Indian Methodism. I pray that there will be a day when there will be a world Methodist Church that will be catholic and universal in its evangelism and that nations and nationalism will be forgotten when we think of The Methodist Church.

I pray that each Methodist society will be willing to be universal in class and color and caste.

We say much about segregated white churches, but how about segregated churches of other colors? A church that is comprised of persons of only one color is liable to have racial pride. A church that is comprised of only one class has a tendency to become a club. A church that is comprised of persons of one nation has a tendency to be nationalistic. There is no place for nationalism, racial pride, or color in the universal gospel.

Democracy and Dictatorship. Will the world have democracy or dictatorship? The universal gospel of Christ puts the importance on the individual. Jesus would have given his life for one person. This is seen when Jesus went to the pool of Bethesda on the Sabbath morning to heal a man. He knew the religious people would plan to kill him for this, but he went.

The universal gospel teaches that a person is valuable because God loves him or her. We are more than material; we are spiritual. We are created in the image of God. Dictatorships take from us our freedom, our liberty. Democracy gives us our freedom, our liberty.

Methodism is against crime, intoxicating beverages, obscene pictures and obscene literature, gambling, riots, lynchings, racial prejudice, social evils, or any political philosophy that harms or destroys the individual or the family.

The gospel of Jesus Christ proclaims the sacredness of each individual and looks upon the family as the basic unit of society. The universal gospel calls for a new world order based on Christian democracy—the kingdom of God on earth.

Let us dedicate ourselves to communicate this gospel of Christ to all persons and to live daily the truths contained therein. Evangelism is for all persons, or it is not evangelism. Methodism believes in the universality of the gospel, and Methodism always has been at its best during pioneer and frontier days. The world population explosion gives a world frontier. Methodism must become a *world* evangelistic movement or a dead sect. Let us be determined to give our time, talents, and wealth to the proclamation and the communicating of the redeeming gospel of Christ.

The gospel is universal because
>   it identifies itself with all persons,
>   it meets the spiritual needs of all persons,
>   it uses all means of communication, and
>   it has the truth for solving all the problems of the
>   social order.

—For The World Methodist Conference
Oslo, Norway, August 24, 1961

SERMONS

All ten of these sermons have New Testament texts, beginning with a personal confession of faith based on Mark 1:14. A series of three sermons on the general theme of "A God-Sent Christ" follows, all three discourses with texts from the Gospel of John.

A proclamation concerning the church as an organism (and not an organization) is based on Matthew 16:18.

Two aspects on the perceptions of Jesus are taken from John 12:21 and John 14:6 as the sixth and seventh sermons.

Peter's experience of preaching at Joppa, as recorded in Acts 11; and Paul's description of the varieties of Christian gifts and the unity of the body of Christ, from the twelfth chapter of First Corinthians, are placed together in this series.

The final sermon provides reflections on the meaning and the importance of the first Pentecost experience of the Christian community, as it is set forth in the second chapter of the Acts of the Apostles.

—This section has been edited by Robert F. Lundy.

Why I Am Here

One day I was sitting in a garage talking to a woman about committing her life to Jesus Christ. A man under the influence of liquor came to the garage and joined in the conversation. Finally he said to me, "What would Jesus do if he were living in this community?" That is a very surprising and striking question, but I said to him, "I believe that Jesus would do in this community what he did in Judea and in Galilee and in Samaria." So I asked myself that question, "What have I come here to do, and why am I here?" I keep thinking about this all the time. I believe that I have come to do what Jesus would do if he were here. I claim to be one of his followers, and therefore, I ought to be Christ-like in what I do.

The text for this morning is "Christ Came into Galilee Preaching the Gospel of the Kingdom of God (Mark 1:14)." Christ came to Galilee to establish the kingdom of God. He did it by preaching the gospel. Repent and believe the gospel. The kingdom means life for all. Christ said, "I am come that they might have life, and that they might have it more abundantly."

All persons desire life. When the hungry people desired bread, Christ gave them bread for their bodies. That meant he was providing physical life for them. Christ is the manna from heaven and that is life for our souls.

When Christ and his disciples were in Samaria, the Samaritans did not receive them because his face was as though he would go to Jerusalem. James and John wanted to bring fire down from heaven and consume these Samaritans, but Jesus rebuked them and said, "For the Son of man is not come to destroy men's lives, but to save them." We see from this that Jesus did not come to destroy life but to bring life.

One day a certain ruler asked Jesus, "Good Master, what shall I do to inherit eternal life?" Jesus said, "Thou knowest the commandments, Do not commit adultery, Do not kill, Do not steal, do not bear false witness, Honour thy father and thy mother." The rich ruler said, "All these I have kept from my youth up." Jesus said, "Yet lackest thou one thing: sell all that thou hast, and distribute unto the poor, and thou shalt have treasure in heaven: and come, follow me."

We know the ruler did not do this. He turned away. He did not want life. He thought he wanted life, but he wanted his gold more than he wanted his life.

"A certain lawyer stood up, and tempted [Jesus] saying, 'Master, what shall I do to inherit eternal life?' [Jesus] said unto him, 'What is written in the law? how readest thou?' And he answering said, 'Thou shalt love the Lord thy God with all thy heart, with all thy soul, with all thy strength, and with all thy mind; and thy neighbour as thyself,' and [Jesus] said unto him, 'Thou hast answered right: this do and thou shalt live.' But [the lawyer, who perhaps did not desire to do this] said unto Jesus, 'And who is my neighbor?' "

And then Jesus told the beautiful story of the Good Samaritan. You see, when you commit your life to Jesus Christ, you become a member of the kingdom and that means life.

We are here to give persons to Christ in order that they might find life. If you are searching for life today, commit your life to Christ, and he will give you life.

In order to be a part of the kingdom, we must do what Jesus said in his message—we must repent and believe the gospel. Repentance means to change your mind. It means to change your mind from the worship of gold to the worship of God. It means to change your mind from the things of the flesh to the things of the Spirit. It means to change your mind from hatred to love. It means to change your mind from racial prejudice to brotherhood. It means to change your mind from the monopoly of things to the giving of things, from selfishness to generosity. And not only must we change our mind, but we must believe. And to believe the gospel means to believe in the good news and that is life. So we change our minds from dying to living. We change our minds from death to living.

In the second place, Christ not only came to establish the kingdom, but he secured persons for the kingdom. And he asked these persons to help him to establish the kingdom. He secured Andrew and Simon, James and John, Philip and Nathanael. He went to the courthouse and secured Levi, a tax collector. At Sychar in Samaria, he secured a woman who brought the whole town to him. One day as he was going to Jericho he saw a small man up a tree. He asked him to come down because he wanted to go home to dinner with him, and he secured Zacchaeus. Another time Jesus went to Gadara, where there was a man who was demon-possessed. Jesus secured him and asked him to publish the good news in the Decapolis.

Jesus Christ went, and he said for his followers to go. He said, "Go" to the twelve, to the seventy, to the one-hundred and twenty, and to the man in Gadara. We must do this. During this Year of Evangelism, how many have you told about Christ and the life they can secure in him? This has been a glorious year, and many persons have found Christ because of the testimony of laymen and laywomen.

I have a friend who is a great surgeon in his city. Also he is chair of the evangelistic committee of his church. He wrote me not long ago and told me of the joy that was his as he sat in his pew on Easter Sunday morning and saw the people stand at the altar and commit their lives to Christ and unite with the church. He realized that he had spoken to some of these, that he had turned aside from pleasure and from the duties of his profession and had gone to their homes in the evening and had sought them for Christ.

I was visiting a place in Paducah, Kentucky, and as the preacher and I approached the institution a man came to greet us and said to us, "He has done it! He has done it! He has done it!" And the preacher said, "What do you mean?" And he said, "Oh! our good friend has surrendered his life to Christ and is going to join the church." Many persons had been speaking to that man and praying for him, and everyone rejoiced when he had made his decision. Do you know the joy of your friend's committing his or her life to Christ because you have spoken to him or her?

Last winter we were having an evangelistic campaign in Chicago. Thousands of laypersons were out visiting every night during the worst of the winter with snow and ice all over the ground, and this story came out of a man's office. One morning he went to his office and told his chief that the Methodists were out to his home the previous evening trying to secure his commitment for Christ in the church. To his amazement his chief said, "Well, I live in another part of the city and the Methodists were in my home last night asking me and my family to commit our lives to Christ and the church." They laughed about it to think that the Methodists were doing this in different parts of the city. Later on in the day, one of the officers of the company arrived from New York, and when the three of them were having lunch they told him what had happened the previous night. He said, "That is strange. I live in New Jersey and last week the Methodists were in my home asking me to become a Christian and unite with the church." And this is the spirit of Methodism. All over the nation, laypersons are going from door to door and from house to house and office to office telling persons about Christ and his kingdom.

Not long ago I was staying in a hotel, and a Negro maid said to me, "Are you a preacher?" And I said, "I try to be." Then I asked, "What church do you belong to?" She said, "I am a Witness." I said, "What is your preacher's name?" She said, "We do not have preachers." I said, "Where is your church?" She said, "We do not have a church. Every person is a witness." I do not agree with what she believes, but I do admire any group where every person considers himself or herself a witness. And that is the spirit we need in this church, that every member will consider himself or herself a witness for Christ.

In the third place, the followers of Christ must live as

he did and that means to live in the spiritual kingdom rather than in a materialistic kingdom. In other words, a Christian is a reproduction of Christ. We must live as he lived. This is the desire of every Christian.

What did Christ do? In the first place, he knew the Scriptures. He was always quoting from the law and from the poets and from the prophets. He said, "I am not come to destroy [the law], but to fulfil [the law]." Therefore, we must read the Scripture and know what he did and what he taught. Read the Gospel of Mark this week or the Gospel of John or the Book of Acts.

I have a friend who does not agree with everything that I say. He runs a very large manufacturing plant and is a very wealthy man. He asked me to come to his city to see him. I am very fond of him and after we had spent a half-day going over his plant, then we had lunch in the cafeteria. I said to him, "What would you like for the church to do?" He said, "I want the church to teach Christianity." I said, "That is a very dangerous thing; the most radical thing I know. Have you read the Sermon on the Mount recently?" He said, "No, but I will." And I say to you this morning that if my millionaire friend can tell me that he wants the church to teach Christianity and that means to teach Christ, that I am going out to do it. But we must know what Christ taught and how he lived.

In the second place, Christ prayed. I sincerely hope that we will spend at least three minutes each morning listening to Christ and that he will tell you what he wants you to do. Not long ago I was holding special services in a church. I met with the officials of the church and asked them what they would like for me to do. One of the officials said that he thought I ought to obey the Holy Spirit. I told him that that was rather costly, but I would try to do it. Of course, I would like for the officials to do the same thing. Now we can never know what the Holy Spirit has for us to do unless we spend some time listening, and so I suggest that we listen.

In the third place, Christ went to the synagogue and the Temple and also to a place of prayer. He went to the synagogue according to his custom. He went to the Temple for all the feast days. He drove the moneychangers out of the Temple in order that the lame and the blind could come. In other words, the poorest of the poor could come to the Temple to worship after Christ had driven out the money-changers.

So many people tell me that they can be Christians without going to church. Well, I know that is true, because there are many invalids who cannot go. You remember the man at the pool at Bethesda. As soon as he was healed the first thing he did was to go to the Temple. That's where Jesus found him. And I believe that those who are invalids long to go. When a man tells me he is a Christian, but that he doesn't have to go to the Temple or the synagogue, then I am not so sure. To be a Christian means to be Christlike, and Jesus went to the synagogue according to his custom, and he went to the Temple to worship.

In the fourth place, Christ healed and helped the bro-kenhearted and those who were hurt. One day when he was in the synagogue, he called a woman who had had an infirmity for eighteen years. He put his hands on her, and she was healed. He put his hands on lepers, and they were cleansed. He went home to eat with Levi, the publican. How many invalids have we been to see? I think that one of the things we ought to do is to visit the people who are not able to come to church. We make a rather big to-do over those that do come to church, but sometimes for months we neglect the people who cannot come. How many have we been to see? How many times have we been to the prison to see people? How many times have we been to those who have sorrow and those who are brokenhearted? Jesus said that he had come to heal the brokenhearted. He did it. And if we are going to be Christlike, we will do it.

In the fifth place, Christ was a servant. He took a towel. If we are going to be Christlike, we are going to be servants wherever we are. This summer I had a wonderful time washing dishes in a camp meeting. I presume the reason

I enjoyed it was because I didn't have to do it, but it was a relaxation; it was recreation because it was different from what I had been doing. Also this summer I was associated with some people who claimed to be very religious, but not a single person would make my bed. I did not ask them to do it. I presume they thought that I could. But one of the things I cannot do is to make up a bed, and I thought it would have been very fine if some of those good Christian women would have made my bed some morning. But I assume that they were busy doing some other things. They were cumbered with much care.

On Mother's Day we come and bring our gifts of love to our mothers, but I think it would be very helpful if we would wash dishes or if we would do some of the hard work she has to do and let her rest awhile.

In the sixth place, Christ had a great faith in God and faith in humanity. He was willing to die because of what he believed. He had committed his entire will and life for God.

Suppose my friend and I are in Niagara Falls, and a man has stretched a wire from the American side to the Canadian side over the falls. He announces he is going to walk across on this quarter-inch wire. I tell my friend I believe he can do it. And then this man not only says he can walk across, but he is going to push a wheelbarrow across. I tell my friend I believe he can walk across, and I believe he can push a wheelbarrow across. Then my friend says, "Do you believe he can walk across on that wire?" I say, "Yes." He says, "Do you believe he can push that wheelbarrow across?" I say, "Yes." Then he says, "Why don't you get in and ride?"

And that is what belief is. And we put our faith in God because God has never broken a promise yet. One time I was speaking in Athens, Georgia, to a large group of men. I asked them to gamble on God. I asked them to stake their all on God. After it was over a very fine Christian man, Mr. Tom Reed, who is a registrar of the university and who is older than I, came to me and said, "Harry, if you do not mind, I would like to make a suggestion to you." I said, "Certainly,

brother Tom." He said, "You asked us tonight to gamble on
God. We do not gamble on God. God is a surety." And how
true that is.

I think it would be rather interesting for us to go home
and write down on a piece of paper what we believe. Do we
believe that Christ can give life to everyone? We know that
every person is searching for life. If we believe that, then we
will go and tell that person. Do we believe that Christ can save
sinners from sin and save men and women from death if they
believe? Do we believe that Christ lives today?

In the seventh place, Christ had a great love even for
his enemies. He loved God. He loved every person. He loved
those who persecuted him. He loved those who put him to
death. And today we need that love. We need to love all
people, regardless of what they do to us.

I was in a city in Kentucky, and I asked a woman to
become a Christian. She told me No. She said she could not
go to church because she hated her neighbor. I said, "Did
your neighbor burn your house down?" She said, "No. I
loaned her my electric iron, and I went to get it, and she said
it wasn't mine." You see this woman was willing to lose her
own soul because of the hatred over an electric iron. She
ought to have been willing to buy a dozen electric irons and
give them away.

So I want to help Christ to establish his kingdom and to
help him secure subjects for his kingdom and to live in a
spiritual kingdom. If I live for a material kingdom, I lose all. If
I live in a spiritual kingdom, I gain all.

A God-Sent Christ Is Sent to the Children

I wish to raise this question for your thinking: Why did Christ come to earth? One of the great sentences in the Bible is "The Word was made flesh, and dwelt among us, . . . full of grace and truth."

In the Gospel of John, the 20th chapter, 21st verse, you find these words: "As my Father hath sent me, even so send I you." Jesus said my Father hath sent me. You find this in the Gospel of John many times: "My Father sent me." To whom did the Father send Jesus?

A God-sent Christ is sent to the children. Jesus must have had a wonderful reputation for loving children. Think of the fathers and mothers who came to him about their children.

A nobleman from Capernaum came to Cana of Galilee to ask Christ to heal his son who was at the point of death. This nobleman came to a Galilean peasant asking for help for his son.

He lived in Capernaum and knew of the healing power of Christ. He loved his son and wanted him to live, so he came to the great physician and was told by Christ that his son liveth.

A ruler of the synagogue by the name of Jairus came to Christ and fell at his feet, saying, "My little daughter lieth at the point of death: I pray thee, come and lay thy hands on her, that she may be healed; and she will live."

This incident reveals a ruler of the synagogue, kneeling at the feet of Christ, asking him to heal his daughter. You remember that the daughter died and when Jesus went to the home of Jairus that the people laughed Jesus to scorn. But Jesus brought life to that little girl.

A Canaanite woman came and besought him saying, "Have mercy on me, O Lord, thou Son of David; my daughter is grievously vexed with a devil." Jesus did not answer. He may have been testing her faith. The disciples said to him, "Send her away." The woman came and said, "Lord, help me." Jesus answered, "It is not meet to take the children's bread, and to cast it to dogs." The woman said, "Truth, Lord: yet the dogs eat of the crumbs which fall from their masters' table." Jesus answered, "O woman, great is thy faith: be it unto thee even as thou wilt." And her daughter was made whole from that very hour.

We see a nobleman, a ruler of the synagogue, and an outcast woman coming to Christ about their children; and he healed them. These desired that their children live.

They brought young children to Jesus. His disciples rebuked them that brought them. When Jesus saw it he was much displeased. And he took the little children in his arms, put his hands upon them, and blessed them.

Jesus made the child the greatest in the kingdom. When the disciples reasoned which of them should be the greatest, Jesus knew their thoughts. He took a child and set *him by him* and said, "Whosoever shall receive this child in my name receiveth me: and whosoever shall receive me receiveth him that sent me: for he that is least among you all, the same shall be great."

Jesus pronounced a curse on anyone who offended a little child who believed in him. "But whoso shall offend one of these little ones which believe in me, it were better for him that a millstone were hanged about his neck, and that he were drowned in the depth of the sea." We need to be very careful what we teach children who believe in Christ. As parents and teachers we should study to know the truth and give it to them.

I wonder if Christ is not displeased today with his disciples because of the way we are neglecting the children.

What is happening to the children? We are too busy making money, and children are being neglected. I have great respect for the woman who has to work to support her children. But I wish to say that any woman who has a husband who makes sufficient money to support the family, and she goes out to work and neglects her children is not patriotic.

I have admiration for a man who holds two jobs in order to help out in an emergency, but if he neglects the spiritual training of his children and if he is doing it to make money he is not doing his patriotic duty.

I have been in homes where children had to get their own meals—breakfast before they went to school and supper after they came home—because father and mother were both working. I have seen children cry to go to Sunday school, but their parents would not take them.

When a mother told me that her twelve-year-old son did not have an appreciation of the Sunday school, I found out that she and her husband were giving Sundays and five nights a week to a fraternal organization. I told her that she and her husband did not have an appreciation of Sunday school. I asked her what the fraternal organization could do for her son. She replied "Nothing." I told her that Christ, the church, and the Sunday school could help her child; and she could take the child to Sunday School.

A mother told me she had quit taking her children to Sunday school and church because of the shortage of gasoline. Later I asked her what the family did on Sunday night. She confessed that they all went to a picture show. I told her that if they could afford gasoline for a picture show on Sunday night, they could afford gasoline for Sunday school and church.

Not only are we busy making money but we are busy with activities that we think are more important than our children. I do not know Dorothy Dix. I do not know if she is a Christian or a church member. I know she gives advice to those who have trouble in their homes and with individual love affairs. She wrote in her column recently that the women of this nation were so busy winning the war that the children were going to hell. What shall it profit a nation to win a war and lose its children?

The people who are doing the finest work today are our school teachers. All could make more money in the war effort, but for the sake of the next generation they are staying on the job teaching. I know that some have quit because of money, but if all of them did we would not have any schools. Then what would happen? We should let the teachers know that we appreciate what they are doing for our children.

A young woman who held a war emergency job in the city of Washington resigned. When questioned why she had done this, she replied, "After this war when peace comes, and I am asked what I did to help win the war; I will say, 'I was a teacher.'"

We talk much about juvenile delinquency today and blame it on the war, but the breakdown of discipline and spiritual training in the home started long before the war started. Why should American cities find it necessary to have curfew laws when we are supposed to have homes? What has happened to the home? The home is the place where a spiritual service should be held each day.

May I tell you about a home? In Alabama there were a husband and wife who loved God and had a Christian home. They were anxious for their children to have an education. They lived before the days of free high schools in Alabama, which was not many years ago. They sent their eldest child to school, and when he returned he taught the others. He went to work and another child went to school. Each child worked and sent another child to college. This family did not produce a single millionaire, but they sent out Christian teachers, preachers, and doctors. A son of that family is one of the great mathematicians in America. Another son is chancellor of Vanderbilt University. In my testament is the signature of that great Christian mother, Amanda Carmichael. They lived in a humble Christian home in Alabama, but that home has blessed the world many times. They are Presbyterians. I imagine there was strict observance of the Sabbath. But that home sent out men and women who have given a strict account of themselves for God and country.

Today I wish to salute the women of our churches who teach in our Children's Division. We need men and women who will quit sitting in adult classes and find children and bring them to Sunday school. If I were the Sunday school superintendent, I would not let an adult in unless accompanied by a child. We are losing the children. Our Sunday school enrollment in The Methodist Church dropped over 300,000 last year. Of course, all of those are not children, but in many conferences there is an increase in the adult division but a decrease in the children's division of the Sunday school.

A preacher in Salisbury, Maryland, said to his congregation one Sunday morning, "I am through helping the Women's Organization of this church with its programs and offerings that are to help children of other lands until you are willing to teach your own children in this Sunday school. I have been telling your children for six months that I could not get teachers. I am through with your program until you help with the program of Christian education of your own children in your own church." The women did not like it, but they knew he was right. Today he has a fine teaching staff.

Your pastor has training classes for your children in church membership. Please bring your children. This is the most important work I know. It is more important than this service.

If your child loves Christ and wishes to join the church, you come with that child to the training classes as the pastor tries to help that child in the Christian life. Why should a pastor or teacher have to ask your child to make a decision for Christ? That is your high privilege as a parent. The decision for Christ should be secured in the home and then the pastor told so the child can be instructed by the pastor.

There is an army of thirty million marching on America. They will take over our legislative halls, our banks, our schools, our churches, our stores, our railroads. They are not Germans. They are not Japanese. They are our children. In thirty years, they will be running America. Will it be a Christian nation? That depends on you and me.

A God-sent Christ is sent to the children. He needs you to be a Christ-sent man or woman to the children of America.

There are groups that are reaching the children. I do not like their methods and beliefs, but if The Methodist Church will not go to the children, I am glad Christ is sending someone to the children.

A God-Sent Christ Takes the Cross

Jesus knew that the cross is more powerful than the sword. While Jesus was praying in the garden of Gethsemane, the mob led by Judas came to take him to the chief priests.

Simon Peter drew a sword and cut off the ear of Malchus, a servant of the high priest.

Jesus said unto Peter, "Put up thy sword into the sheath: the cup which my Father hath given me, shall I not drink it?"

Jesus could have taken a sword, but he knew that to do his Father's will and die on a cross would bring larger and greater results than using a sword. He was not going to put his trust in a sword but in obedience to God, which meant a cross.

The civilized and Christian nations are using a sword. The terrible Turks and the barbarians are at peace today.

Simon did not pray because he had a sword. He put his trust in a sword. Christ was putting his trust in a cross.

The cross is more powerful than force.

Gandhi does not have a battleship, a sword, or an airplane. He is locked up in jail, but he has power.

Christ knew that the cross was more powerful than twelve legions of angels.

He said, "All they that take the sword shall perish with the sword. Thinkest thou that I cannot now pray to my Father, and he shall presently give me more than twelve legions of angels?"

You see, Jesus knew that doing God's will and going to the cross were more powerful than any miracle. If he had called legions of angels that would have been miraculous, but it would not live as much as his going to the cross.

We would like to do healing and do the unusual and have the populace applaud, but the most powerful thing to do is to live the principles of the cross daily.

Jesus knew there was more power in a spiritual kingdom represented by a cross than a material kingdom represented by gold.

In the wilderness, Jesus determined that his kingdom would be a spiritual kingdom rather than a material kingdom.

Pilate said to Jesus, "Art thou the King of the Jews?" Jesus said, "Sayest thou this thing of thyself, or did others tell it thee of me?"

Pilate said, "Am I a Jew? Thine own nation and the chief priests have delivered thee unto me: what hast thou done?"

Jesus answered, "My kingdom is not of this world: if my kingdom were of this world, then would my servants fight, that I should not be delivered to the Jews: but now is my kingdom not from hence." You see, the kingdom that Jesus represents is a spiritual one.

The persons who have turned away from the material and live in a spiritual kingdom are the persons who have spiritual power.

I told you about my friend in Knoxville who has so much spiritual power. I think one reason that he has spiritual power is that he has kept his salary at $2,500. You see, no one wants his job. If he would build the salary to $5,000, someone would want his job.

A young man came to Birmingham, Alabama, more than fifty years ago from Princeton University. He did not come to mine our coal or to dig our ore. He did not come to sell our real estate or to build our skyscrapers. He did not come to be a pulpit preacher or to edit our papers. He did not come to make gold but to be a fool for Christ. He threw his life away. He prayed with my mother before I was born. Early in the morning you found him at the shops. At midnight you found him at the car barns. He would take off his hat and stop an automobile on the boulevard and say, "I just wanted to pray with you." For fifty years he gave his life to Christ and to Birmingham. His church never paid him but always paid his wife. He would give it away before he got home. Everybody called him Brother Bryan. The city had a big celebration to celebrate the fiftieth anniversary of his work in our city as a Presbyterian preacher. I went back to give the address on this occasion. Birmingham gathered in our great municipal auditorium to try to do him honor. He sat in a wheelchair on the stage. He had more power in Birmingham than the mayor of our city. He had more power than the editors of two great dailies. He had more power than the chairman of the Board of Directors of the First National Bank. He had more power than the pulpit preacher. He had more power than the president of the great corporation that employed 30,000. He had spiritual power because he lived the life of the cross. He was a fool for Christ. But I had rather be a fool for Christ than to be a fool for gold.

Jesus knew that there was more power in the cross than there was in the scepter.

They desired to make him king. The people wanted to make him king. Jesus said No. He knew that the scepter represented temporary power while the cross was eternal.

Jesus took the cross rather than the scepter. The spiritual is eternal; the material is temporary; and Jesus knew that.

Jesus knew that the cross rather than a creed would save the world. I do not discount a creed, but a creed is of no avail unless there is a cross.

While he was dying on the cross his enemies said, "He saved others; himself he cannot save." If you save yourself you can never take a thief to paradise.

If you save yourself a Roman soldier will never say, "Truly this was the Son of God."

If you save yourself, you will never live eternally.

There had to be a Calvary in order to be an Easter. There must be a death before there can be life.

"Except a corn of wheat fall in the ground and die, it abideth alone: but if it die, it bringeth forth much fruit."

Jesus gave us a great system of teachings, but the reason his teachings live is because he died for his conviction.

He gave us a creed, but he spilled his blood and that creed lives today.

If he had not taken the cross, his teachings would not have been anything except a system of ethics. Because Christ died on a cross, he is saving men and women from sin and death—if they will repent and accept the Christ and his way of life, which is the cross. He lives, and we too shall live if we will reproduce him.

A God-sent Christ took the cross. He needs men and women who will be Christ-sent and take the cross. You choose.

Judas took silver. Christ took a cross.

Annas and Caiaphas took security in God; Christ took a cross.

Pilate took security with Caesar; Christ took a cross.

The mob took Barnabas; Christ took a cross.

Some of the soldiers gambled; Christ took a cross.

One thief took the hate of hell; Christ took a cross.

After World War I, Woodrow Wilson believed that America should take responsibility for part of this world, which meant that America would have to be unselfish. He died for his conviction. America was not willing to sacrifice, but what is America doing today? When Mr. Wilson outlined his ideals at the peace table, Mr. Clemenceau said, "Mr. Wilson, you talk like Christ." Mr. Clemenceau had his way and ruled with hate and revenge.

I do not think Christ will be represented at the next peace conference, but Mr. Stalin will be there. There will be a sickle and a hammer and not a cross. You choose.

You will let me say what I believe. I do not ask you to agree. There are young men today who were taught by The Methodist Church that war is wrong and sinful. They refused to be drafted. They are being bitterly criticized. But after all, they believed something they were taught. Some of them are engaged in all kinds of work. I had a letter and an article telling about some of their work. They are attendants in mental hospitals. They are assigned to wards. Some of these patients are incontinent. They have no control over their bodies. A man is put in with 300 naked, raving men. He is locked in there with them. He has to feed and bathe and clean them. Would you like to be locked up with 300 insane men?

These young men are using peaceful methods. They do not use broomsticks on the patients but friendliness.

These young men have taken their cross. We laugh at them. I have more respect for them than I have for others who get a soft government job because of political influence.

These young men who are willing to live and die for peace may be the forerunners of a great movement that will affect this world 200 years from now.

You choose. You take your cross or refuse it. Taking your cross is the only way to live.

When Jesus was on the way to Calvary the women of Jerusalem were weeping. Jesus said, "Daughters of Jerusalem, weep not for me, but weep for yourselves, and for your children." He told them what would happen to Jerusalem.

If you are living the life of the cross, you can say, "Daughters of America, weep not for me, weep for yourselves, and for your children." America is on the way out.

I do not want America to rule the world because of having a navy on every ocean.

I do not want America to rule the world because we have 80 percent of the gold.

I do not want America to rule the world because it has more men under arms than any other nation.

I do not want America to rule the world with its air bases and air routes all over the world.

I want America to be powerful because America will take the principles of the cross and serve the world; and if need be, will die for the world.

If it is expedient that one man die to save a nation, why not a nation dying to save the world?

I would rather that America die on a cross trying to save the world than to rot and die because of sin.

I do not want The Methodist Church to be powerful because of its numbers, its wealth, its polity, its cathedrals, its culture, and its training. I want The Methodist Church to be powerful because it is willing to live the life of the cross and die if need be for a sin-sick world.

> Must Jesus bear the cross alone,
> And all the world go free?
> No, there's a cross for everyone
> And there's a cross for me.*

*From the hymn "Must Jesus Bear the Cross Alone" by Thomas Shepherd and others.

A God-Sent Christ Is Sent to Conquer Death

"Then went in also that other disciple, which came first to the sepulchre, and he *saw*, and *believed*" (John 20:8, italics added).

John is writing this Gospel, and he gives his own experience.

Mary Magdalene brought a message to Simon Peter and John that the body of Jesus was gone. She went to the sepulchre early.

Simon Peter and John ran to the sepulchre. John outran Peter and arrived at the sepulchre first. He stooped down, looked in, and saw the linen clothes.

Simon Peter came to the sepulchre, went in, and saw the linen clothes.

Then John went in, and he saw and *believed*.

John saw an empty tomb and believed that Jesus was alive. Mary said that his body had been taken away, but John believed he was alive. For he goes on to say that they knew not the Scripture that he must rise from the dead. What a wonderful thing it is to believe in Christ!

Christ gave us an empty grave. If we believe in him we have an empty grave. You see, we have a dead body that goes back to dust, but the soul that believes in Christ does not die.

We make our graves beautiful with flowers, markers, and monuments. But if our loved ones believed in Christ, that is just their bodies. They are alive just as Christ was alive.

John believed, and he went home. There was no use spending time at a cemetery.

How many Christians stay at a cemetery? Your loved ones are not there. Of course, if they were unbelievers that is all you have.

The disciples went home, but Mary stood without the

sepulchre weeping. She wanted to find the body of her Lord.

She saw a person whom she believed to be the gardener. He said, "Woman, why weepest thou?"

Mary said, "Sir, if thou have borne him hence, tell me where thou has laid him, and I will take him away."

Jesus said "Mary."

Mary said "Master" (John 20:15, 16).

She did not know his resurrected body, but she knew his voice. She knew he was alive. He gave her a message for his disciples.

The living Christ has a message for all who know him. The living Christ appeared to Saul and gave him a message.

That day two of the disciples went to Emmaus, which from Jerusalem was about threescore furlongs. An unknown person drew near and went with them.

"What manner of communications are these that ye have one to another, as ye walk, and are sad?"

"Art thou only a stranger in Jerusalem, and hast not known the things which are come to pass there in these days?"

And he said unto them, "What things?"

And they said, "Concerning Jesus of Nazareth."

"And they drew nigh unto the village whither they went: and he made as though he would have gone further. But they constrained him, saying, Abide with us: for it is toward evening, and the day is far spent. And he went in to tarry with them. And it came to pass, as he sat at meat with them, he took bread, and blessed it, and brake, and gave it to them. And their eyes were opened, and they knew him; and he vanished out of their sight. And they said one to another, Did not our heart burn within us, while he talked with us by the way, and while he opened to us the scriptures? And they rose up the same hour, returned to Jerusalem . . . [to tell] what things were done in the way, and how he was known of them in breaking of bread" (Luke 24:17, 18, 19, 28-33, 35).

If you are on the sad road to Emmaus, the living Christ

makes that sad road one of gladness. If you invite him to tarry with you, you will know him.

> Then the same day at evening, ... when the doors were shut where the disciples were assembled for fear of the Jews, came Jesus and stood in the midst, and saith unto them, Peace be unto you. And when he had so said, he shewed unto them his hands and his side. Then were the disciples glad, when they saw the Lord. . . . Peace be unto you: As my Father hath sent me, even so I send you. And when he had said this, he breathed on them, and saith unto them, Receive ye the Holy Ghost. (John 20:19-20)

He gave us a task and the power to do it.

The living Christ gives us an empty grave. We do not live in the grave; we live with him. He said, "Because I live, ye shall live also" (John 14:19). Believers do not have to weep by a grave; we can go to our homes rejoicing.

So many persons fail to come to church after losing their loved ones, but there is where we hear about the living Christ.

The living Christ turns our sadness into gladness. On the road to Emmaus, the hearts were warm. He will come to tarry with you if you invite him, and you will know him.

The disciples were glad when they saw him. Why should we be sad? Christians should rejoice. Our dead are alive. Missing in action reported dead—then alive. How wonderful that is for all believers.

The living Christ turns our fear into peace. The disciples were afraid. They were hiding from Jews, but Christ brought them peace. No fears: "I will fear no evil: for thou art with me" (Psalm 24:4).

The living Christ has a mission for each of us. Young men in this war go on a mission. It may mean death, but it means life for others.

Mary of Magdala had a mission that first Easter morning. The disciples came back from Emmaus to tell what they had seen and felt. The disciples received his commission: "As my Father hath sent me, even so send I you.... [Then he breathed on them] "Receive ye the Holy Ghost" (John 20:21, 22). They went forth to do his will.

They went to the children; they went to the outcasts; they went to condemn injustice and hypocrisy; they went to comfort and to have compassion; they went to the cross, to prison, and to death; they went to live forever.

The living Christ gives us power to do his mission. Today we give the young people who go on our missions for us the best equipment, training, and power. Christ gives us the power.

We are planning a nationwide evangelistic movement. Bishop Arthur J. Moore said what we need to do is to undertake a big job for the Christ, and he will give us the power. He will give us power for any mission.

Jesus said to Thomas, "Because thou hast seen me, thou hast believed: blessed are they that have not seen, and yet have believed" (John 20:29).

The Church: Not an Organization but an Organism

Christ said, "I will build my church" (Matthew 16:18). The church is not an organization but an organism. It is composed of those who confess that Jesus is the Christ, the Son of the living God, and who live that faith. The church has for its members those who have a great living faith in Christ. The church is Christlike. The characteristics of the church are the same as those of Christ. You can tell a Christian church because its activities are the same as Christ's activities.

A Christlike church will be a singing church. I do not mean that it will have a good choir and congregational singing. This is very fine and good and is necessary. The singing to which I refer is the singing Christ and his disciples did the last night Christ lived in the flesh. The Gospel writer tells us Christ could sing. He knew that Judas would betray him and that Peter would deny him, because he prophesied both. He knew that he would be arrested, beaten, spat upon, illegally tried, lied about, crucified, and deserted. But he could sing.

The Christian church can sing in the face of adversity. However, no one is crucifying us today. We are not attacking the gates of hell.

Christ was persecuted and slain because he thought more of a person than he did of the institution of the Sabbath. While Pharisees healed oxen and sheep on the Sabbath, Christ healed people. We find these words in the fifth chapter of John, "And therefore did the Jews persecute Jesus, and sought to slay him, because he had done these things on the sabbath day" (John 5:16).

The Jews sought to kill him because he claimed God as his Father. Jesus said, "My Father worketh hitherto, and I work" (John 5:17). Therefore, the Jews sought the more to kill him. He had broken not only the Sabbath, but also said that God was his Father—making himself equal with God.

When you claim God as your Father, then you claim all of God's children as your brothers and sisters. When you treat all men as your brothers and all women as your sisters, this will take you to a cross.

Jesus had to leave the country of Gadara because he thought more of a man than he did of 2,000 hogs. If the church would become Christian and go out to live as Christ lived, then the church would be persecuted; but it could sing.

We need to live in order that we can sing. I am afraid we do not have anything about which to sing.

A great bondslave of Christ went out to preach Christ and the resurrection in the face of opposition. He was placed in jail. He was beaten. He was stoned. He was shipwrecked. Thrice he was beaten with rods, 195 times the lash came down on his back. But how he could sing! His theme was, "Rejoice in the Lord always" (Philippians 4:4). "Rejoice evermore" (1 Thessalonians 5:16).

"I have learned, in whatsoever state I am, therewith to be content" (Philippians 4:11).

A Christian who has been persecuted for Christ's sake can sing.

A Christlike church is a *seeking* church. Christ always was seeking those who were neglected. Zacchaeus and Levi were the lost sons of Abraham, and Christ went to find them.

He sent out the seventy two by two. "For the Son of man is come to seek and to save that which was lost" (Luke 19:10). The lost were the ones the Pharisees had neglected.

The man at the pool of Bethesda, in sight of the Temple, was lost. Jesus found him.

The Galileans were lost. No prophet comes out of Galilee. Jesus found the Galileans Andrew and Simon, James and John, Philip and Nathanael.

The woman at the well was lost. The Jews have no dealing with the Samaritans. Even his disciples marveled that he would talk to her.

A Christian church will be seeking those neglected persons who are lost. If a church fails to find the lost men and women, then that church is not Christlike. Sometimes a person can be lost right next door to the church.

Christ was seeking those who needed him. The self-righteous Pharisees can always lose persons, but a living Christ can find them.

A Christlike church will be saving persons. One time when Jesus was in Samaria, he had set his face toward Jerusalem and because of their prejudice the Samaritans would not receive him. James and John, the sons of Thunder, wanted the authority to bring lightning down and burn them up, but Jesus said, "[I am] not come to destroy men's lives but to save them" (Luke 9:56). Here is the philosophy of Christ—not to destroy but to save.

One day the Pharisees brought to Jesus in the Temple a woman taken in the very act of sin and said, "Our law says stone her to death." Jesus ignored them, but they persisted and Jesus said, "If you are without sin you cast the first stone." They went away. The woman was saved from stoning by the higher law of love. Jesus said, "Go, and sin no more" (John 8:11). She was saved from death and from a life of sinning.

The Christian church is in the saving business. We are to preach and teach Christ, who saves persons from drunkenness to sobriety; from greed to generosity; from gossip to good news; from lying to truth; from racial prejudice to brotherhood; from self to others.

The church as an organization cannot save, but the living Christ can. But those who are needed should see the living Christ in the living organization that is the church. Many of you can testify that you are what you are today because of the love of Christ in a mother, father, relative, or friend.

Christlike living attracts attention. The Greeks desired to see Jesus. They had seen the tempter. They had seen the Pharisees. They had seen the moneychangers. They had seen the ritual service. They desired to see Jesus.

People desire to see him today. Christlike living will bring saving power.

This generation could be won for Christ if our church members would become Christ's men and women.

The Christlike church will be the servant of the community: Jesus and a towel; Jesus feeding; Jesus healing; Jesus cleansing the lepers; Jesus casting out demons.

The church serves the community by feeding people, healing people, serving people.

"The Son of man came not to be ministered unto, but to minister" (Mark 10:45).

"He that loveth his life shall lose it; and he that hateth his life in this world shall keep it unto life eternal" (John 12:25).

The reason Christ could live as he did is that he had great faith in God. We need that faith in Christ. A living faith in Christ will sing,

will seek,
will save,
will serve.

Faith brings the victory.

A victorious church
will sing,
will seek,
will save,
will serve.

How Can Anyone See Jesus Today?

"Sir, we would see Jesus" (John 12:21). These words were spoken by the Greeks who had come to Jerusalem to worship. These words were spoken to Philip of Bethsaida of Galilee. This request came to Philip from the Greeks right after the triumphal entry of Jesus into Jerusalem, which is filled with people because of celebrating the Passover.

Evidently Jerusalem is filled with talk about Jesus. All the city asked, "Who is this?" And the multitude answered, "This is Jesus the prophet of Nazareth of Galilee" (Matthew 21:11). The Pharisees are worried tremendously about the influence of Jesus in Jerusalem. This is what the Pharisees said, "Perceive ye how ye prevail nothing? behold, the world is gone after him" (John 12:19).

Jesus so filled Jerusalem with his presence that the Greeks desired to see him. They went to Philip, who was a despised Galilean. I presume these Greeks thought they would get more sympathy from one who was despised as Jews were by the Pharisees. Anyhow, these Greeks did not go to the leaders of Judaism to see Jesus.

Philip went to Andrew and told him that the Greeks desired to see Jesus. They went and told Jesus.

Do you believe that today a city could become so full of the presence of Jesus that people would say "Sir, we would see Jesus?" I do.

The story is told that a censor of soldiers' mail went to a chaplain with this statement and request, "Chaplain," he said, "I read the mail of the soldiers who were at Guadalcanal to their friends and relatives at home. In their letters they talk about Jesus and how much he means to them. I do not know

Jesus, but from reading the mail of these soldiers, I wish to know him. Tell me about him."

Jesus was in the flesh when the Greeks were in Jerusalem and asked to see him. Philip and Andrew could go to him in the flesh.

How can people see Jesus today?

They must see Jesus at church. They must see Christ in the worship service. The music should be sung by those who know him. Sometimes we are guilty of criticizing the singer for display of voice and ability rather than glorifying Christ. We preachers are just as guilty. Sometimes we display our knowledge of the material rather than tell what we know of the spiritual.

In our conference we had one of the great souls of the church in the Reverend Joe I. Williams. He was a man of great native ability. He was not a seminary man unless you are willing to count the College of Hard Knocks, the University of Experience, and the Seminary of Arabia, which are very good schools. Brother Williams was pastor of the First Methodist Church of one of our cities in North Alabama. One of his contemporaries made a trip to the Holy Land. Of course, when he returned he had a lecture: "To the Holy Land and Return." His lecture became very popular. He was the talk of the city. Brother Williams was not to be outdone. He delivered a lecture relating his early experience in the ministry. The name of his lecture was "My Trip to Pea Ridge and Return." Needless to say, this became a very informing and entertaining lecture in Alabama.

Most of us who travel extensively and who have unusual experiences relate them when we should be giving the people the gospel of Christ. The sermon must be Christ-centered. It should be thought-provoking, but also it should reach the heart.

Last year I was waterbound for four nights and three days. During that time you get to know your fellow passengers. One man and I talked at great length. I told him about my work. He said, "I used to go to church. When I go, I desire to get a lift. The music should be rendered properly and correctly, but it should also stir the emotions. The radio has a varied musical program in order to reach all the people. We should sometimes sing hymns that the congregation will enjoy, not just those hymns that the choir and director like."

It is told that soldiers like to sing, "Leaning on the Everlasting Arms" and "The Old Rugged Cross."

A young man, six years of age, was asked by the minister how he liked the sermon that morning. He said he did not like it. When asked why he did not like the sermon, the boy replied, "I kept waiting for you to talk about Jesus."

In a certain city, Holy Week services are held in all the department stores. The employees come thirty minutes early each day to hear these devotional messages. Several of the stores are owned by Jews, and many of the employees are Jews. The only criticism that was made by the Jews was this: "We came to hear you talk about your Christ, and you did not."

All worship services must lift up Christ. One Sunday a minister found this note in his hand after shaking hands with his parishioners, "Sir, we would see Jesus." The next Sunday morning, he gave them Christ as Paul and John Wesley did. Then he received this note: "Then were the disciples glad, when they saw the Lord" (John 20:20).

The teaching in the church school should be about Christ—his activities, his teachings, his power. It was my privilege to hear one of the great scholars of our church preach for months. He is a university professor. I do not think he ever closed a sermon without saying, "Let us see, what did Jesus say about this?" or "What did Jesus do about this?" I know we have to teach church history, Bible geography, and history in our Sunday schools, but we can relate lessons to Christ and his influence.

The fellowship in our churches must be Christian. Fellowship that discriminates between rich and poor, educated and illiterate, background and foreground, white and black, adults and children, officers and privates is not Christian.

The Christian church was created to minister to those who live on Main Street and those who live on the alley, to those who live on the boulevard and the slum streets, to those who live on both sides of the railroad track. Christ knew no boundaries. Rich rulers, Samaritan women, members of the Sanhedrin, women possessed of demons, and men in Gadara, all looked alike to him.

If boys in the alley can die for our freedom, we can give them a Christian welcome to our churches. If we are Christian, we will go to them.

We must see Christ in our church recreation. If our recreation is Christ-centered, it will be re-creative instead of wreck-creative. I do not believe the church should engage in any kind of recreation that harms personality rather than helping it.

Our recreation should teach activities that can be avocational for our people. It is a means to reach people for Christ. When a church has recreational activities that are an end instead of a means, then that church is dying. Why should we teach boys and girls the harmfulness of tobacco and then have banquets at which time our people smoke?

We can see Jesus in our daily worship service in our homes as we read the Bible, pray, and meditate.

For the past five years I have read my Bible morning and night. I know that Christ is more real to me than he was then. My experience of him grows richer and richer. As I read his life and his teachings, I am a better Christian. The periods of silence that I have when I listen to his voice are the richest experiences. There are all kinds of devotional books you can use as an individual or as a family. May I mention a few: *The Upper Room*, "How to Conduct Family Worship at the Table," *The Christian Home*, "The Abundant Life." Let me insist that you use your Bible in connection with these.

You can see Christ in Christian literature and art. Many persons have paintings of Christ in their homes and offices. What a joy it is to have a place to meditate and pray where there is a painting of him and a cross!

Can we see Jesus in the flesh today? Yes. The best place for people to see Jesus is in our flesh. We go everywhere. People see us at church, at school, at home, at work in the shop or on the farm. They see us in the social room, the banking room, the court house, and on the street. They may not read The Gospel According to Matthew, Mark, Luke, or John, but they read the gospel that you and I are writing every day. It was said of the early disciples, by their enemies, that they had been with Jesus.

A friend of mine said that we do not follow Christ or imitate Christ, but that we reproduce Christ. The disciples were first called Christians in Antioch of Syria. Of course, it was said in derision, but they reminded people of Christ. What happened at Antioch?

- They preached the Lord Jesus to the Greeks.
- The hand of the Lord was with them.
- They had the grace of God.
- Paul was captured.
- They sent an offering for the poor at Jerusalem.
- Missionaries were sent out under authority of the Holy Spirit.

This is a good picture of a Christian church.

We see Christ in individuals. Saul of Tarsus saw Christ in Stephen as he prayed when dying. He saw Christ when he was called Brother Saul by Ananias of Damascus, whom he went to persecute. He saw Christ in Barnabas, who befriended him before the church council in Jerusalem and who came and took him to the great spiritual meeting at Antioch.

Christ must have human beings through which to work today. How many people have been won for him by Christ-living men and women? Also the other is true: thousands of men and women have been kept from Christ by the un-Christ-like living of some of his followers. Many stories could be told for both sides.

How will Christ live in us? We must do like Paul and

die daily or like John the Baptist. I must decrease. He must increase.

The more my spirit becomes the spirit of Christ, the more my flesh becomes his flesh. The more of Christ I take, the more of me he takes. "They twain shall be one" (Mark 10:7).

When Phillips Brooks died they found a worn-out note in his pocketbook. This note was written to the great preacher by a bricklayer's helper of Boston. This was what the bricklayer wrote to the first citizen of Boston: "I cannot think of you steadily for three minutes without seeing Christ."

"Except a corn of wheat fall into the ground and die, it abideth alone: but if it die, it bringeth forth much fruit" (John 12:24).

The Greeks had a desire to see Jesus. Men and women have that desire today. We have tried every plan, panacea, and program of government. Why not try God?

People may be in foxholes, rubber rafts, under the water or above it, but there comes a desire to see Jesus. Let us give them Jesus. He will take away their fears. He will give peace not as the world giveth. He will bring life instead of death. He will bring salvation instead of sin. He will bring boldness instead of cowardice. He will bring love instead of hate. He will bring good instead of evil. He will bring purity instead of impurity.

Let people see Jesus in our words, our living, our giving. There is one person in the world today who is glorifying Christ and revealing Christ to others. He is the Holy Spirit. Christ said, "I will send him unto you, and when he is come, he will reprove the world of sin, and of righteousness, and of judgment. . . . He shall glorify me" (John 16:7-8, 14). The Holy Spirit is glorifying Christ today. When we glorify Christ, we are coworkers with the Holy Spirit, and he baptizes us with power. Also he reveals truth to us. Do you know a greater work today than glorifying Christ? "Sir, we would see Jesus." Can the world see Jesus in you, in me?

Jesus as the Way of Life

Recently I was entering a city by car, and I saw the four words *I am the way* in very large type on a billboard. These are the words of Jesus and were said by him the last night he lived in the flesh. You find them in the sixth verse of the fourteenth chapter of John.

They were spoken in the upper room where Jesus and his disciples were observing the Feast of the Passover. Jesus is telling the disciples that he is going away and he says, "You know the way where I am going." Thomas said, "Lord, we do not know where you are going; how can we know the way?" Jesus replied to Thomas, "I am the way" (John 14:4-6).

Jesus did not say, "I am *a* way." He said, "I am *the* way, . . . no man cometh unto the Father, but by me" (italics added).

In this life, we either accept Jesus as the way of life, or we live our own selfish way.

Jesus Is the Way of Salvation

Zacchaeus, the tax collector of Jericho, tried to find salvation in the accumulation of money by taking advantage of the poor and other citizens by false accusations about assessments. He represented himself and Caesar of Rome, who occupied and ruled his country.

However, Zacchaeus had a spiritual hunger. He had heard of the strange teacher of Nazareth who did not have as much home as the foxes and the birds of the air. He sought to see Jesus. He desired to see this strange person who befriended all. Zacchaeus was chief of the publicans and was rich. He had position and power that place and wealth could give him. Yet what he had heard about Jesus caused a great desire to see him.

262

Zacchaeus heard that Jesus had entered and passed through Jericho. He was a small man physically and could not see Jesus because of the crowd. He was determined to see Jesus, so he ran ahead and climbed up into a sycamore tree. He knew that Jesus was to pass that way. It must have been the only road leading out of Jericho, or the road to the well, or the road to Bethany.

Now this man of wealth and position was prepared to see Jesus. I am not sure Jesus was anxious to see him, but he was anxious to see Jesus.

But when Jesus came to the place, he looked up and saw Zacchaeus. Jesus always saw persons. He never saw a tax collector. He did not see a publican. He did not see a sinner. He did not see a man of wealth. He saw a person. Jesus knew his name. He knew Zacchaeus had a house, and Jesus spoke to Zacchaeus, a publican, before the throng. He recognized him as a person.

Jesus said, "Zacchaeus, make haste and come down; for to day I must abide in thy house." The carpenter who could build houses but did not have one is going to the house of a sinner, according to the people of Jericho.

Zacchaeus did exactly what Jesus invited him to do. He made haste. He came down. He received Jesus. But he received Jesus joyfully. Zacchaeus was full of joy. Jesus had spoken to him, a publican. He was going home with him who was called a sinner and shunned by the people of the community. He had been recognized by the one the crowds were thronging to see. Now he will find out the secret of the life of Jesus. He was joyous.

The people of Jericho saw that Jesus was going to be a guest of a sinner, and they murmured. I presume that they had never been to the house of Zacchaeus. They had been to the tax office, which perhaps adjoined the house, but that was business. They had never been on a social or spiritual visit to this house. Now this strange teacher had gone to the house of a sinner to be his guest. They murmured. We always murmur when someone performs a spiritual deed that we know deep in our hearts that we should be doing.

What an interesting and strange picture! The rich man of Jericho escorting the poor peasant of Galilee to his house and the crowd murmuring. And stranger still is the fact that the poor teacher of Nazareth invited himself to the home of the chief publican. That was the beginning of a very exciting day in Jericho.

There is no record of what Jesus said to Zacchaeus in that house. I do not think Jesus condemned him. He did not explain the plan of salvation to Zacchaeus. He did not preach to him. Jesus recognized Zacchaeus as a son of Abraham. That caused Zacchaeus to see himself and to realize who he was. When you come to Jesus to see who he is, you see yourself as you are. As they sat together in the house, Zacchaeus had a great yearning to make this person the Lord of his life. What was wealth and position if he could be like Jesus instead of being as he was?

Zacchaeus stood before Jesus and said, "Behold, Lord, the half of my goods I give to the poor; and if I have taken any thing from any man by false accusation, I restore him fourfold" (Luke 19:8).

He called Jesus Lord. He has changed his mind. That is repentance. He is making Jesus the Lord of his life and not the getting of wealth and position. He is going to restore four times as much as he has taken by false accusation from his fellow citizens. That is repentance. Instead of robbing the poor, he is going to share with the poor. That is repentance. That is a new life.

Jesus spoke these joyous words to Zacchaeus: "This day is salvation come to this house, forasmuch as he also is a son of Abraham" (Luke 19:9).

This day—think what happened in one day. Jesus found a sinner. The sinner found a Savior. Salvation came to a house. Jericho had a new citizen, and society became new.

Salvation started when Zacchaeus had a spiritual desire to see who Jesus was. Jesus saw him and gave Zacchaeus a gracious invitation. He accepted the invitation. They went to the house. There Zacchaeus committed himself to the way of Jesus and found salvation for himself, for this house, and for a society in which he lived.

Zacchaeus changed his mind. God changed his heart; Jericho had a changed man. Jesus is the way of salvation for all persons. He is the way to God for all persons. Living my way separates me from God, but living the way of Jesus brings me to God, my Father. All this happened to Zacchaeus in one day—perhaps in a few hours.

Many persons are up a tree today. They have wealth and position but not salvation. Jesus invites himself to your house today. Make haste and come down from your tree and receive him joyfully.

As Jesus and Zacchaeus started the journey to the house, I do not think any words were spoken. Zacchaeus was too happy to speak. Jesus did not have to speak with his lips. His act of going with Zacchaeus was speaking. That journey and visit brought salvation. You can start today walking with Jesus to your house. Zacchaeus put his faith in Jesus and called him Lord. If you will make Jesus the Lord of your life and commit yourself to him and make his way of life your way of living, salvation will come to you this very minute. You change your mind, and God changes your heart. God cannot change your mind, but you can. You cannot change your heart, but God does when you change your mind. Today is the day for your salvation. Society cannot be changed unless persons are changed.

Jesus is the way of salvation. Try his way.

One day Simon, a Pharisee, asked Jesus to eat with him. Jesus accepted the invitation and went into the Pharisee's house and sat down to meat.

A woman who lived in that city was a sinner. When she knew that Jesus was in Simon's house, she brought an alabaster box of ointment and stood weeping at the feet of Jesus and behind him. She washed his feet with her tears and wiped them with the hair of her head and kissed his feet and anointed them with the ointment. (See Luke 7:36-38.)

The self-righteous Pharisee who had invited Jesus to dinner in his house began to talk within himself about Jesus, *This man, if he were a prophet, would have known who and what manner of woman this is that toucheth him: for she is a sinner* (Luke 7:39).

Thank God, Jesus did know that she was a sinner and was willing for her to touch him. He never called her a sinner. She was a person who needed love. Simon had law. Jesus had love.

Jesus said, "Simon, I have somewhat to say unto thee." Simon said, "Master, say on." Jesus said, "There was a certain creditor which had two debtors: the one owed five hundred pence, and the other fifty. And when they had nothing to pay, he frankly forgave them both. Tell me, therefore, which of them will love him most?"

Simon answered and said, "I suppose that he, to whom he forgave most." And Jesus replied, "Thou hast rightly judged."

And Jesus turned to the woman but spoke to Simon the Pharisee. No doubt he desired that Simon see her as a person. Perhaps Simon knew her. Jesus makes a comparison between Simon the self-righteous Pharisee and the sinner.

Jesus said unto Simon, "Seest thou this woman? I entered into thine house. You did not give me water for my feet, but she has washed my feet with tears and wiped them with the hairs of her head. You, Simon, gave me no kiss, but this woman since the time I came in hath not ceased to kiss my feet. You did not anoint my head with oil, but this woman anointed both my feet with ointment" (Luke 7:40, 41-42, 43-46).

Simon had invited Jesus to eat in his house but had forgotten the common courtesies due his guest. The woman was doing what Simon failed to do.

"Wherefore, I say unto thee [Simon], Her sins, which are many, are forgiven; for she loved much: but to whom little is forgiven, the same loveth little. Then [Jesus] said unto her, Thy sins are forgiven. And they that sat at meat with him began to say within themselves, Who is this that forgiveth sins also? And [Jesus] said to the woman, Thy faith hath saved thee; go in peace" (Luke 7:47-50). The sinner found a Savior.

I have wondered why Simon, the Pharisee, invited Jesus to dinner. I do not think he desired fellowship with Jesus. If he had, he would have cared for his guest by having his servant bathe the feet of Jesus. He would have saluted Jesus with a kiss and anointed his head. Perhaps he desired to see how Jesus would behave toward the woman. Perhaps the woman had been coming regularly to Simon's house for forgiveness and did not receive it.

Jesus first tells Simon that the woman's sins, which were many, are forgiven. He tells the woman also, and the others at the table could not understand why Jesus would forgive.

Jesus showed us the forgiving love of God. God is more anxious to forgive than we are to repent. This woman wept because of her sins. She humbled herself. She demonstrated love for Jesus by bathing his feet and kissing them and anointing them. Her faith, not her works, saved her. Jesus said to her, "Thy faith hath saved thee; go in peace."

This woman found salvation in Jesus Christ and not in Simon, the Pharisee. Jesus Christ is love. Simon represented law.

Jesus is the way of salvation for all persons—the rich publican, Zacchaeus, or the poor woman of the streets.

A young man gave this testimony: "I was reared in a Christian home. After finishing school I went to a large city to work. I had not been there long before I was living a sinful life. After losing my job, I returned home. The young people of the church were having an institute. I took a course on what it means to be a Christian. The Holy Spirit convicted me of my sins. I repented and believed in the Lord Jesus Christ and found salvation. Today I am in school studying for the ministry. I praise God that I found forgiveness and salvation in Christ."

Jesus is the way of salvation for all persons. He gave himself to all persons. They can find salvation by putting their faith in him. What he has done for others he will do for you and me. He is the way of salvation.

I heard a layman speak to a large group of laymen assembled for a weekend retreat. He gave a real testimony of what Christ had done for him. Later this man took me to the airport. I said to him, "Tell me about your Christian experience." He said,

> I have been a member of the church for many years. Last year a city-wide revival was planned for our city. Church members were asked to open their homes for neighborhood prayer meetings. I told the committee on arrangements that a prayer meeting could be held in my new home. I was not anxious to have the prayer meeting, but I desired people to see my new home which had cost $40,000. At the close of the prayer meeting, one of the preachers who was present said to me privately, "Do you know Jesus Christ as your Savior?" I told him that I did not. He said that he would wait and talk with me. He did. He told me about Christ as Savior. I yielded my life to Christ and knew him as a Savior. Nine other members of my family have done the same. I have a joy and a peace I never had before.

This man found salvation in Christ because a man loved him and witnessed to him.

Simon Peter Makes His Defense

Simon Peter has become a liberal, or whatever the conservatives of the Jerusalem church called those who associated with Gentiles. The leaders of the Jewish Christians in Jerusalem hear that the Gentiles have received the word of God. The unclean and common have heard the word, and the same Holy Spirit has fallen on the Gentiles that had fallen on them the day of Pentecost.

Simon Peter had been impulsive once too many times. He should have stayed on the conservative side of the railroad tracks. He had no business going to Joppa to live with Simon the tanner. That was a mistake. If he had not gone to Joppa, he never would have gotten as far as Caesarea. If he had not been at Joppa, Cornelius would not have sent for him.

The charges against Simon were two. "You wentest in to men uncircumcised, and didst eat with them" (Acts 11:3). They thought that the baptism of repentance and the baptism of power were only for the Jewish Christians. The Gentiles were not even to have the crumbs that fell from the table.

Simon starts his defense with my text, "I was in the city of Joppa praying" (Acts 11:5). Simon Peter had learned a great fundamental the hard way. He had learned to pray. It took him a long time to master the lesson of prayer.

When Jesus was praying on the Mount of Transfiguration, Simon went to sleep. When Jesus was praying in the garden of Gethsemane, Simon as usual went to sleep. By bitter experience he had learned what happens when you do not pray; and by wonderful experiences, he had learned what happens when you do pray.

After Peter had shared in the great transfiguration experience of Jesus on the mountain, he and the other disciples were unable to help a father and his demon-possessed son. When they asked Jesus why they were spiritually helpless in this acute situation he answered, "This kind goeth not out but by prayer and fasting" (Matthew 17:21).

He knew what happened in the garden of Gethsemane. Christ said to him, "Could you not watch with me one hour? Watch and pray" (Matthew 26:40-41). He could not, for he had a sword. Christ depended on prayer. Simon depended on a sword. He denied his Lord. He cursed and swore that he did not know Jesus. He wept bitterly because he followed afar off instead of praying.

Simon knew the power that came on the day of Pentecost because of obeying the living Christ and tarrying in prayer until the power came. He could never forget that day of all days, Pentecost, when persons cried out, "What shall we do?" (Acts 2:37), and he told them, "Repent, and be baptized every one of you in the name of Jesus Christ for the remission of sins, and ye shall receive the gift of the Holy Ghost" (Acts 2:38). Simon Peter had learned that it is better to pray ten days and preach ten minutes and have three thousand converted than to pray ten minutes and preach ten days and get no one.

Perhaps the mystic, John, was of great help to Simon. I imagine that one day Simon Peter said to John, "Let us go and heal someone. We need a committee on healing. I will be chairman, and you will be secretary. We will have a healing mission. Let us do something that will stir Jerusalem. Pentecost was a great day. We will have to do something bigger." John said, "Simon, it is the ninth hour. Let us go to the Temple to pray." They found a lame man at the Gate Beautiful. Simon Peter could never forget that experience. The lame man leaped and walked into the Temple, praising God. There was another short message, and five thousand men came to march under the banner of the living Christ.

The day he stood before the Sanhedrin, after being in jail all night, would never be forgotten because he issued his declaration that day when he said, "Whether it be right in the sight of God to hearken unto you more than unto God, judge ye. For we cannot but speak the things which we have seen and heard" (Acts 4:19-20).

He remembered, after hearing the threatenings of the Sanhedrin, that the members of the little church prayed until the house was shaken, and they were all filled with the Holy Ghost, and they spoke the word with boldness.

He could never forget the night when the angel of the Lord delivered them from prison so they could teach all the words of life in the Temple the next day and be whipped by order of the Sanhedrin for doing it.

He knew the value of prayer to such an extent that when his membership on the Jerusalem Community Chest and the Board of Directors of the Rotary Club and the panel board of rationing took so much of his time, he had seven laymen elected to do this work in order that he could give himself continually to prayer and the ministry of the Word.

He knew how prayer was answered at Joppa. Two men brought him to Joppa because Dorcas was dead. The widows needed Dorcas. She was a person who was greatly missed when she died. The widows showed Simon Peter what Dorcas had done for them. Peter put the widows out of the room. He knelt down and prayed and called on Dorcas to rise, and she did.

No wonder Simon Peter started his defense before the church council in Jerusalem, "I was in the city of Joppa praying." He knew what praying would do. He knew when you did not pray, you denied your Lord; and when you did pray, you glorified your Lord. He knew that if you do not pray, persons will continue to be demon-possessed. He had learned to pray.

We need to learn that lesson. Great spiritual movements have been born when persons prayed. The Student Volunteer Movement was born in a prayer meeting. The Foreign Mission Movement was born in a prayer meeting. Young people have heard the voice of the Lord because persons have prayed. Young people have given themselves to Christ as ministers, for the singing of the Word, for the preaching of the Word, for teaching the Word, and to the power of the Word to heal. The reason we have a shortage of preachers is that we have stopped asking the Lord to call them, and God did.

"I was in the city of Joppa praying...I saw a vision." He is telling the story of his experience to his critics. In the house of Simon the tanner by the seaside he saw a vision. He was not in the Temple. He was across the railroad tracks. He ought not to have been in the house of a tanner. When we leave the accustomed routine, we get a vision of the need today.

I do not presume that you read classical literature such as Dagwood and Blondie. If you do, you will remember that this week the postman delivered the mail to all the back doors instead of the front doors, and he exclaimed that a whole new world had been opened to him. I am sure that if we would get off the boulevard, we would see a new world. We talk a great deal about one world, and we think of China, India, Japan. But one world includes the slums of our own cities.

It was the sixth hour when Peter went up to the housetop to pray. He became very hungry and would have eaten, but while they made ready he fell into a trance and he saw a vision. If Peter had eaten, he never would have seen the vision. Full stomachs have always kept us from seeing the spiritual truths of God. Fasting is not only good for the health of our bodies, but it is also good for the health of our souls.

He saw a great sheet descend from heaven, and it came to him. He saw the four-footed beasts of the earth and wild beasts and creeping things and fowl of the air; and he heard a voice saying, "Arise, Peter; stay and eat" (Acts 11:7). Remember, Peter is hungry. This is a vision, but Peter is still a good legalistic Jew. He said, "Not so Lord: for nothing common or unclean hath...entered into my mouth" (Acts 11:8). Then the voice answered, "What God hath cleansed, that call not thou common" (Acts 11:9). This was done three times.

Simon Peter was being prepared to go to the house of Cornelius, whom he thought was common and unclean because he was a Gentile. However, the record says that Cornelius was a devout man who feared God with all his house and who gave much alms to the people and prayed to God always.

Simon Peter was prejudiced against Cornelius because he was a Gentile. When Jesus lived in the flesh, he told his disciples that the greatest faith he had seen in all Israel was possessed by a Gentile, another centurion. Simon had forgotten that statement. His Jewish legalism and training were dominant. He marveled when Jesus talked to a Samaritan woman, but he had grown in Christian grace to the place where he could put his hands on the heads of the Samaritans while they were baptized of the Spirit. Christ wanted him to make another step and that was to eat with the Gentiles. So there had to be another vision.

We have prejudices today against people because of their color, their economic conditions, their nationality, their illiteracy, and other conditions. We talk about the riff-raff. We discuss the underprivileged; we lift our eyebrows and shrug our shoulders when we talk about certain sections of the city. We sometimes hate people on account of their color, and we dislike them because of their religion. God never labels. We do that. God is colorblind—we see color. Whenever we hate Jews, we hate God. Whenever we hate Japanese, we hate God. To be Christlike we must love all. We can hate what people do, but to love Christ means to love all the children of God and to see that they hear the good news of the word of God. Sometimes we shun those who live in certain sections of the city or certain parts of the country. We are guilty of believing that some are hopeless. We think that drunkards should be turned over to Alcoholics Anonymous. We think harlots should be turned over to the Salvation Army.

Do we believe that the word of God and the miracle of grace are for all persons regardless of their sins, their color, their economic condition, their education, and their social standing? "[The fields] are white already to harvest" (John 4:35) was said in Samaria.

"I was in the city of Joppa praying. . . . I saw a vision. . . . I heard a voice."

While Peter doubted in himself what this vision meant, the messengers from Caesarea arrived and made inquiry for Simon the tanner's house. They stood before the gate and inquired if Simon Peter lodged there. While Peter thought on the vision, the Spirit said unto him, "Behold three men seek thee. Arise therefore, and get thee down, and go with them, doubting nothing: for I have sent them" (Acts 10:19-20).

When one prays, one not only sees visions but one hears the voice of the Spirit. The best part of praying is listening. We should put ourselves in the attitude of listening. To do this we must shut out all other voices.

If Simon Peter had listened to the voice of the flesh and eaten, he would not have heard the voice of the Spirit. If Simon Peter had listened to the voice of racial prejudice, he would not have heard the voice of brotherhood. If he had listened to the voice of legalism, he would not have heard the voice of love. The law of Judaism would not let him go to the house of Cornelius, but the love of God compelled him. He said to Cornelius, "You know it is not lawful for me to be here." Simon was under the great law—the law of love.

At our place of prayer, when we have eliminated all the voices, we can hear the voice of the Spirit telling us what to do.

We need a place to pray where every physical voice can be shut out. Then we need to shut out the voices of self, jealousy, fear, pride, pity, greed, anger, and hatred. Then we are ready to open the door and let Christ come in, for he is knocking and ready to sup with us. We need the discipline of shutting out voices and listening to the voice of the Spirit. Simon Peter did this.

How well do we know God's voice? Do you hear all that God has to say to you? Simon Peter heard. Cornelius heard. Isaiah heard. Moses heard. Ananias heard. Paul heard. The church at Antioch heard.

"I was in the city of Joppa praying, . . . I saw a vision, . . . I heard a voice, . . . I went with them to Caesarea."

As you know, the messengers tell Simon Peter what Cornelius had commissioned them to do. "Cornelius the centurion, a just man, and one that feareth God, and of good report among all the nation of the Jews, was warned from God by an holy angel to send for them into his house, and to hear words of thee" (Acts 10:22).

Then Simon Peter called them in and lodged them. "And on the morrow Peter went away with them, and certain brethren from Joppa accompanied him" (Acts 10:23).

The die is cast. He is going to break from Jewish law and tradition. He is going to obey the voice of the Spirit. We need to break with tradition.

When the company reached Caesarea, they went to the house where Cornelius, his kinsman, and near friends were waiting. Simon Peter says, "Ye know how that it is an unlawful thing for a man that is a Jew. . . but God hath shewed me that I should not call any man common or unclean" (Acts 10:28).

Simon has learned another lesson. Through prayer he has learned that God is no respecter of persons. "But in every nation he that feareth him, and worketh righteousness, is accepted with him" (Acts 10:34). When we pray, we learn many lessons about the children of God.

"I was in the city of Joppa praying, . . . I saw a vision, . . . I heard a voice, . . . I went to Caesarea, . . . I began to speak."

When they entered the house, Cornelius said, "Four days ago I was fasting until this hour; and at the ninth hour *I prayed in my house*, and, behold, a man stood before me in bright clothing and said, Cornelius, thy prayer is heard, and thine alms are had in remembrance in the sight of God. Send therefore to Joppa, and call hither Simon whose surname is Peter; he is lodged in the house of one Simon a tanner by the sea side: who, when he cometh, shall speak unto thee. Immediately therefore I sent to thee; and thou hast well done that thou art come. Now therefore are we all here present before God, to hear all things that are commanded thee of God" (Acts 10:30-33, italics added).

Here we have another praying man who had a vision, who heard a voice, and who obeyed that voice. No wonder the Spirit fell on them. He is anxious to hear the words whereby he and his house shall be saved.

Simon Peter has a message. A praying person who sees the field, hears a voice, and obeys, has a message:

a. The word came from God.

b. It was published throughout all Judaea and began from Galilee.

c. It came after the baptism that John preached.

d. God anointed Jesus with the Holy Ghost and power.

e. Jesus went about doing good and healing all that were oppressed of devils.

f. God was with him.

g. We are witnesses of all things that he did, both in the land of the Jews and Jerusalem.

h. Jesus, whom they slew and hanged on a tree.

i. God raised him up on the third day and showed himself openly.

j. God showed Jesus to witnesses chosen before God.

k. Jesus was shown to us who did eat and drink with him after he arose from the dead.

l. He commanded us to preach to all people.

m. It is he who was ordained of God to be the judge of the quick and the dead.

n. To him all the prophets give witness that *through his name*, whosoever believeth in him shall receive remission of sins. (See Acts 10:35-43.)

While Peter preached, the Gentiles believed and the Holy Spirit fell on them—to the astonishment of the Jews. The Christian Jews were not expecting anything to happen.

Simon Peter says "The Holy Ghost fell on them, as on us at the beginning" (Acts 11:15). This was not crumbs for the dogs—this was manna from heaven for all God's children.

We are to preach Christ—calling on all to repent. They believe, and the Holy Spirit works. Persons do not repent and believe, and the Holy Spirit does not fall when we are having a book review or a motion picture show or a forum.

This atmosphere was godly. Cornelius said, "We all are here before God, to hear all things that are commanded thee of God" (Acts 10:33).

If our congregations realize that they are in the presence of God and that the messenger has the word from God, the Holy Spirit will fall on us. If the messenger realizes that he or she is from God and has a word from God, the Holy Spirit will fall on him or her. What a glorious experience it is to feel the power of the Holy Spirit as you preach and to see the power of the Holy Spirit in the congregation!

Simon Peter the preacher prayed, Cornelius and the congregation prayed. No wonder the Holy Spirit fell. When the person in the pulpit prays and the congregation prays, something is bound to happen.

"I was in the city of Joppa praying, . . . I saw a vision, . . . I heard a voice, . . . I went to Cornelius, . . . as I spoke the Spirit fell. . . . Remembered I the word of the Lord."

Simon Peter said, I remember that the Lord said, "John indeed baptized with water; but ye shall be baptized with the Holy Ghost" (Acts 11:16).

We seem to have forgotten the word of the Lord in this particular. This was his last message to his disciples before he ascended.

We preach that he said to live, to go, to deny, to take up the cross.

We need to remember that there are two baptisms—the baptism of repentance and the baptism of the Holy Ghost. Think what happened to these men, the disciples, after the baptism of the Holy Spirit. They learned to pray, to share, to suffer, to obey, to believe.

They had boldness. They witnessed to a living Christ. They were put in prison and beaten. They were stoned. They were put to death.

They preached to the Samaritans, the Ethiopians, the Gentiles, the Greeks.

They preached before rulers—kings.

They preached in the Temple, in jail, on the streets.

They turned the world upside down.

Simon Peter said to Cornelius, "I am a man." Paul said, "I am a man."

They were possessed men. They were men of power. They had been with Jesus. They had received two baptisms: one of water, the baptism of repentance; one of the Spirit, the baptism of power.

Jesus made the promise, and he has never broken one. He said, "Tarry. . . until ye be endued with power from on high" (John 24:49). This promised power and baptism that came to the early church comes from prayer and obedience. The Holy Spirit gives us atomic power.

"I was in the city of Joppa praying. I saw a vision. I heard a voice. I went to Cornelius. As I spoke the Holy Spirit fell. Remembered I the word of the Lord. What was I, that I could withstand God?"

Simon Peter is summing up his defense before the keepers of the law, the conservatives, and he said, "Forasmuch then as God gave them the like gift as he did unto us, who believed on the Lord Jesus Christ; what was I, that I could withstand God?"

We cannot withstand God—when we preach the word.

Are we withstanding God by not praying, seeing, listening, hearing, obeying, preaching, remembering?

Let us give God, Christ, and the Holy Spirit a chance. Let us be branches.

We can block God—the Jews did.

Paul went to the Gentiles. The Methodists can. The Methodists will be a channel.

"I was in the city of Joppa praying. . . ."

The Christian Has Particular and Special Gifts

Paul wrote the words in 1 Corinthians 12 to the church at Corinth. He is trying to get the Corinthian Christians to understand that they are the body of Christ but that the Holy Spirit has given particular and special gifts to each Christian.

First, Paul says that no one can say that Jesus is the Lord except under the influence of the Holy Spirit. You have to be under the influence of the Holy Spirit to know that Jesus is Christ.

He says "Now there are diversities of gifts, but the same Spirit. And there are differences of administrations, but the same Lord. And there are diversities of operations, but it is the same God which worketh all in all" (1 Corinthians 12:4-6). We have one congregation but many persons. You are a member of the congregation; I am a member of the congregation.

We have many talents but the same Spirit. We are different, but the same Holy Spirit is speaking to each of us.

We have something special to do but the same Lord. This is done in different ways but the same God worketh in all.

Second, Paul says we have been baptized into one body by the Holy Spirit. If we have been baptized by the Holy Spirit, we are the body of Christ. I am anxious for you to know the wonder and beauty of being the body of Christ. It does not make any difference if I am Jew or Gentile, free or bond, black or white, Japanese or American. If we have been baptized by the Holy Spirit, we are the body of Christ. Paul compares the body of Christ to the human body. The body is not one member but many.

"If the foot shall say, Because I am not the hand, I am

not of the body: is it therefore not of the body? And if the ear shall say, Because I am not the eye, I am not of the body; is it therefore not of the body? If the whole body were an eye, where were the hearing? If the whole were hearing, where were the smelling?...And if they were all one member, where were the body? But now are they many members, yet but one body" (1 Corinthians 12:15-17, 19-20).

We have feet and hands, toes and fingers, eyes and ears, nose and mouth, teeth and lungs, heart and tongue—but one body. The body is comprised of these members.

If I lose any member of my body, I become different according to the extent of my loss. I can never run as fast with artificial legs as I can with the ones God gave me. Artificial teeth are not as good as God's teeth except for cleaning purposes. Glass eyes are not as good as the eyes God gave us except that someone coming to borrow might find a look of sympathy in a glass eye. Bifocals are good but not as good as the eyes God gave us. A wig never looks as good as real hair or as good as a bald head. There is something very real about a bald head.

We never realize the value of a particular member of our bodies until we suffer the loss of one of them. If I have a paralytic stroke, and one side of my body becomes dead; I go through life dragging that dead body. Am I an artificial member of the body of Christ or a real member? Am I a dead member of the body of Christ or a live member of the body of Christ?

We see the work of the individual in all activities of life. Today we talk about mass production, the machine age, and the assembly line. But if the individual fails or does inefficient work, the finished product on the assembly line is marred or ruined.

One day we stood at the altar of the church and took our place on Christ's assembly line. Are we doing the work God desires to have done? We know that it takes the team-work of eleven to win a football game. If one fails in the line or if another fails to tackle, the runner is stopped before getting started. The church is a team, and each member must play where the signals are called. Most of us wish to pay and sit in the grandstand and watch the preacher do it all. Christ is calling the signals. Are you in your place?

In an orchestra we know that one person whose instrument is out of tune can bring discord. If you desire harmony, all must be in tune. The curtain is going up; Christ is lifting the baton. He is the maestro. Are you ready to play the particular instrument belonging to him?

In the business world, we know that an individual employer can wreck a business because of greed and dissipation. We know that an individual employee can spread dissatisfaction and strife.

In our nation we are individuals. America will be great, not if we are the richest nation, not if we have the largest number of airplanes, automobiles, or ships. America will be great in the proportion that we as individuals live great lives.

America is going to be great in the proportion that I am great. Americans make America. If I am greedy, America is greedy to that extent. America is drunk to the extent that I get drunk. If I am unselfish, America will be unselfish to that extent. The lust for power and gold on the part of individual Americans will destroy us long before our war enemies will.

A man who gets rich during a war is not a patriot. One person gives his or her life, another gets rich, and that destroys us. America needs discipline. It must begin in Washington.

The church is the body of Christ. As an individual member of the body of Christ, am I helping or hurting? As a particular member of the body of Christ, what can I do?

There is no rationing on Christian fellowship. All of us can do that.

I went to see a man who was an invalid. He told me how two men who were members of the church came to see him regularly every week. They belonged to the body of Christ and the whole members were helping the weak member.

I have a friend who prays for me many times each day.

He was very sick. His family expected him to die. I went to Birmingham to see him. We prayed together. He got well. He wrote me and told me how many people came to see him while he was sick. I wrote him that this is not strange. For many years he read the church bulletin every Sunday and noted those who were sick or who had had sorrow, and he went to see them. They went to see him. We reap what we sow.

There is no ceiling on Bible reading and praying. I see so many homes with a sign that says "We are prepared," which means they have a bucket of sand and other items in case of an emergency. But I wonder if they are prepared for other emergencies.

It is through prayer and Bible reading and meditation that we know what the head of the Body desires us to do.

In two cities I went into over seventy homes. I asked three questions. Do you read the Bible? No. Do you pray? No. Do you have grace at the table? I found one family that had grace at the table.

As a particular member of the body of Christ, we must be governed by him through meditation, prayer, and Bible reading.

There is no ceiling on your giving to Christ. The government allows you to deduct 15 percent for giving. But the Lord lets you do as you please. You can give nothing or you give all. The rich ruler kept all and lost all. The widow gave all and kept all.

I know a multimillionaire who gives the church $25 per month. I do not know how he can afford it. I know a soldier officer who tithes his income and sends his church $25 per month. Both belong to the same church. One knows the joy of giving and one does not know.

I know an official of a church who told me he paid income tax of $30,000 per year. Yet he gave the church $100 per year.

You do not have to hold a priority card to witness for Christ. We all witness for Christ every day or against Christ every day.

A young man came to me one night after service and said, "I desired to say something tonight, and you would not let me." He said, "This afternoon I was impressed by the Holy Spirit to go and see a man. I secured permission from my employer to leave work early. I went to his home. His wife said, 'I have been praying all day for someone to come. My husband is drinking and is going out tonight to kill a man.' I went in and prayed with this man. He was in no condition to come to church, but he promised me he would not go out last night, and he promised me he is coming to church with me tomorrow night."

The next night I saw this young man and his wife come in, and they had a couple with them. When the invitation was given, this strange couple came to the altar for prayer. The young man and his wife came with them. Others came for prayer. I went to the strange young man and asked him if he desired to repent of his sins. I asked him to pray. Do you know what he prayed? He first thanked God for his friend who came to see him. He then prayed for forgiveness. Christ forgave him. His wife repented and prayed for a Christian home. Christ forgave her. They both rejoiced in their new-found life and applied for church membership.

A pastor was preaching in a certain city. One night he preached on repentance. A woman of the church came and knelt to pray. She said, "I do not think I am guilty of social sins, but I have come to repent for doing nothing for my Lord."

Are you a real member of the body of Christ?
Are you an artificial member of the body of Christ?
Are you a live member of the body of Christ?
Are you a dead member of the body of Christ?
Are you a particular member of the body of Christ?
Are you a parasite member of the body of Christ?

With One Accord in One Place

"And they were all filled with the Holy Ghost" (Acts 2:4).

Today is Pentecost Sunday. We commemorate today what happened to the early church.

May I remind you of what took place.

On Ascension Day Jesus commanded them to "not depart from Jerusalem, but wait for the promise of the Father, which, saith he, ye have heard of me. For John truly baptized with water; but ye shall be baptized with the Holy Ghost not many days hence" (Acts 1:4-5).

Jesus also said, "But ye shall receive power, after that the Holy Ghost is come upon you: and ye shall be witnesses unto me both in Jerusalem, and in all Judaea, and in Samaria, and unto the uttermost part of the earth" (Acts 1:8).

They returned to Jerusalem from Mount Olivet and went to an upper room and for ten days continued with one accord in prayer and supplication.

"And when the day of Pentecost was fully come, they were all with one accord in one place. And suddenly there came a sound from heaven as of a rushing mighty wind, and it filled all the house where they were sitting. And there appeared unto them cloven tongues like as of fire, and it sat upon each of them. And they were all filled with the Holy Ghost" (Acts 2:1-4).

I would like you to notice that before they were filled with the Holy Spirit they did the following:

They obeyed Christ. He told them on Ascension Day not to depart from Jerusalem and to wait for the promise. They did this.

Simon Peter in one of his sermons said, "And so is also the Holy Ghost, whom God hath given to them that obey him" (Acts 5:32). We can never be filled with the Holy Spirit until we obey Christ.

These men did not depart from Jerusalem. It took courage to do this. I would like you to know that these are the men who ran from the Sanhedrin in Jerusalem the night Jesus was taken by a mob.

They displayed unusual boldness by staying in Jerusalem. The men who put Jesus to death were there. It would have been lots easier to go to Galilee in their fishing boats, but they obeyed Christ by staying and waiting.

Sometimes you can wait when you are very busy, but they were waiting for the promise.

Philip, a layman, is the only man in the Bible called an evangelist. He obeyed the Spirit. He went to the Samaritans. He went in the desert to an Ethiopian. He preached Christ. He demanded a belief in Christ, and there was always joy wherever he went. It says of Samaria: "And there was great joy in that city" (Acts 8:8). And the Ethiopian went on his way rejoicing.

Barnabas was a good man, full of faith and of the Holy Spirit. Barnabas obeyed.

Obedience to Christ always brings the infilling of Spirit.

They continued with one accord in prayer and supplication. One hundred and twenty persons had one place, an upper room, where they went to pray.

One reason we are not filled with the Holy Spirit is that we are not in accord in our praying. Suppose this church would meet every day and pray for a revival. We would have one.

They were desperate. Their leaders were gone. Jesus had been lynched. They had been given a great task. They came together with one accord to pray.

They were to witness in Jerusalem in front of their enemies, which meant death. They were to witness in Samaria, which was very hard on a Jew. They were to leave Palestine and go into all the world. They were driven to prayer.

If this church would take the words of Jesus seriously, we would be driven to prayer.

Suppose this church would feel its responsibility for all the people living in this community. Suppose this church would feel its responsibility for those who drink and gamble in our clubs. Suppose this church would feel its responsibility for telling every man, woman, and child about Christ.

We came together to pray with one accord. Praying with one accord brings results.

You remember the first constitutional convention of this nation? It looked as if the nation would split over a centralized federal government and decentralized state government. Benjamin Franklin asked the convention to recess for prayer to ask for the divine wisdom of God. In a few days, all of their troubles were smoothed over and the Constitution was written.

Many homes seem hopelessly divided; but when the family prays together, many troubles disappear, and the home rejoices in the Lord. This early church had to elect a successor to Judas. They prayed and did not have any trouble.

They believed in the Holy Spirit. These men had great faith. They believed the promise would be fulfilled. They did not depart. They waited in Jerusalem. The living Christ had ascended, but they believed his words about the sending of the Holy Spirit, the Comforter. We will never be filled with the Holy Spirit until we believe the words of Christ.

I know a prominent luncheon club that has for its motto: "Service above self." Do they believe it? Some do. Christ taught that as you would that person would do to you do so unto them.

Do we believe in a living Christ today? If so, we will obey him.

When Jesus was in the flesh he was looking for faith. Today the living Christ is looking for faith.

I have a friend who was a school teacher before her marriage. She was to go to the hospital for a major operation. She testifies today that Christ healed her.

We trust God for eternal life. Why not trust God for temporary life?

They had a common purpose, which was witnessing to a

living Christ, all with one accord. What is the common purpose of this church? What could we get this congregation to agree on?

All of us could agree on my messages. I get too many anonymous letters.

What could all of us agree on?

All of us do not believe in the Sunday school. If we did, we would work on it.

All of us do not believe in children's joining the church when they love Jesus.

All of us do not believe in tithing, which the Bible teaches.

All of us do not believe in the Ten Commandments. If we did, we would keep them.

All of us do not believe in reading the Bible. If we did, we would.

All of us do not believe in revivals.

All of us do not believe in Sunday evening services.

There ought to be one thing that this congregation believes.

Do you believe that everyone is searching for life?

Do you believe that Christ is the only one who can give life?

Do you believe that the one purpose of the church is to tell people about Christ?

We must teach Christ; we must give the world Christ.

All of us believe that we do not want the preacher to talk on
economic issues
racial tension
world order
liquor
war and peace
social evils
gambling
drinking.

All believe that the business of the church is to give

them Christ. You believe that every member should do that in his or her own tongue, his or her own way. Devout Jews heard in their own tongues. If you are a lawyer, you can speak the language of a lawyer. If you are a merchant you can speak the language of a merchant.

I am selling Christ. You believe that is the business of the church. Any church can win people for Christ if its members are at one place with one accord.

They were filled with the Holy Spirit. These Galileans eliminated fishing boats. The tax collector forgot his tax books. They were filled with the Spirit.

Jesus said to Nicodemus, "The wind bloweth where it listeth, and thou hearest the sound thereof, but canst not tell whence it cometh, and whither it goeth: so is every one that is born of the Spirit" (John 3:8).

You cannot tell what makes the wind blow and where it comes from and whither it goes, but you know it blows. You have been in a house when it stood. You knew it was blowing.

You cannot explain how you are filled of the Spirit, but you know it. *The wind blows;* we are filled. Spirit-filled persons do not make much noise, but their lives make a difference.

Part Three

MEDITATIONS

INTRODUCTION

In an entry in his *Journal* (June 11, 1739) John Wesley explained what he meant when he said, "I look upon all the world as my parish." He wrote this:

I look upon all the world as my parish; thus far I mean, that, in whatever part of it I am, I judge it meet, right, and my bounden duty to declare unto all that are willing to hear the glad tidings of salvation.

"The world is my parish" had a somewhat similar connotation for Harry Denman, but his was a much larger parish than Wesley's. For Harry Denman it meant carrying the gospel across America and around the globe. He developed a special interest in Ewha University in Seoul, Korea, an internationally acclaimed school for girls. He was invited by Dr. Helen Kim, Ewha's president, to conduct evangelistic services on the campus, which he did on numerous visits. He also had ready access to speak in the government-operated high schools there. Students on both the secondary and collegiate levels looked upon him as a special and beloved Christian friend.

Harry Denman was a remarkably multifaceted man. He was a layman. He never married. He earned baccalaureate and graduate degrees, but he was not a seminarian. He took no courses in the art of preaching or theology, but the persuasiveness of his pulpit style and his dedication to biblical preaching were widely respected and acknowledged. He was winsome in his appeals, plainspoken in his presentation of the gospel. He had a remarkable gift in quickly establishing easy and friendly rapport with his audiences. He even antici-pated interruptions from audiences and seemed to enjoy engaging in impromptu repartee. He was never unnerved by anyone who felt inclined to ask for clarification or even to differ with him. He never lost his cool. When he was sharply challenged he would say, "Thank you, brother" or "Thank you, sister" and keep on going.

At a camp meeting service, he was building up to a summation of his message when the lunch bell began ringing. He knew that the audience's attention would erode quickly, so he stopped preaching and closed the service. I have listened to the tape of that service and regret that his sermon was cut off so abruptly. I am sure that some of those present in the tabernacle regarded the ringing of the bell as an intrusion and that something much more important than food for the body never found its way into their hearts.

When I told a young pastor friend of mine that I was working on a book of meditations written by Harry Denman, I asked, "Did you ever hear of him?"

The reply was, "No. Who was he?"

It is hard to imagine that this "Mr. Methodist" of the mid-twentieth century, who wielded such widespread, benev-olent influence in Methodism and ecumenically, would be slipping into anonymity. I was in my early twenties, and he was in his midforties when he invited me to join the staff of Metho-dism's Board of Evangelism. In that relationship I witnessed close up his dedicated imagination and spiritual vitality that remind me of those lines written by Bishop Ralph S. Cushman:

> Set us afire, Lord!
> Stir us, we pray!
> While the world perishes
> We go our way,

> Purposeless, passionless,
> Day after day.
> Set us afire, Lord,
> Stir us, we pray!*

Harry Denman's life and work was a spiritual flame. He emanated warmth and Christian love. He was adept at turning strangers into friends, perhaps causing some of them to ask when he left them, "Who was that man?"

Harry Denman was the effective chief administrator of the General Board of Evangelism for many years. He did not lay a heavy hand on his staff, but he chose men and women who had the gifts and dedication he wanted and then trusted them to carry out their assignments. I never got the feeling that he was looking over my shoulder. Instead, he was always sending memos of appreciation and encouragement. He always passed on ideas he picked up in his travels that might be the seed for some fresh print "copy" to be used across the denomination.

Professors of preaching sometimes talk about developing "the homiletical mind." They try to show young men and women how to find sermon material through the observation of everyday life experiences. Harry Denman was a master of that art. Illustrative of that was his recollection of a preacher named Simpson. He wrote:

> The first Methodist preacher I can remember was Will Simpson, who vaccinated me for smallpox while my mother held me in her arms. In those days the Preacher had other ministries beside preaching the Gospel. He was trying to keep me from having a contagious disease of the body. I thank the Heavenly Father for all the Methodist preachers who have tried to keep me from having contagious diseases of the soul.

*From *A Pocket Prayer Book*, compiled by Ralph Spaulding Cushman (Copyright ©, 1941 by the General Board of Evangelism of The Methodist Church), p. 6.

Many persons who saw Harry Denman for the first time may have had the impression that he was stern, perhaps even unapproachable. He was, in fact, a large man. But housed in that great frame was marvelous warmth and a delightful sense of humor. One of his stories illustrates this side of his character:

A man had a rich relative who died and left him a million dollars. The man who was to receive this inheritance had a weak heart. The lawyers were afraid to tell him about this million dollars. They thought the shock might bring about sudden death. They decided to have his minister tell him about this inheritance. The preacher went to see him. During the conversation he casually said to the man, "Suppose you had a million dollars. What would you do with it?" The man thought a while and said, "If I had a million dollars I would give you half of it"—and the preacher dropped dead.

Harry Denman cared about young people. He enjoyed visiting and speaking in high schools and colleges. He caught the attention of one of his younger audiences by asking and answering the question: "What would I do if I were sixteen years old?" Here was his answer:

1. I would take care of my body. I would eat food that has vitamins in it. I would get plenty of sleep at night, plenty of sunshine during the day. I would be careful about what I put in my mouth.

2. I would make friends. That is all we ever have. Our parents are our best friends. I would help others.

3. I would develop my mind. I would acquire knowledge. I would learn to read and write. I would seek to master a subject.

4. I would know God. I would find him in the beauty of the world he has created. I would find him in music, in prayer, in the Bible, in Christ.

It is very likely true that many persons "found Christ" under the preaching and by responding to Harry Denman's evangelistic appeals. He was very modest in recalling his own transforming experience:

> I do not remember the day I joined the church. I only know that one day, in revival, the pastor's wife, Mrs. Theo Copeland, came to me and asked me if I did not want to live the Christian life and she went with me to the altar. One night Brother Rudisell came to our home when I was about sixteen years old. He was our pastor. My mother told him I was a church member but that I was not living the Christian life. He prayed with me. That night I went to the altar and surrendered my life to Christ.

It is somewhat remarkable that a man who had witnessed some very dramatic conversions under his preaching would have recounted the story of his own experience of accepting Christ in such mild and modest terms. But those who knew him were convinced that that experience made Harry Denman the great proclaimer of the gospel that he became.

—*Thomas Chilcote*

Why I Am a Christian
Scripture: John 14:1-6

Christianity offers the way of life. In his last words to his disciples Jesus said, "I am the way." He said this in response to Thomas who asked, "Lord, we do not know where you are going; how can we know the way?" (RSV).

There are different ways of life: There is the high way, and there is the low way. There is the way of unselfishness, and there is the way of selfishness. There is the way of giving, and there is the way of getting. There is the way of love, and there is the way of hate. There is the way of serving, and there is the way of being served. There is the way of faith, and there is the way of unbelief. There is the way of purity, and there is the way of impurity. There is the way of hope, and there is the way of despair. There is the way of peace, and there is the way of fear. There is the way of optimism, and there is the way of pessimism. There is the way of forgiveness, and there is the way of revenge. There is the way of humility, and there is the way of pride. There is the way of heaven, and there is the way of hell. There is the narrow way, and there is the broad way.

Christ lived the way of God. When the time came for him to choose between God and the Evil One, Christ took the way of God. The disciples observed this in his life, remembered it when he was taken from them, and courageously followed in his steps. Those of us who now profess that we are his followers can do no less if we intend to be true and persuasive witnesses.

Help us, our Father, who call Christ "Lord of our lives" to conduct ourselves after the manner of his life, thereby convincingly commending him to our generation and receiving spiritual enrichment that comes from our obedience to him. Amen.

Christ's Way of Living
Scripture: John 1:10-14

Christ lived a life of faith, of love, of hope, of courtesy, of peace, of purity, of gratitude, of doing good. He revealed God's way for us. At the Pool of Bethesda, he healed a man. In that act we saw God doing good.

When he called Levi, the tax collector, we see God having faith in a man. When he bent down and wrote with his finger on the ground to keep from embarrassing a sinning woman, we saw God being kind, considerate, courteous, and hopeful. When Christ knelt to bathe the feet of the disciples, we saw God as a servant. When we saw Christ on a cross, taking a thief to Paradise, we saw God loving a sinner. When we saw Christ healing the ear of Malchus, the servant of the high priest, his enemy, we saw God forgiving.

Christ said, "I am . . . the truth (John 14:6)." He came to reveal the truth of God. Christ gave the people, the religious leaders, and sinners the truth of God.

When we hear Christ say, "Blessed are the meek: for they shall inherit the earth," that is God giving us truth.

When we hear Christ say, "Love your enemies, do good to them which hate you, bless them that curse you, and pray for them which despitefully use you"—that is God giving us truth (Luke 6:27-29).

Christ could say, "I am . . . the truth," because he lived the truth revealed to him by God. Standing before Pilate he said, "To this end was I born, and for this cause came I into the world, that I should bear witness unto the truth" (John 18:37). Christ lived the truth. He lived only what God revealed in him.

As much as we desire to know, speak, and live the truth, our Father, we acknowledge it is sometimes difficult to be committed to the truth. Help us today to seek the truth and to proclaim it in word and deed. In Christ's name we pray. Amen.

Running for God
Scripture: Acts 8:26-40

Do you obey the Spirit today? Will you do what God tells you to do? He may have a running job for you. In fact, all work of the kingdom is so important that we should be runners. The only place for a sitter in the kingdom is to take time to meditate, to hear the commands and instructions of God—and then run to execute them. Let us be runners.

We read that Philip was running. Why? He was the leader of a great spiritual awakening in Samaria. In fact, this layman, under the leadership of the Holy Spirit, was having such a great revival in Samaria that news reached First Church, Jerusalem. So it was decided to send Peter and John to see about this movement among the underprivileged Samaritans across the tracks. Thank God, First Church, Jerusalem sent their best leaders to help.

In the midst of this wonderful spiritual outpouring "the angel of the Lord spake unto Philip, saying, Arise, and go toward the south unto the way that goeth down from Jerusalem unto Gaza, which is desert. And he arose and went: and, behold, a man of Ethiopia, a eunuch of great authority under Candace, queen of the Ethiopians, who had the charge of all her treasure, and had come to Jerusalem for to worship, was returning, and sitting in his chariot read Esaias the prophet. Then the Spirit said unto Philip, Go near, and join thyself to this chariot. And Philip ran thither to him." Philip ran.

He ran because the errand was urgent. The opportunity to bear gospel witness to the Ethiopian would not come again, and God had no one else to run this errand. He ran because he was under orders from the Holy Spirit. There was no higher authority for him to submit to than that.

Help us, our Father, to look upon our opportunities to share the good news of Christ as divine calls to enlarge the kingdom of God. Give us rejoicing hearts as we proclaim thy love and goodness wherever we can bear testimony to Christ, our Lord. Amen.

The Christian Use of Money
Scripture: Matthew 6:19-21

The right use of money, someone once observed, implies foresight—to be ready for losses; self-control—to be able to go without things that we should like but cannot afford; patience—to know how to wait for what we wish; discretion—clearly to perceive what will suit us best; self-denial—that we may help others; conscientiousness—that in all we spend we may please God; good sense—to draw the right line between extremes on either side; a joyous liberty of heart—to trust the kindness of God, knowing that he wants us to be happy.

I believe in the life everlasting. I must, then, lay up treasures in heaven. Where my treasure is, there will my heart be also. I believe my soul is to live eternally with God, my Creator. Therefore, I must have treasures there. While here on earth I will give to God the best part of my life. Malachi, the prophet, asks, "Will a man rob God?" (3:8) and God answers by saying that persons rob God "in tithes and offerings."

I will not rob God. He is my Father and my benefactor. He gives me all my material and spiritual blessings. In determining what my part will be in giving to any cause, I must determine the need. Sometimes I must do without luxuries and, if possible, even necessities in order that the kingdom of God can be extended.

Also, I must remember that the church is the only agency commissioned to bring spiritual life to all the human family. Therefore, I must put the church at the top of the list in my giving. No matter how small or how large my income, the first part of it should be given to my heavenly Father through his institution, the church. Christian generosity is measured by what we have left over.

Give me a spirit of generosity, O God, so I may gladly share as much as I can of my material wealth to serve persons and to support causes that will bless life both locally and globally. In Jesus' name I pray. Amen.

Being an Example for Believers
Scripture: 1 Timothy 4:12-16

"Let no one despise your youth, but set the believers an example in speech and conduct, in love, in faith, in purity." Paul wrote this to Timothy. He told his young friend what he could do as a Christian.

1. Set the believers an example of speech. Talk about spiritual things. Testify to your Christian experience. Witness to Christ. Youth can do that. Say grace at table. Say gracious, encouraging, and kind words. Speak words of purity.

2. Set the believers an example of behavior. Unite with the church, attend regularly, and pray for the church. Invite others to participate in worship and Sunday school. Behave in a Christlike way at home and at school. Get all the education you can. Participate in community activities.

3. Set the believers an example of love. Love God and Christ with all your being. Love the beautiful. Love good music and good literature. Love the Bible. Love your home, your church, your country. Love people who do not like you.

4. Set the believers an example of faith. Believe in Christ, in the Bible. If God calls you to the ministry or to the mission field, have faith and answer Yes. If God calls you to make money for him, show believers how to give money away for God. Give generously. Be a tither.

5. Set the believers an example of purity. Read pure books, think pure thoughts. Be careful about what you put in your body, which is the temple of the Holy Spirit. Let your speech and inward thoughts be acceptable to God. Read some Scriptures daily. Write down your thoughts.

Show each of us, O God, regardless of our age or health, how we can reflect your goodness and love to those around us, possibly leading us to some person who needs the radiance of our Christian life to help him or her through this day. Amen.

Simon Peter, Pioneer Missionary
Scripture: Acts 10:30-35, 44-48

Simon Peter said, "I was in the city of Joppa praying" (Acts 11:5). The great Gentile movement started in a prayer meeting.

1. I saw a vision. Simon Peter saw a certain vessel descend as a great sheet let down from heaven by four corners. On the sheet he saw four-footed beasts of the earth and wild beasts and creeping things and fowls of the air.

2. I heard a voice, "Arise, Peter; slay and eat" (11:7). But I said, "Not so, Lord, for nothing common or unclean has at any time entered my mouth." The voice answered me: "What God has cleansed call not thou common."

3. While Peter was pondering the vision, the Spirit said to him, "Behold, three men are looking for you. . . . Accompany them without hesitation; for I have sent them" (Acts 10:19-20). Peter went down to the men and said, "Why have you come?" And they said, "Cornelius, a centurion, an upright and God-fearing man, who is well spoken of by the whole Jewish nation, was directed to send for you to come to his house and to hear what you have to say." Defending his action before the Jerusalem apostles, he said, "Forasmuch then as God gave [the Gentiles] the like gift as he did unto us, who believed on the Lord Jesus Christ; what was I, that I could withstand God?" (Act 11:17).

"When they heard these things, they held their peace and glorified God, saying, Then hath God also to the Gentiles granted repentance unto life."

Our heavenly Father, show us how important and necessary it is for those who profess their love for thee to regard all of thy children as brothers and sisters, even as Simon Peter had to examine his own prejudices against Gentiles. Amen.

Persons Christ Transformed
Scripture: Mark 1:16-18

"I will make you to become." That promise of Jesus came true in the lives of men and women he met along the way.

He gave this promise to Simon. Simon was weak, vacillating, fearful. At Caesarea Philippi he said of Jesus, "You are the Christ, the Son of the living God" (Matthew 16:16). He protested when Jesus said he was going to Jerusalem and to the cross. He heard Jesus' rebuke: "Get behind me, Satan. . . . You are not on the side of God, but of men" (Matthew 16:23). Peter asked, "Lord, why cannot I follow you now? I will lay down my life for you" (John 13:37). Jesus answered, "Will you lay down your life for me?" Peter denied his Lord; but later (after Pentecost) he stood before the mob in Jerusalem; he stood before the mob at Solomon's portico; he stood before the Sanhedrin. He went to Samaria and to the house of Cornelius. He became a rock, a fisher of people, a missionary, an evangelist, a preacher, a man of power, a man of boldness, a healer in the name of Jesus, a sufferer. The Jewish religious leaders perceived that Peter and the other apostles had been with Jesus.

Others too were transformed by Christ: Zacchaeus became the most liberal man in his community; Levi became a Gospel writer; Mary of Magdala became one of the first messengers of the resurrection; a madman in the Decapolis became tamed, gained his right mind, and went out to publish the good news of what the Lord had done for him; Saul of Tarsus, once a proud Pharisee, came to love all persons.

Our Father, when the Christian faith was in its beginning, men and women experienced transformations that startled the world around them. May it always be true that those who give Christ control over their lives cause those around them to marvel. Amen.

Today's Choices for Tomorrow
Scripture: Matthew 16:24-27

What do you desire to become? A gambler? Do not come to Christ. He will never make you a gambler. He wants your treasures to be in heaven. A drunkard? Do not come to Christ. You may become intoxicated with the Holy Spirit and God's love but not alcohol. A libertine? Do not come to Christ. He wants you to treat every woman as you would every man— your wife, sister, mother, sweetheart. A gossiper? Do not come to Christ. He wants you to tell the good news of salvation.

Do you desire to have a temper? Do not come to Christ. He may call you to battle unrighteousness but not persons. Do you desire to be a swearer—to profane the name of Christ? Do not come to Jesus. He will expect your devotion. Do you desire to be jealous? Christ never made a jealous person. He will make you jealous for his kingdom. Do you desire to become a Christian parent? Christ helped parents—the nobleman, the ruler of the synagogue, the outcast woman. Do parents today help their children become Christians by becoming Christians themselves?

Do you desire to become a preacher, a missionary, a teacher? Come to Christ. Learn of him.

What do you have to do in order to become? If anyone will come after me, said Jesus, let him (1) "deny himself" (glorify Christ), (2) "take up his cross," and (3) "follow me." If we glorify self we renounce Christ. Self gets between you and Christ. He will make you to become what he wants you to become.

Show us, our heavenly Father, how to shut out the cares and anxieties of everyday life for a moment or two each day so we can quietly examine our efforts to seek and obey thy will. Amen.

You Shall Have Power
Scripture: Acts 1:6-9

Christians seek power—the power to be good. Barnabas is described as a good man. He was an encourager. He stood for Saul at Jerusalem when Saul was being questioned by the apostles. When Saul abandoned his missionary work and returned to Tarsus, Barnabas found him and set him to work anew. He stood up to Paul in support of John Mark.

We have the power to be good. Peter and John rejoiced when they were beaten that they were counted worthy to suffer for Christ.

We have the power to glorify Christ. Philip went down to Samaria and preached Christ there. He preached Christ to the Ethiopian eunuch. Daily in the Temple and in every home, the apostles taught and preached Christ. Peter said publicly, "Be it known to you all . . . that by the name of Jesus Christ of Nazareth, whom you crucified, whom God raised from the dead, by him this man is standing before you well" (Acts 4:10).

The baptism of the Holy Spirit endues us with the power to give. Barnabas, having land, sold it and brought the money and laid it at the apostles' feet. He wanted to do this. When we are baptized with the Holy Spirit, all belongs to the Lord. He can have it all or any part.

The baptism of the Holy Spirit gives the power to go. Philip, John, and Simon Peter went to Samaria to the home of Cornelius, a Gentile, because they had come to believe that God is no respecter of persons. Paul reached out to Jews and Gentiles, to women, a jailer, a runaway slave.

We need your help, O God, to make sure that the power we seek is the power to show kindness, the power to bestow Christlike love, the power to go on divine errands of helpfulness. Give us that power today, through Christ, your Son our Lord, in whose name we pray. Amen.

Who Is Worse than an Infidel?
Scripture: 1 Timothy 5:8

Paul said that a person who has denied the faith is worse than an infidel. Who is this person? Paul wrote a letter to Timothy in which he made this statement: Who is one who denies the faith? He is the one who does not provide food and raiment for his relatives and family.

1. Conscientious fathers are concerned about their children. They are concerned about the bodies of their children.

2. Conscientious fathers are interested in the mental lives of their children. They will sacrifice to give their children an education. Why not be interested in what your children see at the movies, hear on the radio, watch on television?

3. Conscientious fathers are concerned about the spiritual lives of their children.

But fathers may worship money. They work for money. They need to worship God and work for God. They need to pray for their children and with their children. We give physical birth to our children; do we want them to experience spiritual birth?

If a man denies the faith he is worse than an infidel because he fails to provide food for his family. What would you say about a man who failed to provide spiritual food for his children? Children have souls. Their bodies die, but their souls live forever. We want our children to have the best of life. Why not be interested in their spiritual lives?

Children learn from parents by what parents do. Are we proud to say, "I am a Christian father"?

Our heavenly Father, put it into the hearts of all earthly fathers that theirs is a holy task—to provide for their children, not only what is needed for their physical and mental health, but what is critically necessary for their spiritual nurture. And let all fathers know that this is a responsibility and role shared by both parents. In Jesus' name. Amen.

Simon Peter's Weakness and Strength
Scripture: Acts 9:37-43

The early church leaders charged Peter that he went in to men uncircumcised and ate with them. Peter, in his defense, said, "I was in the city of Joppa praying" (Acts 11:5). He sought divine direction by praying.

1. On the Mount of Transfiguration he fell asleep. When he awoke he wanted to build tabernacles.

2. He fell asleep in Gethsemane when Jesus was praying. Jesus said to him: "Could you not watch one hour?" (Mark 14:37).

3. Simon Peter did obey the last appeal of Jesus: tarry in Jerusalem until you are endued with power from on high. He and 119 others prayed for ten days. They were of one mind.

What happened in the work of the early disciples?

1. New converts entered into the fellowship. "They continued stedfastly in the apostles' doctrine and fellowship, and in breaking of bread, and in prayers" (Acts 2:42). The early church was a praying church.

2. When Peter and John went up into the Temple at the hour of prayer, they were arrested and jailed.

3. They went to a prayer meeting. They prayed for signs and wonders to be done in the name of Jesus. They were all filled with the Holy Spirit and spoke the word with boldness.

4. Peter and John went to Samaria. When they arrived they prayed for them that they might receive the Holy Spirit.

5. Dorcas died at Joppa. Peter was at Lydda, and they sent for him. At Dorcas's bedside Peter knelt down and prayed, and she opened her eyes.

6. One day Peter was lodging with Simon the tanner in Joppa. He went up on the housetop to pray. It was noon. He became hungry, but he prayed. On the housetop he had a vision.

The farther we journey in our Christian pilgrimage, our Father, the more we feel compelled to join our deeds to prayer. May thy spirit indwell in us and then outflow through us as we reach out to persons in need. In Jesus' name. Amen.

Jesus on that First Palm Sunday
Scripture: Luke 19:41-44

"When [Jesus] was come near, he beheld the city, and wept over it."

On Palm Sunday we recall Jesus' triumphal entry into Jerusalem. On that day Jesus shed tears over the city. Here stood the Temple in its splendor. Here sat the Sanhedrin, composed of the leaders of Judaism. But Jesus saw traders—representatives of the priests—on the Temple porch, robbing the poor. He saw the sick and lame at the Pool of Bethesda. He knew that Barabbas, a murderer and insurrectionist, was in jail. He knew the multitude would clamor for the release of Barabbas and insist on Jesus' crucifixion. He saw children being ignored. He knew that the publicans were despised, that his disciples would desert him, that Pilate would yield to the demands of the religious leaders. Jerusalem would reject him.

Not only did he weep over the city, he did something about it. At the Temple porch he said, "My house shall be a house of prayer; but you have made it a den of robbers" (RSV). After he drove the moneychangers away, the lame and blind came to pray and worship.

Jesus wept over Jerusalem and said: "O Jerusalem, Jerusalem, . . . how often would I have gathered your children together, . . . and you would not!" (Luke 13:34, RSV). He shed God's tears.

Jesus' weeping over Jerusalem showed us, our Father, your concern for those who are entrusted with holy things and who occupy holy offices for the work of thy kingdom. May each of us who serves in the church in any capacity look upon these as sacred and privileged obligations. Amen.

The Agony of Jesus
Scripture: Luke 22:63–23:1

When Jesus came to the Passover observance, he said to his disciples, "With desire I have desired to eat this passover with you before I suffer: For I say unto you, I will not any more eat thereof, until it be fulfilled in the kingdom of God." In that room at that time, he took a towel and basin and assumed the role of a servant.

He went to the Mount of Olives. His disciples followed him. He left eight of them at the garden gate. Judas had already broken ranks with Jesus and his friends. He took Peter, James, and John and asked them to pray. He went a little farther and prayed alone: "Father, if thou art willing, remove this cup from me; nevertheless, not my will, but thine, be done" (Luke 22:42, RSV). And being in agony he prayed more earnestly, and his sweat was as great drops of blood falling down to the ground. He agonized in prayer. Three times he prayed that prayer. His spirit was crucified on the night before the crucifixion. His body was crucified on the cross at Calvary; his spirit was crucified in the Garden of Gethsemane.

Christ shed his blood. He suffered. The soldiers slapped him. He was taken before Annas and Caiaphas. He was called a blasphemer. He was taken to Pilate, Herod, and back to Pilate. They placed a crown of thorns on his head. He was scourged. He was taken to Calvary, bearing the burden of his cross up the steep slope. He was crucified. Nails were driven into his hands and feet. A spear was thrust into his side. He shed his tears, his sweat, his blood. It takes tears, sweat, and blood to bring in the kingdom.

The brutalities heaped on Jesus on that memorable day when he was released to the mob and the soldiers dismay us, O God. They were so unspeakably cruel—and Jesus was totally innocent of any crime. So we stand in his presence amazed at his composure and grateful for his sacrifice on our behalf. Amen.

What Things?
Scripture: John 13:12-17

"If ye know these things, happy are ye if you do them." Jesus was thinking about the fundamentals of life.

1. What are you going to do about God? Jesus made him to be his Father. He made himself to be the Son of God. Philip said to him, "Show us the Father," and Jesus replied, "He who has seen me has seen the Father" (John 14:8). He taught his disciples to address God in prayer as "Our Father."

2. What are you going to do about persons? No two are alike. When you make God your Father, then every person becomes your brother or sister. We belong to God's family. How did Jesus treat persons? He spoke to the Samaritan woman, surprising both her and his disciples. He ate with Zacchaeus, and the religious people murmured. He healed a man on the Sabbath and the religious people decided to kill him. He healed a demon-possessed man and had to leave the land of Gadara.

3. What are you going to do about property? Jesus believed that property was sacred as long as you controlled it. Food was sacred: "Gather up the fragments," he ordered his disciples after the feeding of the multitude (John 6:12). We are judged by what we throw away.

4. What are you going to do about time? Jesus was always busy, always working.

5. What about death? What did Jesus do about death? Even though he was young he said, "I lay down my life . . . (John 10:15), I go to prepare a place . . . (John 14:2), I am the resurrection and the life" (John 11:25).

6. Have you a purpose in living? Jesus had a purpose: His cause was establishing the kingdom of God.

Our Father in heaven, help us as your sometimes bewildered children to discover anew each day that the Christian life is an ever-enlarging experience that keeps adding new dimensions and meanings for our earthly pilgrimage toward the Celestial City. In Jesus' name we pray. Amen.

"Son of Consolation"
Scripture: John 1:35-42

One of Jesus' great words was *Come*. When James and John started following Jesus, he asked them, "What do you seek?" The two men said, "Where are you staying?" They wanted to be with him. Jesus said, "Come and see." That signaled the beginning of the evangelistic movement.

Saul of Tarsus consented to the stoning of Stephen, the first Christian martyr. Then he met the living Christ and became a disciple. The Jerusalem disciples feared him. Barnabas took him to them and stood up for him.

A great revival began in Antioch (Syria). When this news reached Jerusalem, the apostles sent Barnabas to conserve this revival. There he saw the grace of God at work and departed for Tarsus to seek Saul.

He found him and took him to Antioch. The name *Barnabas* means "son of encouragement" or "son of consolation." Later he and Paul went to Jerusalem, taking gifts for the poor because there was a famine in Palestine. When they returned to Antioch, they brought with them John Mark, the nephew of Barnabas.

On their first missionary journey, John Mark left the team at Perga in Pamphylia. Later Paul rejected Mark when he wanted a second chance. But Barnabas took Mark and sailed to Cyprus. He believed in the Gospel of the Second Chance. Barnabas was always helping people by encouraging them. He is described as a man who was full of the Holy Spirit, full of God, full of love.

With so much harshness in our world, O God, help us to become like Barnabas, offering encouragement and consolation at every opportunity. Help us lift someone's burden of guilt or sorrow today. In Jesus' name. Amen.

Zacharias and Elisabeth, Chosen Parents
Scripture: Luke 1:5-25

"Thy prayer is heard; and thy wife Elisabeth shall bear thee a son, and thou shalt call his name John." The angel delivered this message to Zacharias, an aged, devout, and faithful priest in the Temple.

The angel said, "Thy prayer is heard." Imagine! In advanced age Zacharias and Elisabeth prayed for a son! They were both righteous and blameless before God. They were persons of perseverance. They were advanced in years, but they were faithful in their prayers.

They became parents. "Thou shalt have joy and gladness; and many shall rejoice at his birth." They were parents of a son: "Thou shalt call his name John."

John was born with the promise of becoming influential: "He shall be great in the sight of the Lord." He was born a son of purity. "He...shall drink neither wine nor strong drink." He was born with power. "And he shall be filled with the Holy Ghost, even from his mother's womb."

Zacharias and Elisabeth were the parents of a son born with a purpose—to prepare the way of the Lord. Do you want your child to be a Christian? Yes? Will you be one?

May the spirit of lovingkindness prevail in our families, our Father, so that we may be truly regarded as the children of God, who looks upon every member of the human family as God's child. Amen.

The Kingdom of God
Scripture: Matthew 4:12-17

"The kingdom of God is at hand."...It is within you. Jesus proclaimed this at the beginning of his ministry.

The kingdom of God is spiritual; the kingdom of self is material. Jesus said, "Seek ye first the kingdom of God, and his righteousness; and all these things shall be added unto you" (Matthew 6:33). The kingdom of God is within you when you have Christ in your heart. He lives in us. The choice is ours: Christ or self.

Jesus went about doing good (he fed the hungry, gave sight to the blind, cleansed lepers, drove demons out) and said to his followers, "Let your light so shine before men that they may see your good works, and glorify your Father which is in heaven" (Matthew 5:16).

Jesus said to Nicodemus: "Except a man be born of water and of the Spirit, he cannot enter into the kingdom of God" (John 3:5). Nicodemus had carved out a small world in which he comfortably lived. He did not love Samaritans, publicans, Galileans, harlots, lepers, persons possessed of demons. God's bigger world included every person, no exclusions. Jesus showed us that God loves all of us.

Christ brings life to whosoever believes in him. (*Whosoever* is a God-word. It is all-inclusive.) He said, "I am come that [you] might have life, and that [you] might have it more abundantly" (John 10:10). Each of us is precious to God.

Jesus' invitation to the fishermen, "Follow me," is given to all of us. We, like them, are ordinary persons.

We must assume responsibility for our sin. Jesus assumed my sins. God has forgiving love for every one of us.

We can well imagine, our Father, the wonder and surprise of those early disciples when Jesus called them to follow him. May we experience something of that same amazement as we respond to his call to live alongside him in our time. Amen.

Showing Thankfulness through Sharing
Scripture: John 5:2-18

We have more automobiles, television sets, telephones, radios, refrigerators, food, and per capita wealth than any other nation. We can show our gratitude for such largesse by sharing. With all our wealth, we are dependent. We are rich in material goods, but are we spiritually rich? We buy books on happiness, the power of the mind, etc. We are hungry for power—material power. When our pioneer fathers and mothers landed on these shores, the oil was here, the gold was here, the rich soil was here, the iron ore was here, the coal was here, the forests were here, the atom was here, the water power was here. We took what we found here and became wealthy, but are we rich toward God?

We are thankful for our material blessings, but they do not feed our souls. Our souls must have bread from heaven. Jesus said, "I am the bread of life; he who comes to me shall not hunger, and he who believes in me shall never thirst" (John 6:36). When we put our faith in Christ, we have life. Are you rich toward self or toward God? Thank God for giving life to your soul.

Consider the plight of the impotent man at the Pool of Bethesda. "Sir, I have no man," he said to Jesus. He had tried for years to gain release from his infirmity, but he had no one to help him. Then along came Jesus, who was ready to make this man's need his own priority. Jesus had compassion. He "suffered with" persons who were distressed. Jesus showed courage when he healed this man "on the Sabbath." The orthodox Jews witnessed the happening and threatened to kill him.

We are grateful, O God, that your Son was unflinching in doing what was right, even when it meant arousing the hostility of powerful forces that insisted that their religious traditions were more precious than human life. Amen.

"*I Will Build My Church*"
Scripture: Matthew 16:13-20

1. The church has for its founder and creator Jesus Christ, the son of the living God. Simon Peter did not say to Jesus, "You are a great rabbi, a great philosopher, a great man, a great teacher, a great psychologist, a great evangelist." He said, "You are the Christ, the Son of the living God." Jesus does not sleep in a grave under the Syrian sky. He is alive—forever. He wants to live in human beings. Paul said, "I am crucified with Christ: nevertheless I live; yet not I, but Christ lives in me: and the life which I now live in the flesh I live by the faith of the Son of God, who loved me, and gave himself for me" (Galatians 2:20).

2. The church believes a creed: "I believe in God." We are to live for God. "I believe in the life everlasting." The grave is the beginning. Our treasures are in heaven.

3. The church has a commission. Jesus instructed his disciples to tell every person about the living Christ: "Go ye therefore, and teach all nations . . . to observe all things whatsoever I have commanded you" (Matthew 28:19-20). We are to do it.

4. The church is in a crusade against unrighteousness. We are against anything that harms and hurts.

Jesus came healing. Jesus came visiting. Suppose Jesus had only preached. He never would have found James and John, Simon and Andrew, the woman at the well, Philip, Levi, the demon-possessed man in Gadara. He taught and trained disciples—twelve, then seventy. He did not try to do it all.

Keep us humbly aware, our Father, that it is Christ and not ourselves who builds the church. At best, we may think of our task as that of extending the kingdom of God rather than creating it. In Jesus' name. Amen.

Sent by God
Scripture: Matthew 9:10-13

A God-sent Christ was sent to the outcasts. He went to the publicans and sinners. He needs followers who will care about the outcasts. "As my Father hath sent me, even so send I you," he said to his disciples (John 20:21).

Think of the compassion of Jesus: "He must needs go through Samaria" (John 4:4). Why? Why not? He was without prejudice. A woman came to him as he sat at the well. Is he going to speak to her? It would surprise her that he, a Jew, would speak to her—a woman and a Samaritan. He did speak to her and revealed to her that he was the Messiah.

Do we speak to Samaritans? Do we befriend persons in the community who have made mistakes and want friendships restored?

I went visiting with a preacher from house to house. At the first house this is what we found: two young women—fifteen years of age who had quit school and were not working; one young woman—seventeen years of age, married, and with a one-week-old baby; another young woman—seventeen years of age, married, and expecting a baby. They were related to one another. All had been to the Methodist Sunday school but had not attended in four years. None of them had made a profession of Christ. They did not have Bibles. We talked to them about Christ. We read to them about Christ. We secured Bibles for them. We took the Methodist pastor in whose community they lived and went to see them. They promised to come to Sunday school and unite with the church. The pastor told me that some of the young people in his church said these young women were cheap girls. I thought, *No, they are dear to Christ. He went to the cross for them.*

May we not be judgmental of other persons, our Father, lest we miss opportunities for divine friendship with children who are precious in thy sight. Amen.

"I Was in the City of Joppa Praying"
Scripture: Acts 9:43; 10:21-23

The leaders of the Jewish Christians in Jerusalem heard that Gentiles responded to Simon Peter's preaching and received the word of God. The same Holy Spirit had fallen on those Gentiles as they themselves experienced on the day of Pentecost.

Simon Peter had no business "crossing the tracks" to go to Joppa, where he was the guest in the home of Simon the tanner. If he had not gone to Joppa he never would have gone to Caesarea. If he had not gone to Joppa, Cornelius, the Roman centurion, would never have sent for him. The Jerusalem church leveled two charges against Peter: You went in to a man uncircumcised and ate with him. They thought that the baptism of repentance and the baptism of power were reserved only for Jewish Christians. Peter started his defense by saying, "I was in the city of Joppa praying" (Acts 11:5).

Simon Peter had learned to pray. He had learned a fundamental lesson. When Jesus was praying at the Mount of Transfiguration and later in the Garden of Gethsemane, Simon went to sleep. He learned what happens when you do not pray; and by wonderful experience he learned what happens when you do pray. When Peter and the other disciples were unable to help a father and his demon-possessed son, they asked Jesus why they were helpless. He answered, "This kind of faith goes out after much fasting and prayer" (Matthew 17:21). Christ depended on prayer. Simon depended on a sword. Power came to him on the day of Pentecost because he obeyed and tarried in prayer until the power came. He learned what happens when you do not pray, and by wonderful experience he learned what happens when you do pray.

May we go to school in learning better how to pray effectually, seeking to discover for ourselves how Jesus made prayer so meaningful in day-to-day living. Amen.

When Peter Learned to Pray
Scripture: Acts 3:1-10

Simon Peter may have learned to pray from the disciple John. One day Peter may have said to John, "Let us go and heal someone. Let us do something that will make Jerusalem talk." John said, "Simon, it is the ninth hour. Let us go to the Temple and pray."

They found a lame man at the Gate Beautiful. Simon Peter would never forget that day—how the lame man leaped and walked into the Temple, praising God. Then there was another short message, and 5,000 men came into the kingdom.

He could never forget saying to the Sanhedrin after being in jail all night: "Whether it be right in the sight of God to hearken unto you more than unto God, judge ye. For we cannot but speak the things which we have seen and heard" (Acts 4:19-20). He remembered that after hearing the threatenings of the Sanhedrin, the little church prayed until the house was shaken, and they were all filled with the Holy Ghost, and they spoke the word of God with boldness.

He would never forget the night when the angel of the Lord delivered them from prison, and they resumed their public witnessing.

He knew how prayer was answered at Joppa. He was brought to Joppa by two men because Dorcas was dead. The widows needed Dorcas. Peter asked the mourners to leave the room. He knelt down and prayed and called Dorcas to arise—and she did.

Standing before the Sanhedrin, Peter began his defense by saying, "I was in the city of Joppa praying." He knew what praying could do. He had learned to pray. He had seen victories wrought by prayer.

We sometimes find it hard to believe, our Father, that prayer can change circumstances and even persons. May we be more confident in calling on Thee for daily help. Amen.

I Have Come to Call Outcasts
Scripture: Matthew 9:9-13

"I have not come to call respectable people, but outcasts" (TEV).

When Jesus said to the tax collector, Levi, "Follow me," Levi responded and became one of the twelve disciples.

On Jesus' way to Jerusalem, where crucifixion awaited him, a blind beggar, sitting by the road, cried out: "Jesus, son of David, have mercy on me" (Luke 18:35). "What do you want me to do for you?" Jesus asked. "I want to see again." In Jericho a very rich man, an outcast because he was a Jew who collaborated with the Romans, caught his attention: "I must stay at your house today." Zacchaeus welcomed him with great joy.

In Jerusalem after he drove the moneychangers from the Temple porch, the lame, halt, and blind came for healing. The church too has a ministry to outcasts.

After Jesus spent forty days in the wilderness fasting, he was determined to live according to the will of God. He was going to worship and serve God only. The early Christians voluntarily shared a common life. Those with resources shared with the had-nots. No one was in need. The fellowship was enriched at the table. One hundred and twenty followers of Jesus prayed for ten days and were baptized with the Holy Spirit. The new fellowship became a force. They were persecuted, but their numbers grew. On the day of Pentecost Peter told his hearers about Jesus. They asked, "What shall we do?" He replied, "Repent, and be baptized . . . for the forgiveness of your sins" (Acts 2:37-38), and some 3,000 were added to their number that day.

Our Father, may we accept the obligations of disciplined living as the means by which we obtain fullness of life. Help us to resist the temptation of living only for pleasures or for thrills that have no lasting worth or value. Amen.

Jesus Becomes the Son of Love
Scripture: Matthew 4:1-11

At the age of twelve Jesus became a son of the Law; at thirty he became the son of love.

He presented himself to his cousin, John the Baptist, for baptism in the Jordan River. But John did not want to baptize him. Jesus insisted. After the baptism "a voice from heaven" announced, "This is my beloved son" (Matthew 3:17).

After Jesus fasted for forty days, the Tempter came and said, "If you are the Son of God turn these stones into bread." Jesus replied, "Man does not live by bread alone but by every word God utters." Then the tempter took him to the temple in Jerusalem. "Cast yourself down" he said, "for it is written that the angels will bear you up." Jesus said, "You shall not put the Lord your God to the test."

Then the devil took him to a mountain. "Worship me," he said, "and I will give you the kingdoms of the world." "You shall worship the Lord your God," Jesus replied, "and serve him only."

Jesus loved all kinds of persons—the sick, the blind, the deaf, the dumb; he gave life to the dead and food to the hungry; he cast out demons; his heart went out to the rich and the poor, the Samaritans, the Galileans, the centurion.

After the Resurrection, Jesus said to Peter, "Do you love me." He answered, "You know I love you." Jesus said, "Feed my lambs.... Feed my sheep."

> *O Love that wilt not let me go,*
> *I rest my weary soul in thee;*
> *I give thee back the life I owe,*
> *That in thine ocean depths its flow*
> *May richer, fuller be.**

*From the hymn "O Love That Wilt Not Let Me Go" by George Matheson.

A Little Boy's Advice
Scripture: Ephesians 4:29-32

Kindness is a Christian characteristic that is needed daily in this world. We can do so many things that will help make the day brighter for people. I wonder how many times we say please and thank you to those with whom we are associated day after day in the home, community, and business. I have found that kindness brings the largest dividends and peace to your own soul. A dog responds to kindness. A child responds to kindness.

The story is told that on a busy icy street a horse fell down and could not get up. The driver beat and kicked, but the horse made no effort to arise. A crowd gathered. A newsboy offered his services, but the policeman who was trying to help the driver and keep the crowd back told the boy to keep quiet. The driver whipped the horse, but the horse made no effort. The boy begged again, but the policeman said no. The driver tried again and pushed but got nowhere fast. The boy said for the third time, "Let me try." The crowd said, "Give the boy a chance. You're not getting anywhere." So the officer told the boy to try. The boy put his newspapers on the curb, took two lumps of sugar from his pocket, and rubbed them on the horse's nose. Then he backed away. Then he let the horse smell the sugar again. A slight tremor went through the horse. The boy came again with his sugar and backed away. The horse made a great effort, came to his feet, and took two or three steps toward the boy who had the sugar. The boy picked up his newspapers and when leaving said over his shoulder to the driver, "Try sweetness."

We are surrounded by so much harshness, O God, that it can infect us without our realizing the infection has set in. Help us keep our hearts fixed on your love so, like the little boy, sweetness will be our gift to the world. Amen.

"What More Are You Doing than Others?"
Scripture: Matthew 5:43-48

In the Sermon on the Mount Jesus asked a disturbing question: "If you salute only your brethren, what more are you doing than others? Do not even the Gentiles do the same?" This is a searching question.

What makes Christians different? They are encouraged to do more than those who do not claim to be followers of Christ.

A Christian lives a positive life. We hear Christians say, "I do not do this, or I do not do that." The principal question is "What do you do?" What do you more than others?

1. A Christian does not resist evil. Whoever smites you on your right cheek, turn to him the other also. You reject the old ethic—"an eye for an eye, and a tooth for a tooth." If a person injures you, you do good in return.

2. "If a man sues you at law and takes away your coat let him have your cloak also." Be sure to do more than anyone demands that you do. Many say, "I kept the law. What I did was legal." Christ says, "Do more."

3. "If a man compels you to go a mile, go with him two." If custom demands that you write a letter, do more—send a present. If your neighborhood is helping a family, do more than your customary part. When you give to the church, measure your giving by the standards of Christ.

4. As children of God we love our enemies, bless them that curse us, do good to them that hate us, and pray for them who despitefully use us. If we have enemies, we pray for them, we do good to them, we bless them, we love them.

May we not resent the expectation of us as Christians that we live exemplary lives. Let us look upon such an expectation as a way for us to give glory to Christ. Amen.

Divine Expectations
Scripture: Matthew 5:48

We must be perfect as our heavenly Father is perfect—perfect in our love for all persons, loving the good and the evil, the just and the unjust. God is perfect in his love toward us. Christ loved the penitent thief on the cross; he would have loved the other felon too had he requested it.

Jesus went about doing good, for God was with him. "I always do those things that please him," he said. "What do you more than others? Whosoever shall break one of these least commandments, and shall teach men so, he shall be called the least in the kingdom of Heaven. . . . Think not that I am come to destroy the law, or the prophets: I have not come to destroy, but to fulfil." In these words Jesus gave us a description of those who are to be great in the kingdom of heaven. You may not be great in the kingdom of earth, but you can be great in the kingdom of heaven. Consider two words in this text:

(1) *Whosoever* means anyone. It doesn't make any difference about your mother and father or your ancestry. All you have to do to qualify is to be a member of whosoever. A child can qualify.

(2) Look at another word—a very important word: *Do.* This is a word of action. It means keeping and doing what God commands. The Pharisees asked Jesus one day why he and his disciples did not keep the traditions of Moses. He said, Why do you not keep the commandments of God? If we are to be great in the kingdom of heaven we must be persons of action. We appreciate persons who live according to what they profess. Love God with all your mind, strength, soul, and heart and your neighbor as yourself.

We are grateful, our Father, for the way in which Jesus brought the kingdom of God into clear and sharp focus for us. May we enter that kingdom with gladness of heart and eagerness to give it vital meaning in our own time. Amen.

Breaking Down Barriers
Scripture: Acts 11:19-26

"And a large company was added to the Lord" (RSV).

This is a remarkable statement. It was said during a revival at Antioch in Syria. After the martyrdom of Stephen, some of the followers of Christ went to Phoenicia and Cyprus and Antioch. However, they preached the word only to the Jews. But some of the new converts were from Cyprus and Cyrene. When they journeyed to Antioch, they spoke to the Greeks, preaching the Lord Jesus; and a large number of the Greeks believed.

When news of this reached the church in Jerusalem, the leaders sent Barnabas, that he should go as far as Antioch. When he arrived there and saw the grace of God at work, he was glad and exhorted them all that with purpose of heart they should cleave to the Lord. He was a man of persuasiveness because he was a good man and full of the Holy Spirit and of faith, and a large company of people was added unto the Lord. If we want large numbers of persons to be added to the Lord, we must have a Barnabas or persons with his winsome characteristics.

The name Barnabas means "son of encouragement" or "son of consolation." Following his conversion, Saul of Tarsus preached in Damascus. When he went up to Jerusalem, the leaders of the church there would have nothing to do with him, but Barnabas stood up in supporting him. A good man can see the good in everyone. It is not surprising that when Barnabas reached Antioch and saw the grace of God at work among the Gentiles there, he was glad. A good person rejoices when the Lord uses other persons for winning souls.

When we see the remarkable accomplishments of such a modest man as Barnabas in winning others to Christ, we take heart in believing that even the humblest testimony can be effective in winning persons for our Lord. Amen.

The Attractiveness of Goodness
Scripture: Matthew 5:13-16

To be good is to be like God. When a person lives a good life, relatives and friends do not want that person to die. When we do good and are good, people see the Lord in us and are drawn to him.

Barnabas was full of the Holy Spirit and many people were added unto the Lord. The big word in this sentence is the word *full.* Barnabas was full of the Holy Spirit. On the day of Pentecost, the Word says that they were all filled with the Holy Spirit. We become full of the Holy Spirit by becoming obedient to the Christ.

Small things keep us from being full of the Holy Spirit. Someone has said that if you will turn over every sin, you will find a four-letter word—*self.*

I was in Atlanta, riding in a cab. I asked the driver if he was a Christian. He turned around and asked me if I had been baptized of the Holy Spirit. He then told me of his experience: He told me that he went to a revival and that the church was asking for a liberal offering. He said he had one dollar, and the Lord told him to give it. But he kept it. After the sermon the invitation was given to those who sought the baptism of the Holy Spirit to come forward and pray. He said he went forward to pray, but he could not receive the blessing because that dollar was in his pocket. He had disobeyed Christ. He told me that he gave the dollar and received the blessing. It was not the dollar, but his willingness to obey, that brought the blessing.

When we think of Barnabas and his devotion to the needs of the early church, we see a demonstration of cheerful generosity. May our gifts to thy kingdom, O God, be just as joyfully rendered. Amen.

Jesus' Revolutionary Way of Life
Scripture: Galatians 2:17-21

Paul said he lived by the faith of the Son of God. He lived in a materialistic age. The priests made money in the Temple by selling oxen, doves, and sheep and by changing money. They were robbing the poor. Some Jews, in order to acquire wealth, became tax collectors, collaborating with the Roman Empire. Zacchaeus was one, Levi (Matthew) another. The rich ruler could not separate himself from his gold when Jesus gave him the test for his discipleship. The disciples advised Jesus that it would be costly to feed the hungry multitude. When Mary of Bethany anointed Jesus, some of the disciples murmured at the waste of money. Judas betrayed him for thirty pieces of silver, but what he did tormented him until he took the money back.

Jesus taught, "Seek first the kingdom of God and his righteousness and all these things shall be added unto you" (Matthew 6:33). He practiced what he preached. He did not worry about food. He accepted invitations to eat. He refused to use his miracle-working power to satisfy his own physical needs. He owned virtually nothing. He borrowed a colt on which to ride. He borrowed a boat from which to preach. He borrowed a room in which to eat the last supper with his disciples. He asked John to take care of his mother. He was entombed in a sepulcher belonging to a rich disciple.

Not only did Jesus have faith that God would provide for his material needs but also for his spiritual needs. Jesus lived by the words that came from God. He did not tempt God. He did God's will.

Society changes little in its demands on life, our Father. So help us learn from Saint Paul and others who have gone before us that living by faith in the Son of God, though difficult, is rewarding, even as it was for them. Amen.

Christ Befriended the Friendless
Scripture: John 8:3-11

One day the scribes and Pharisees brought to Jesus a woman taken in adultery. Jesus said, "He that is without sin among you, let him cast the first stone." They who heard it, convicted by their own conscience, went out one by one; and Jesus was left with the woman. Then he asked the woman: "Where are your accusers? Has no man condemned you?" She said, "No man, Lord." And Jesus said: "Neither do I. Go and sin no more." Religious people brought this woman to Jesus.

Not long ago a woman committed suicide. She said she had served a jail sentence, and no one would help her. Everyone turned against her. Another woman in Pennsylvania had been out of jail for a year, and no one had spoken to her.

Judas came with the mob to take Jesus to the house of the chief priest to be put on trial. He had betrayed Jesus for thirty pieces of silver. Yet Jesus called him "friend." Jesus knew that soon the men who conspired with Judas would turn against him. Judas lost his place with the disciples. He lost his place with the scribes and chief priests.

Jesus died on the cross between two thieves. Around the cross was the sneering mob, gambling soldiers, arrogant priests. One thief said to the other: "We die justly, this man unjustly. Lord, remember me" (Luke 23:40-43). Jesus answered, "This day you shall be with me in Paradise." The thief found a friend in Jesus.

Jesus calls us friends if we do what he commands us. "I call you not servants, for the servant knows not what his Lord does" (John 15:15). Jesus said, "But I call you friends because I have imparted to you all that I have learned from my Father."

So many of your children, our Father, think they are in a friendless world. May they find in us friends to help them along life's toilsome way. Amen.

Jesus Must Have Persons
Scripture: Luke 6:12-16

"The day following Jesus went into Galilee and found Philip and said to him, Follow me" (John 1:43).

Jesus did not say, "Follow my way" or "Follow my truth" or "Follow my life" but "Follow me."

Philip told his neighbor Nathanael that he had found the Messiah and invited him to come see this person. When Christ invited Levi (Matthew) to follow him, this tax collector invited his friends to come and have dinner with Jesus.

In Sychar he encountered a woman who invited others to him. To accompany him to Paradise, he enlisted a thief. His ambassador that first Easter morning was Mary of Magdala. On the day of Pentecost the mantle of the church's leadership fell across the shoulders of Simon Peter of Galilee—a province from which no religious leader had ever come before. He wanted an apostle to the Gentiles and secured a person who had a reputation for despising Gentiles—Saul of Tarsus.

Jesus wanted witnesses. He taught, preached, healed, sang, visited, crusaded against the evils of his day, magnified children, fed the hungry, and used all methods to reach people. He loved the outcasts; he put his hands on lepers. He touched untouchables, tamed those who were wild, taught the unteachable, and loved the unlovable. He sought the unsought, saved the unsaved, cleansed the unclean.

What were Christ's witnesses to do? You "shall be witnesses unto me" he told them (Acts 1:8). We do not witness to a church or a Sunday school class or a youth group or a program or a new world order. We witness to a person.

What a variety of persons Jesus befriended! Let it be our prayer this day, our Father, that we may find someone in need whose life will be brightened by our expression of love and concern. Amen.

Love Gives
Scripture: John 3:12-17

It is the nature of love to give. Love demands only the right to give. We see this in the very nature of God. Jesus told us that God so loved us that he gave his only Son that if we would believe we would not perish but have everlasting life.

Christ loved and gave. He loved everyone—the Samaritan woman, the Pharisees, his enemies (even healing Malchus), the scoffing penitent thief (even taking him with him to Paradise), the criticizing and unbelieving priests (praying for them). He gave himself to all persons—to the woman who had an infirmity for eighteen years, to the Canaanite woman (and healed her daughter when the disciples sent her away), to children (when the disciples would have driven them away), to the poor (getting rid of the moneychangers from the Temple porch who were exploiting them).

I am to love as Christ loved. A Christian is to be Christlike. A Christian is to love as Christ loved and give as Christ gave.

I read about a mother in Chicago whose son was sent to prison. She believed he was innocent. She got a job scrubbing floors and started saving money. Finally she had $5,000 and advertised that there was a $5,000 reward for the apprehension of the guilty person. A newspaper reporter took an interest and proved that her son was innocent. He was released after serving seven years. The guilty ones were apprehended. This mother loved and gave.

God has bestowed great love on us by giving the life of God's Son. So we are to bestow our love and to do this we must love all persons and give ourselves to them. Our personality will grow richer as we give it away.

We sing, "O Love that wilt not let me go," and we also experience the support of your tender embrace. Help us to find ways to give back to you the love we owe, our Father, that it may become richer and fuller. Amen.

Christ Saves the Unsaved
Scripture: Luke 23:39-43

One of the thieves crucified with Jesus wanted to be saved from death. He said to Jesus, "If you are the Christ, save yourself and us." Jesus said, "Today you shall be with me in Paradise."

This one thief knew that he had done wrong. He was receiving the due punishment for his deeds. He admitted the purity of the life of Jesus. He knew Christ was coming into his kingdom. He asked only to be remembered. Jesus assured him that he was going with him to Paradise.

Christ is saving the unsaved today. One afternoon I called with a pastor to see an elderly man. He admitted that he was not saved. We talked to him about Christ. We read the Bible. We prayed. He would not repent of his sins and yield his life to Christ. As we were leaving he said, "I will be at church tonight." As I sat behind the pulpit that evening, I saw him sitting in the congregation near the front. After preaching I gave the invitation. We sang one hymn. He did not respond. I saw him hold on to the bench to keep from coming. I announced another hymn. Then I did what I seldom do. I went to this man and said to him, "Let us do this tonight. Come and go with me." He came as a little child. He knelt and prayed. I left him praying as I went to other men in the congregation who came and joined this first man in prayer. Before I could get back to the first man, he arose from prayer with a smile on his face. Tears ran down his cheeks as he praised Christ for forgiveness and salvation.

Christ saves the unsaved when we pray, visit, preach, believe, and love, and when they pray, repent, and believe.

Refresh in our hearts, our Father, the knowledge that life is sacred and needs redemption. Then may we search our hearts to see if there be any wicked way in us—and prayerfully and penitently seek thy redeeming grace. Amen.

Barnabas
Scripture: Acts 4:32-37

We are introduced to Barnabas in Acts 4:36. His name was Joseph, but the apostles called him Barnabas (son of encouragement).

He was a most conscientious Christian. In the early church those who chose to do so could share some or all of their wealth with the poor. Barnabas gave it all.

What then shall we give? First, we must pay what we owe. God requires the tenth. After we render that, we begin giving.

Barnabas invested in persons. Saul of Tarsus persecuted the Jerusalem Christians, even consenting to the stoning of Stephen. On the road to Damascus, Saul met the living Christ and became a disciple. In Jerusalem the apostles were afraid of him and did not believe he was a disciple. But Barnabas believed in him and brought him to the apostles. When news that a great revival was occurring in Antioch (Syria) reached Jerusalem, the apostles sent Barnabas to get a firsthand report. When he saw the working of the grace of God there, he went to Tarsus, found Saul, and took him to Antioch. Later he and Paul went to Jerusalem, taking an offering for the poor because there was a famine in Palestine. When they returned to Antioch, they took John Mark (Barnabas's nephew) with them. On their first missionary journey, John Mark left the team. Paul rejected Mark's overture to rejoin their missionary effort; but Barnabas welcomed him, and they sailed for Cyprus. Later John Mark became profitable to Paul and wrote the first Gospel, based on Peter's preaching.

Barnabas believed in the Gospel of the Second Chance. He was a good man, full of the Holy Ghost and of faith.

Give us the sensitivity in the church, our Father, to seek and find laypersons like Barnabas who can become useful in the work of extending thy kingdom. In Jesus' name. Amen.

Go Back Home and Witness There
Scripture: Mark 5:15-20

This man was demon-possessed when he met Jesus. He seemed to be something of a madman. The citizens put him in fetters and chains. As soon as Jesus stepped out of the boat, this man named Legion ran and knelt before Jesus. Jesus relieved him of his distresses.

The people came and saw the man sitting quietly. He was clothed and in his right mind. They were afraid. They entreated Jesus to depart. The man wanted to go with Jesus. But Jesus said, "Go home to your friends and tell them how much the Lord has done for you." What had happened to this man?

Since he had been with Jesus, he had regained his right mind and could go home. He could go to his friends, and he had something to tell. Instead of being demon-possessed, he now was spirit-possessed.

Have we something to tell? Yes, if we have really seen and confessed the living Christ. We are many persons. We are known at the church as one person, in our homes as another kind of person, in the office or shop as someone else, in public places as still another person. When Christ reigns in our lives, our families and friends see and know the difference.

We are to tell what Christ has done for us. A young man tried to commit suicide and prayed, "O God, let me die." Then someone told him about Christ, and he prayed, "O God, let me live." When the demon-possessed man was freed from his demons he prayed, "Jesus, let me go with you." But Jesus told him to go back home and witness there.

May this story of one man's transformation after he was confronted by Christ help us look for opportunities to present our Lord to a world that needs the goodness and grace he has to offer troubled and bewildered men, women, and youth. Amen.

The Blessings of Christian Obedience
Scripture: Matthew 15:21-28

Mothers are concerned about us. They took care of us when we could not take care of ourselves. They fed us, bathed us, nursed us, put us to bed, stayed up all night when we were sick, sacrificed for us, did without so we could go to school, prayed for us, taught us. They were concerned about where we went and what we did.

But someone else is more concerned about us than our mothers: God. God loved us so much that he gave us Jesus Christ, who died for us. God wants us to be like Christ.

In Capernaum four men brought a man sick of the palsy to Jesus. "Rise," he said, "take up your bed and go home" (Luke 5:24). He got up. The people were amazed and glorified God saying, "We never saw it in this fashion."

When we obey Jesus, our eyes are opened. Jesus said to the blind man, "Go, wash in the pool of Siloam" (John 9:7). The man obeyed and came seeing. "Whereas I was blind, now I see," he proclaimed to his friends who wanted him to disclaim Jesus.

Obedience to Christ means life. Lazarus had died. When Jesus arrived on the scene he commanded, "Roll away the stone from the tomb" (John 11:39-44). When they took it away, Jesus called out: "Lazarus, come forth." And Lazarus came forth. Jesus said, "Loose him, and let him go." Then many believed on him.

Salvation comes when we obey. "Zacchaeus, make haste, and come down; for to day I must abide at thy house" (John 19:5). And he made haste and came down and received him joyfully. Zacchaeus met the conditions. "This day is salvation come to this house," Jesus said (John 19:9).

When we become distraught over some loss that we think is greater than we can bear, may we think about the living Lord of Life who conquered death and the grave. In Jesus' name. Amen.

"Satan Has Desired to Have You"
Scripture: Luke 22:31-34

"And the Lord said, Simon, Simon, . . . Satan hath desired to have you, that he may sift you as wheat." Jesus spoke those words to Simon Peter at the Last Supper.

1. Satan first confronted Jesus in the wilderness when he started his ministry. Later he met him when the people wanted to make him king. He met him in the garden of prayer, Gethsemane. He met him on the cross.

2. He knew Satan had possessed Judas. ("Then entered Satan into Judas surnamed Iscariot, being of the number of the twelve," Luke 22:3). Satan captured Judas through money.

3. He knew that Satan was trying to get James and John. They wanted recognition and positions of power. That very night, at the Last Supper, Christ took upon himself the role of a servant.

4. Jesus said to Simon: "Satan hath desired to have you." On what grounds was he going to try to get Simon?—on his zeal for his Lord. Simon declared, "Lord, I am ready to go with thee, both into prison, and to death." But Jesus said, "Peter, the cock shall not crow this day, before you shall three times deny that you know me." Peter could not stay awake in Gethsemane when Jesus asked him to pray. He did indeed deny Christ, as Jesus foretold. His faith failed.

5. Christ is praying for us. He wanted Simon, and Satan wanted Simon. Simon did not think he had to pray because he had a sword. When he saw Jesus condemned, notwithstanding his innocence, he went out and wept bitterly. Later, after Jesus' resurrection appearance to him, Peter followed faithfully. Satan cannot get us when we obey Christ. The Holy Spirit empowers us.

Sometimes, like Simon Peter, we are inclined to speak more boldly of our loyalty to Christ than our words or deeds justify. Help us, our Father, to make our profession of our faith in him consistent with our service to him. Amen.

Jesus' Secret Disciples
Scripture: John 12:37-43

Who were some of these secret disciples who preferred the approval of men more than the approval of God?

1. Joseph of Arimathea. John tells us that he was a secret disciple. He came after Jesus was dead and asked Pilate to let him have the body of the crucified Galilean. This request was granted. He and another secret disciple by the name of Nicodemus prepared the body for burial and put it in his own newly hewn tomb. It is said of Joseph that he was a good man, a just man, and a counselor. He was a rich man.

2. Nicodemus. He came to Jesus at night. He probably could not come during the day because of his duties as a ruler of the Jews. He was one of the seventy who ruled the nation. Jesus said to him: "Are you a teacher in Israel, and yet you do not understand this? (John 3:10). He called Jesus a teacher. He said, "Rabbi [teacher], we know that you are a teacher come from God, for no one can do these signs that you do, unless God is with him." Nicodemus was a Pharisee. He knew and interpreted the law. "It is our law to judge no man without hearing him," he said to the Sanhedrin in defense of Jesus (John 7:50).

As far as we know, Joseph of Arimathea and Nicodemus never enlisted any followers for Christ. They were going to strictly observe the Sabbath. They knew where the Pool of Bethesda was. When Jesus asked the man if he would like to be healed, he replied, "Sir, I have no man." Where was Joseph of Arimathea? Where was Nicodemus? They were busy looking after ceremonials. They were busy keeping the law. They were busy teaching young men who were candidates for the rabbinate.

How difficult it must have been for Joseph of Arimathea and Nicodemus to befriend Jesus when their religious careers were so involved with Judaism. But we are grateful for Nicodemus's desire to learn of Jesus and for Joseph's tender concern in giving him fitting entombment after the crucifixion. Amen.

Jesus' Public Disciples
Scripture: John 1:43-47

Now let us look at some of Jesus' public disciples.

1. A young man named Andrew was a disciple of John the Baptist. When he heard John say one day, "Behold, the Lamb of God," he and an unknown disciple followed Jesus. Then he told his brother, Simon, "We have found the Messiah (which means Christ)." He brought him to Jesus. He brought a member of his family to Jesus. Public disciples always bring their families to Christ.

A man named T.C. Young gave this testimony: Not a single member of his family was a Christian. His father ran a saloon. He and his brothers were bartenders. His mother was to have a surgical operation. She was not a Christian, but she told God if he would spare her life she would serve him and win her family for Christ. God spared her. She became a public disciple. She won her husband and every member of her family for Christ. He is a spiritual leader in a great church. He has two brothers who became preachers in California.

2. There was another young man, Philip, whom Jesus found and said, "Follow me." He was a neighbor of Andrew and Simon. He found a friend, Nathanael, and said, "We have found him of whom Moses in the law and also the prophets wrote, Jesus of Nazareth." Philip was a public disciple. He enlisted his neighbor for Christ. Among the public disciples who won their neighbors for Christ is a woman. Jesus found her drawing water at the well. She was a Samaritan. She was looking for the messiah. "I who speak to you am he," said Jesus (John 4:26). She brought the men to Jesus, and they believed because of her testimony. Secret disciples look for a teacher; public disciples look for a Savior. Are you a private or public disciple of Jesus?

Help us not only to see the necessity for being public disciples of Jesus, O God, but also to feel the exhilaration of publicly acknowledging him at every opportunity. Amen.

Passion Sunday
Scripture: John 13:2-17

On Passion Sunday we think of Jesus' weeping over Jerusalem on Palm Sunday. Devout Jews from all over the world had come to joyfully celebrate the Passover. Why did he weep?

He wept. He knew the Jewish leaders would demand his death because he cared more about persons than class, race, religion, or property.

His passion for the sacred prompted him to take a scourge of cords and drive the moneychangers and those who sold oxen, sheep, and doves away from the Temple. After this dramatic act, he ministered to the lame and the blind.

His passion caused him to take a towel and a basin of water and bathe the feet of his disciples—an example of servanthood.

He said that those who ministered to the hungry, ill-clad, sick, strangers, and prisoners would receive an inheritance from the heavenly Father.

He was an obedient and willing son. His passion led him to die on the cross.

A Christian desires to be rich toward God. The hospital at Lambarene (Albert Schweitzer's jungle clinic in Africa) is known because a man lost himself for God in order to help some of God's neglected children.

The sinner separates himself from God by renouncing Christ. The Christian renounces self. May we pray that we will be rich toward God, renounce self, and follow Christ.

Difficult as it may be for us, our Father, help us to look always at the world and the persons around us through the eyes of Christ. Help us to resist the temptation to expect others to serve us. Instead may we become skillful and generous in ministering to the needs of others. Amen.

The Church Is Born
Scripture: Acts 2:1-4, 38-41

In the calendar of the Christian church, May 24 is known as Whitsunday or Pentecost. On this day we celebrate the birthday of the Christian church.

After his resurrection, Christ commanded his disciples to wait in Jerusalem "for the promise of the Father" (Acts 1:4).

After his ascension the apostles returned to Jerusalem, and on the day of Pentecost "they were all filled with the Holy Ghost" (Acts 2:4).

A primary participant was Simon Peter. He was one of the three disciples to whom Jesus gave special attention, James and John being the others. The Gospels tell us that on the last night Jesus lived, Peter followed afar off and denied his Lord.

But this was not the end, because Peter became the rock of the early church. On the day of Pentecost he preached a sermon. When he finished, the multitude said, "What shall we do?"

"Repent," Peter said, "and be baptized every one of you in the name of Jesus Christ for the remission of sins, and ye shall receive the gift of the Holy Ghost" (Acts 3:37-38). In that moment a great evangelistic movement was born.

The church today, if it is to experience spiritual renewal, must prayerfully tarry for the promise of the Father. The early Christians went everywhere telling every person about the living Christ and his power to bring life. The Christian fellowship today needs a dynamic faith to help Christ redeem the world. The main business of the church is to call persons to repentance and to baptize them in the name of Jesus Christ for the remission of sins.

We give thanks, our Father, for the faith and willingness of the early Christians to obey the command of Christ to tarry in Jerusalem until the day of Pentecost, enabling the Holy Spirit to transform them into sons and daughters of God. Amen.

May 24, 1738—A Memorable Date
Scripture: Ephesians 1:3-14

On May 24, 1738, the Wesleyan Evangelistic Movement began. The leader of this movement, John Wesley, was born June 28, 1703, at Epworth, England, the fifteenth child of Samuel and Susannah Wesley. At six years of age, he was snatched from the burning rectory. His family, and John himself, regarded the event as an act of God's saving him for a special task.

He studied at Charterhouse School and then at Christ Church (College), Oxford, where he became the leader of the "Holy Club," a group derisively called Methodists because they followed regimens of holy living.

On that memorable May 24, Wesley wrote in his *Journal*:

> In the evening I went very unwillingly to a society in Aldersgate Street, where one was reading Luther's preface to the Epistle to the Romans. About a quarter before nine, while he was describing the change which God works in the heart through faith in Christ, I felt my heart strangely warmed. I felt that I did trust in Christ, Christ alone for salvation, and an assurance was given me, that he had taken away *my* sins, even *mine*, and saved *me* from the law of sin and death.

For the next fifty-three years, he traveled the British Isles preaching, praying, organizing, writing, and leading the movement that became world Methodism.

John Wesley sought salvation through good works but to his dismay. Then Peter Böhler, a Moravian, told him about trusting Christ, Christ alone, for salvation. A heartwarming experience changed him. Through him society became transformed.

The Christian experience of one person cannot be duplicated exactly in the life of someone else, but we know, our Father, that all of us can find spiritual joy when we open our hearts to the lordship of Jesus Christ, in whose name we pray. Amen.

Battling One's Self
Scripture: Colossians 1:19-29

If we are full of self, we will witness to self. We will never seek others if we are full of self. Jesus said, "He who loves his life loses it, and he who hates his life in this world will keep it for eternal life" (John 12:25, rsv).

We will never save others if we are trying to save ourselves. We will never serve others if we are trying to get others to serve us. Christ reaches out to others when we become his channels of service by letting him come alive in us.

The church must show its crucified hands, its suffering. What does the church have to show the world?

On that first Easter night, Jesus appeared to the disciples and showed them his hands and his side. Then they were glad when they saw him.

His first message to them was not a message of words but the signs of his having suffered. He did not say with his lips, "I have been to the cross." He showed them the evidence of his faith and sacrificial love. He showed them the evidence, and then he spoke to them. He said, "Peace be unto you: as my Father hath sent me, even so send I you" (John 20:21).

Self-righteous persons do not want a Savior. They depend on themselves. Many self-righteous persons are in our churches. They are depending on their works for their salvation.

The church is Christ alive in the world. Christ was sent, as he himself said, "to seek and to save that which was lost" (Luke 19:10). Jesus believed that the gospel must be lived out in everyday relationships. Even more, he made it evident that salvation is for all persons, so it must be expressed everywhere.

As we witness among Christian friends, our Father, we find it easy to be Christlike in our words and actions. May we know that our more important witness for Christ is among those who do not acknowledge him. We need your presence and guidance to make that witnessing effective. Amen.

The Certainty of Today
Scripture: Luke 4:16-21

It is my opportunity and obligation to do the things that should be done each day—write letters of love, make visits of sympathy, offer prayers for others. This is also your opportunity and obligation.

Jesus did not postpone. When he saw Zacchaeus up in a tree where he was trying to get a glimpse of Jesus, he said to him, "Make haste and come down; for I must stay at your house today" (Luke 19:5). Not tomorrow, but today.

We ask for things in Jesus' name and do not live under his will. The only certain thing in our life is the uncertainty of tomorrow. Jesus could preach love because he practiced love.

We can bring light and joy to others only by doing good with a compassionate heart. Are we carrying good or bad tidings? All too often we tell about someone who has made a mistake or slipped. Why not try for one month to tell only the good things we know? Like Jesus, we are sent "to heal the brokenhearted."

Consider how indifferently we live. We indulge ourselves, even damaging our delicately balanced bodies. We allow self-centeredness to blind us to the needs of others that we could ameliorate.

The program of my Lord and King is "to preach the gospel to the poor, . . . to heal the brokenhearted, to preach deliverance to the captives, and recovering of sight to the blind, to set at liberty them that are bruised" (Luke 4:18). Some kingdoms have been extended by the sword—and sometimes even the church (as with Charlemagne) has done that. But that is not the way to extend the kingdom of Christ.

May we find loving and kind ways to draw persons into the Christian fellowship, our Father, even as you have drawn us to your own heart by cords of love. In Jesus' name. Amen.

God's Call
Scripture: John 5:30-34

God wants us for a purpose. No one can take our place. Let God find you. You may not love God, but he loves you.

Let our tongues become servants of praise and servants of kind words for others. Say kind words or nothing.

Life does not consist in seeing how many can wait on us but on how many we can wait. The Christian religion does not promise us perfect lives on earth or freedom from suffering. It does guarantee us the strength to bear suffering. The Christian religion does not expect us to be free from sin or mistakes in judgment; it does promise us forgiveness for our mistakes.

The Christian religion expects us to continue making conscientious efforts on behalf of others. It does not guarantee that we ourselves or anyone else can arrange the lives of other persons as we please.

If Christ lives in our hearts, we will obey God as he did. We will seek persons as he did. He was obedient to God, even unto death. He cast himself into the role of a household servant when he bathed his disciples' feet.

If Christ lives in our hearts, persons will know it by the way we live. Are we known as Christians by the way we live and by what we profess? Do people see us or our Savior?

The kingdom of God is a youth movement, or is for those who have young souls. The disciples were young men; Jesus was young. The kingdom is for busy persons, for those who work and work diligently. If we are busy, Christ needs us for his kingdom. Some Galilean fishermen were mending their nets. He called them to mend people.

When we hear you calling us, our Father, may we know that your call is a call to serve others. Give us a willingness to become concerned about others rather than about ourselves. In Jesus' name. Amen.

Repent
Scripture: Luke 16:19-26

John the Baptist came preaching, "Repent and be baptized, every one of you." Jesus came preaching, "Repent, and believe in the gospel." Sin separates us from God.

We need to talk honestly to God about our giving and our service. If he asks us to do something, he will give us the power to do it. We need to talk to him about our time. Do we set aside time for prayer, for Bible reading, for family devotions? We grow spiritually only when we devote some time regularly to cultivating spiritual disciplines. Do we find time to visit the sick, the stranger, the prisoner? Do we find time for our family? We need to talk to him about our unbelief. Jesus looked for faith in persons. When he found it, he was able to change lives for the better.

Peter on the day of Pentecost declared, "Repent, and be baptized every one of you" (Acts 2:38). To repent means to turn around, quit gratifying self, and start following the Savior.

In Jesus' story about a rich man and a beggar, the rich man repented too late. He failed to do anything for Lazarus when he had the opportunity. Later in torment, he wanted Lazarus to do something for him. His crime was that he did nothing when he had the opportunity.

In the parable of the Good Samaritan, the priest and Levite did nothing, but the Samaritan did something. It is easy to sin by doing nothing. We do not witness. We neglect reading the Bible. We are indifferent to devotional meditation and reflection. We rarely visit the sick. We fail to speak words of encouragement. Are we masters at condemning or commending? Like Jesus we can go about doing good.

Give us clarity of vision, our Father, to see the needs around us and then give us the willingness to reach out to persons who need lovingkindness and tender care. Amen.

Practicing Christian Stewardship
Scripture: Proverbs 3:9-10

"I believe in the life everlasting." I re-declare this affirmation in God's house every Sunday. It follows, then, that I will lay up treasures in heaven where neither moth nor rust corrupts. My treasure is where my heart is. I believe my soul is to live eternally with God, my Creator. Therefore, I must have treasures there for God and my soul. So I will give to God's church and God's kingdom here on earth.

I will give God the best part of my income and life. Malachi, the prophet, asks us, "Will a man rob God?" He answers for God by saying, "You have robbed me . . . in tithes and offerings" (Malachi 3:8).

God is my benefactor. God gives me all the material and spiritual blessings of my life. I will not rob my benefactor.

In determining what my part will be in giving to any cause, I must determine the need. If the need is great, then I must do without luxuries—and even necessities—to help prosper the kingdom of God. The church is the only agency commissioned to bring spiritual life to all God's children. So I must put the church at the top of the list in my giving. Regardless of the size of my income, I will give the first part of it to my heavenly Father through the institution of the church.

The wise Solomon taught, "Honor the LORD with your substance and with the first-fruits of all your produce; then your barns will be filled with plenty."

Saint Paul, writing to his young friend Timothy, said, "The love of money is the root of all evils" (1 Timothy 6:10). If I love the money that comes to me more than I love my heavenly Father, then I will become selfish and evil. Therefore, I must give liberally.

Let us find holy excitement, our Father, in your call to us to be generous in support of thy kingdom here on earth. As good and faithful stewards, help us to have the courage to set aside the first-fruits of our labors in support of that task. Amen.

"Do the Work of an Evangelist"
Scripture: 2 Timothy 4:1-5

Paul wrote these words to Timothy, his son in the gospel: "Do the work of an evangelist." What is the work of an evangelist?

1. Establish persons in the faith. Paul did this. He had great faith in Judaism until he met the living Christ on the road to Damascus. Then his faith was in the person of Christ: "For to me to live is Christ. . . . I live by faith in the Son of God. . . . I am not ashamed of the gospel. . . . I have kept the faith." An evangelist—one who eagerly shares the good news of Christ—will get persons committed to this faith.

2. Establish persons in the fellowship of the church. Paul did this. He organized the church. Wesley was not the great preacher that Whitefield was, but he organized societies that conserved the newly won Christians. An evangelist will get persons committed to the Christian fellowship.

3. Establish persons in the fraternity of proclaiming the good news—by preaching, by witnessing. Witnessing is a means of grace. Recruitment follows. Andrew said, "We have found the Messiah." The woman at the well said, "Come and see a man who told me all things I ever did."

4. Establish persons in the fundamental work of the kingdom. Create a Christian home, a Christian community.

The Lord has done so much for us. He has offered life instead of death. He has made our salvation possible. What are we doing for him? A Christian is busy doing the work Christ would have him or her do.

In the full sense of the word evangelist, *help us to see, our Father, that every Christian is a proclaimer of Christ and his message—and help us this day to demonstrate to the world around us that we are in this proclaiming business. Amen.*

A Roman Calls on a Jew
Scripture: Acts 10:30-35

Here we have another praying man who had a vision, who heard a voice, and who obeyed that voice. No wonder the Spirit fell on them. Cornelius was eager to hear the words whereby he and his house would be saved.

Simon Peter had a message. A praying man who hears a voice and obeys has a message. What did he include in his message? (1) The word came from God; (2) the word was published throughout all Judaea, beginning at Galilee; (3) after the baptism which John the Baptist preached, God anointed Jesus with the Holy Ghost and with power; (4) then he went about doing good and healing all that were oppressed of devils; (5) God was with him; (6) we are witnesses of all things that he did both in the land of the Jews and Jerusalem; (7) whom they slew and hanged on a tree; (8) how God raised him up on the third day and showed himself openly; (9) not to all people but unto witnesses chosen before God; (10) even to us who did eat and drink with him after he rose from the dead; (11) he commanded us to preach to all people (12) that it is he who was ordained of God to be the judge of the quick and the dead; (13) to him gave all the prophets witness that through his name whosoever believes in him shall receive remission of sins.

Sometimes we are called upon to do difficult work for you, our Father, as Simon was called upon to help the Gentile Cornelius. May we do your bidding willingly and gladly whenever we discern it. In Jesus' name. Amen.

"As I Spoke the Spirit Fell"
Scripture: Acts 10:30-36

While Peter preached, the Gentiles believed, and the Holy Spirit fell on them to the astonishment of the Jews. Simon Peter said, "The Holy Spirit fell on them just as on us at the beginning." All this happened because the atmosphere was godly. Cornelius said: "We are all here in the sight of God, to hear all that you have been commanded by the Lord."

What a glorious experience to feel the power of the Holy Spirit as you preach and to see the power of the Holy Spirit on the congregation. Simon Peter, the preacher, prayed. Cornelius and the congregation prayed. No wonder the Holy Spirit fell.

Peter remembered the Lord's promise to the disciples: "You shall be baptized with the Holy Spirit." After the baptism of the Holy Spirit, they learned to pray, to share, to suffer, to obey, to believe. They had boldness as they witnessed. They were imprisoned and beaten, stoned, put to death. They preached to the Samaritans, the Ethiopians, the Gentiles, the Greeks. They preached before rulers and kings. They preached in the Temple, in jail, on the streets. They turned the world upside down. They were persons possessed of power because they had been with Jesus.

This is how Simon Peter defended his actions before the Jerusalem Christians (who believed that the new Way was for Jews only): "Forasmuch then as God gave them the like gift as he did unto us, who believed on the Lord Jesus Christ; what was I, that I could withstand God?" (Acts 11:17). There are so many ways to thwart God's way, but God wants us to be channels instead.

Dear Lord, help us to keep from letting our own desires stand in the way of seeking out and doing thy will. May the manner of our speech and the quality of our daily living be an encouragement to others to love and serve Christ. Amen.

A Man Named Joseph
Scripture: Genesis 47:1-10

A man named Joseph had eleven brothers. Ten of his brothers disliked him because he was having dreams and visions. They did not like Joseph to have these dreams because he dreamed about their falling down and worshiping him.

The opportunity came for them to sell him to some traders for twenty pieces of silver. Those who bought him took him to Egypt and sold him to an Egyptian by the name of Potiphar. Joseph worked hard and the spirit of God was on him. Whatever he did prospered. He was so successful that Potiphar put him in complete charge of all his affairs.

One day Potiphar's wife tempted Joseph to commit sin with her. Joseph said, "How then can I do this great wickedness, and sin against God?" Joseph made a great decision that day. That decision took him from Potiphar's house to the penitentiary and from the penitentiary to the palace and from the palace to be prime minister of the nation.

Because of his ability to reveal secrets and to organize, he saved the people from starvation. He could not save them from their sins, but he could save them from perishing with hunger.

Joseph could have saved the Egyptians and let the Israelites perish. They had sold him into slavery, but he fed them. We do not find any record that he let Mrs. Potiphar go hungry because she had lied about him. Joseph made his decision not to sin against God, and God used him to save persons from starvation.

Help us to see that this ancient story of Joseph and his brothers in Egypt may in other ways be repeated in all our lives. Give us a generous heart whenever we have opportunity to do good. In Jesus' name. Amen.

Moses and Esther, Deliverers of Their People
Scripture: Exodus 12:29-33; Esther 4:10-16

God needed a person to take the children of Israel from the slavery of Egypt to the Promised Land of Canaan. Moses heard the voice of God at the burning bush and became the great emancipator and lawgiver. Moses was having an easy time looking after Jethro's sheep, but he could not get away from the fact that his people were in slavery. After many trials and testings, he started with them to the Promised Land. They rebelled against him and God time and time again.

There came a time of great soul anguish for Moses. He said to the Lord, "Oh, this people have sinned a great sin, and have made them gods of gold. Yet not if thou wilt forgive their sin—; and if not, blot me, I pray thee, out of thy book which thou hast written" (Exodus 32:31-32). Take me out, but save the people. Moses was willing to be blotted out in order that his people might live. Moses saved the children of Israel from slavery and gave them freedom, but he could not save them from the slavery of sin and give them freedom from death.

A young woman by the name of Hadassah was selected by the king to be the queen of the beauty contest and to become his queen, Esther. Her people were being persecuted because of their nationality. All of them were to be put to death. Mordecai reminded Queen Esther that she was a Jew and that she had a responsibility to save her people. She reminded Mordecai that if she did go in to see the king and he did not receive her it meant death for her. But she said, "If I perish, I perish." She made her great decision. She was going to do her best to save her people from perishing.

May the examples of uncommon courage that we see in the lives and actions of Esther and Moses inspire us to boldness in standing tall in support of Christ in our world today. In his name we pray. Amen.

When a Christian Prays
Scripture: Matthew 6:5-15

1. We pray the *Pater Noster*: We call on our Father in heaven. He hears and answers every sincere prayer. Sometimes he says "Yes," sometimes "No," and sometimes, "Wait." Jesus, living in the flesh, never refused a simple petition of anyone when that person met the conditions of obedience and faith.

2. We pray the prayer of praise: God loves us, and God waits for his loving children to offer praise for God's goodness and mercy. We pray, "Hallowed be thy name" (Psalm 107:8).

3. We pray for peace: We are searching for peace of mind and soul. All we need to do is to pray, "Thy kingdom come" and live for his kingdom to come in our lives. Christ wants to give us his peace.

4. We pray for power: All of us need spiritual power. This comes by praying, "Thy will be done, on earth as it is in heaven." Christ had power because he prayed, "Not my will but thine." The early disciples also had power because they prayed.

5. We pray for daily provisions: We need daily spiritual food. We pray, "Give us this day our daily bread."

6. We pray for pardon: Father, forgive us our sins, for we also forgive everyone who is indebted to us. Forgiving those who have sinned against us is a cleansing process.

7. We pray for purity: "Lead us not into temptation, but deliver us from evil." We want to avoid even the appearance of evil.

8. We pray for persons: Jesus said to pray for laborers. God will answer our prayers and send them.

9. We pray for perseverance. We ought always to pray.

Help us, our Father, never to weary in praying for all that we must receive in order to extend your kingdom on earth. Give us the desire to make your kingdom the most important concern of our daily living. Amen.

Laypersons at Work for God
Scripture: Acts 20:28-32

When we have a golden calf and other gods, we are taking God out of religion. When we fail to belong, attend, and support the church with our prayers, service, presence, and substance, we are taking the church out of society. When we minister more to the physical needs of people than we do the spiritual needs of people, we are taking the soul out of humanity.

God is not dead. The church will live. We will always have a soul. God breathed on us. God put the church here. And God is here. God needs us to help with the church and to minister to human souls. The preacher can preach and visit a few people, but God needs laypersons to reach one or more of the unreached for Christ and the church.

How can laypersons do this work? Read the four Gospels until you discover how Jesus was concerned about those whom the religious leaders of his day were neglecting. Read how Jesus was concerned about all persons—adults and children, Samaritans and sinners, Pharisees and publicans, men and women, poor and rich, lepers and leaders. Pray until you have the concern that Christ had. Then you will go as he did. We are to go to the people who are being neglected today. Pray until you are willing for self to die and until your living Savior lives in you.

Read the Book of Acts and pray until you believe that Jesus is the Christ and that he is alive and that he can bring life to all because he brought life to you when you repented and believed.

May we, through prayer, our Father, catch a vision of tasks undone that we can undertake. Your kingdom, as yet so very modestly in evidence in the world around us, awaits the contributions which we, your children, are expected to make to bring it to greater fulfillment and expression. Amen.

Changing One's Mind
Scripture: Romans 12:1-3

Repentance means to change your mind. St. Paul wrote, "Do not be conformed to this world but be transformed by the renewal of your mind, that you may prove what is the will of God, what is good and acceptable and perfect." What do we have to change our minds about?

1. If we have set our minds on gold, we must make an about-face and fix our minds on God. We are not to be enslaved to material possessions. We want God to be supreme in our affections.

2. If we have been concentrating on the flesh, we put our minds on the Spirit and become citizens in God's kingdom.

3. If we have had our minds on sin, we change and put our minds on salvation. We become redeemed rather than self-minded persons. We work for the health and welfare of God's kingdom.

4. If we harbor hatred, we change. We entertain thoughts of love for our king and care for other members of the human family.

5. If we are disturbed by doubts and distraught by fears we change and cultivate faith, trust, and belief in God. We become believers in and for the kingdom, doubting nothing.

6. We change our minds about other persons, regarding them as our brothers and sisters. We want to serve them and do not expect them to serve us. This was the mind of Jesus.

7. We also change our minds about material things, dedicating all that passes through our hands to God's kingdom.

8. Finally, we change our attitudes about other human beings. We believe each person is entitled to his or her own convictions, beliefs, and freedoms.

As the years of our lives advance, may we know that our spiritual understanding and our spiritual needs change. So may we seek your guidance, our Father, so that our thinking will change to better fulfill your purpose for our lives. Amen.

The New Testament Disciples
Scripture: Acts 11:22-26

The New Testament says, "The disciples were called Christians first in Antioch." The preceding sentence reads, "And it came to pass, that a whole year they assembled themselves with the church, and taught much people."

They were engaged in a teaching mission for a year! They taught the people about Christ and his love. They lived it and were called Christians.

How can we live as Christ lived unless we know how he lived? We need teachers in the home, the pulpit, the Sunday school, the social room, the classroom, the courthouse, the business room—teachers who will be priests of Christ and his love.

Jesus was a great teacher—to three, to twelve, to seventy. Today we have a teacher. Jesus called him "The Comforter." He said, "The Comforter, which is the Holy Ghost, whom the Father will send in my name, he shall teach you all things, and bring all things to your remembrance, whatsoever I have said unto you" (John 14:26). The Holy Spirit will teach us.

We are beginning to recognize the work of the Holy Spirit in the life of the church and in our individual Christian lives. The Holy Spirit is God's representative in our world and among us, bearing witness to God in our minds and hearts.

Paul said to the Galileans, "I certify you, brethren, that the gospel which was preached of me is not after man. For I neither received it of man, neither was I taught it, but by the revelation of Jesus Christ" (Galatians 1:11). May we teach the true God and his law, the living Christ and his love.

May we find comfort, strength, and guidance as we yield to the influence of the Holy Spirit, our Father. We marvel at your giving us such an Encourager, who helps us experience your daily presence. In Jesus' name. Amen.

"Master, Eat"
Scripture: John 4:31-34

"I have meat to eat that ye know not of." When the people heard Jesus say that they asked, "Has anyone brought him something to eat?" Jesus continued, "My meat is to do the will of him that sent me, and to finish his work." Christ did the will of his Father. A committed Christian will follow his example, seeking and doing God's will.

The will of God for Christ one day was to speak to one woman—a sinning woman! What happened? She believed. She testified. Her friends believed because of her testimony, and a revival broke out in Sychar! Peter and John spoke to one man at the Gate Beautiful—and something wonderful happened. In prison, Paul and Silas spoke to the jailer, and he was converted.

We know the will of God. Christ did. He prayed, "Thy kingdom come. Thy will be done." We may not understand, but we can obey, pray, visit, apologize, give, participate in family worship, attend church. Paul heard the command, "Arise and go." Ananias heard the same command.

Partnership with God includes our help in finishing his work. God created us, he redeemed us, and he judges us. "Lift up your eyes, and see how the fields are already white for harvest" (John 4:35). When we look around us, we see needs everywhere.

Jesus said that it was his meat to do the will of his Father. What is your "meat"—to follow others' conduct, the will of self, the will of your family? Or is it to do what God wants you to do?

Help us learn more perfectly from Jesus that when we seek to do your will, our lives will be uncomplicated. May we busy ourselves, not seeking to be understood, but to understand. Amen.

"One Thing You Lack"
Scripture: Mark 10:17-23

The rich young ruler was not lacking in goodness, helpfulness, riches, or morality. But everything he did was attached to this present world. He needed to set his sights on eternal life.

1. We follow Christ by having faith in God and people. Jesus had faith in the woman taken in adultery, telling her, "Go, and sin no more" (John 8:11). No one else believed that a sinless life was possible for her. He had faith in the man at the pool of Bethesda, saying to him, "Rise, take up thy bed, and walk" (John 5:8). No one else believed that could happen. He also had faith in the man with palsy, "Your sins are forgiven. . . . Take up thy bed and walk." No one else saw any such future for him. He had faith in the penitent thief on the cross. No one else cared about him.

2. Follow Jesus in his love of God and people. He loved God with the totality of his being. He was willing to die for any and every person he ever saw. Everyone was worth redeeming. He loved as God loved.

3. The church needs the faith and the love of Christ. The faith of God is in us, the love of God is for us, the gift of God (Christ) is to us.

4. Jesus gave himself to God and people. "No one takes my life from me," he said, "I give my life of my own accord." He freely gave himself to each one of us. The woman with an infirmity in the synagogue, the daughter of Jairus, the servant of the Roman soldier in Gethsemane, the Syrophoenician woman—all of them benefited from the self-giving love of Christ.

How thankful we are, our Father, that you are not a vindictive but a loving God. We are convinced of that because of the way in which Jesus, your Son, reached out and ministered to all kinds of persons in need. Amen.

What It Means to Be a Methodist
Scripture: Romans 5:1-10

1. Methodist theology is Christ-centered. Faith in Christ brings life and salvation: "Thy faith hath saved thee"—not water, not the church, but Christ. Faith in Christ means that we join hands and heart with others who have faith in Christ.

2. Methodism is an authoritarian church. We speak with authority when we proclaim that (a) All are sinners who have not been reconciled to God through faith in Christ. They are lost. They must repent and believe. (b) All can be saved. "God so loved the world!" God's grace is for all.

3. All persons can know that they are saved. This is the authority of experience. Wesley said, "I felt I did trust in Christ, Christ alone for my salvation, and an assurance was given me, that he had taken away *my* sins, even *mine*." God's anxiety for our salvation exceeds our desire for our salvation.

4. A Methodist is methodical. We do things decently and in order. We have fixed times for study, prayer, scripture reading, visitation, witnessing.

5. Methodists believe in holiness and perfect love. They also know the reality of backsliding (falling from grace). Holy living—loving God with all one's heart—seeks to spread scriptural holiness and to change society.

6. Methodism is a connectional church. We have an episcopal, not a congregational, form of government. We have bishops and district superintendents through whom the local church is connected with the world.

We give thanks to thee, our Father, for raising up men and women who help us discover for ourselves the experiences needed to vitally relate our lives to thee. May we welcome heartily the spirit of Christ into our hearts. Amen.

After the Ascension of Jesus
Scripture: Acts 1:12-14

After the disciples witnessed Jesus' ascension on Mount Olivet, they returned to Jerusalem and went to the upper room where they were in the habit of meeting. Prior to the ascension they had had fellowship with the living (resurrected) Christ for forty days. During this time together he had taught them about the kingdom of God.

He may have recalled for them his resistance of temptation in the wilderness, declaring that he would worship and serve God only. After he came out of that experience, he began preaching the gospel of the kingdom of God.

He concluded this teaching about the kingdom of God by saying, "John truly baptized with water; but ye shall be baptized with the Holy Ghost not many days hence. . . . Ye shall receive power, after that the Holy Ghost is come upon you: and ye shall be witnesses unto me both in Jerusalem and in all Judaea, and in Samaria, and unto the uttermost part of the earth" (Acts 1:5-6). Then he was taken up, and they were left alone. Where were they going to go?

They went to the upper room where they had only so recently fellowshiped with Jesus. There he had demonstrated servanthood and had given them his farewell message about love. Perhaps it was there that they went on the night when they were afraid, but he (now the resurrected Christ) appeared to them. He spoke peace to their hearts and gave them a commission.

Just as Jesus gave reassurance to his bewildered disciples, we pray that we may receive encouragements from you, our Father, for our daily living. It is hard to make right decisions, to speak fitting words, to express Christlike love without your inspiration and presence. Amen.

Made Courageous through Prayer
Scripture: John 20:21-29

What did the disciples do after Jesus' ascension? They felt forlorn and helpless. But in obedience to their Lord, they went back to the upper room to wait for the promise of the Father. They turned to prayer. They remembered how Jesus prayed.

Now as they tarried in the upper room, the day of Pentecost finally arrived, and they were filled with the Spirit and with power. Jesus at the start of his ministry spent forty days in soul-searching. Now the disciples spent forty days with the resurrected Christ and ten more days in prayer. They, too, were filled with the Holy Spirit. They were empowered to boldly proclaim Christ, to give all they had, to suffer and die.

After Pentecost they preached openly in Jerusalem what they had seen and heard. They had the power to witness to all persons about Christ: "Ye shall be witnesses unto me" (Acts 1:8). In the upper room they waited for the promise of the Father, engaged in prayer, felt the presence of the living Christ, and experienced the power of the Holy Spirit.

Think of all that crowds into our lives. We engage in play for the health of our bodies. Do we engage as enthusiastically in prayer for the rejuvenation of our souls? We are up-to-date on current news, but do we take time to become acquainted with the news of the eternal? We need rest for the body and restoration for the soul. We have baggage for the body, but have our souls been clothed by the Spirit?

Tarrying is not one of our most faithfully practiced disciplines, our Father. Help us to see that if we did linger sometimes for thy guidance we would be more effective in our Christian living and witnessing. In Jesus' name. Amen.

Listening
Scripture: James 5:13-16

"A good man's prayer is powerful and effective" (James 5:16, NEB). These are the words of the writer of the Book of James.

Who is a good man? The Book of Romans, written by Paul, advocates salvation by faith. The Book of James emphasizes salvation by works. These two writings complement and supplement each other. Paul wrote, "By my deeds I will prove you my faith."

Faith unsupported by deeds is unproductive: "Faith divorced from deeds is lifeless as a corpse" (James 2:18-26, NEB). James could have used the experience of the disciples in the upper room as an example.

Eleven men met in an upper room in Jerusalem. Their names are recorded in Acts 1:13. These good men found it hard to believe that Jesus, their crucified leader, had been raised from the dead. Even after the risen Christ had taught them for forty days about the kingdom of God, they still hoped that he would restore the political kingdom of Israel.

These eleven men received from the living Christ a worldwide commission. And he told them not to leave Jerusalem. "Wait," he said, "for the promise made by my Father, about which you heard me speak . . . you will be baptized with the Holy Spirit, and within the next few days" (Acts 1:4-5, NEB). They obeyed. They waited. They prayed constantly for ten days. On the day of Pentecost they were filled with the Holy Spirit and became witnesses for Christ.

Waiting is always difficult for us, our Father, even as it must have been for Jesus' disciples. But the blessings that come when we turn aside from daily encounters in order to meditate on your purpose for our lives, make our lives more joyous and productive. Help us to practice the art of waiting. Amen.

Waiting
Scripture: Matthew 6:6-8

How can we know God's will for our lives unless we listen to God? "From time to time [Jesus] would withdraw to lonely places for prayer" (Luke 5:16, NEB). He waited and listened. We too must wait and quietly listen to God. I believe in corporate prayer, family prayer, group prayer, and individual prayer.

A man with a deep spiritual hunger lived in England. He received Christian nurture from his parents. Later as a student he pursued a disciplined, methodical life to enrich his mind, to develop his inward life, and to become sensitive to society's needs. He lived life in three dimensions—inward, upward, and outward. He became a missionary to the American Indians, but he lacked an inner witness. Distressed, he returned home. Then one night (May 24, 1738), he went to a group meeting on Aldersgate Street in London. A layman was reading Martin Luther's preface to the Book of Romans. As he listened, he experienced a spiritual transformation. He knew his sins were forgiven and that he trusted in Christ alone for salvation.

He had been a witness to Christ, and now he became a witness for Christ. He began caring for neglected people. He wanted everyone to know Christ and experience the forgiveness of their sins. He wanted everyone to experience a warm heart and a desire to help reform society. He helped to bring about a spiritual and social revolution in England that spread to many other parts of the world. His name was John Wesley.

We give thanks, our Father, for John Wesley and the spiritual miracle that enabled you to commandeer his enormous energy, intellect, and love to work miracles in the deteriorated society of his day. May we be so committed to thy purposes that we will see such changes in our society in our time. Amen.

What Did Jesus Believe?
Scripture: John 9:1-7

Jesus believed that "man shall not live by bread alone, but by every word that proceeds from the mouth of God."

He believed in the will of God: "My meat is to do the will of [my Father]." His life and work reflected that belief: "The works of God were made manifest through him."

He believed in the exaltation of God. "You shall worship the Lord your God and him only shall you serve."

He believed in the law of God: "Think not that I am come to destroy the law, or the prophets: I am not come to destroy, but to fulfil."

He believed in the love of God: "By this all men will know that you are my disciples, if you have love for one another." He loved as God loves.

We must believe that Christ spoke truly when he said, "Unless a grain of wheat falls into the earth and dies, it remains alone; but if it dies, it bears much fruit. He who loves his life loses it, and he who hates his life in this world will keep it for eternal life. . . . If any man will come after me, let him deny himself, and take up his cross, and follow me. For whosoever will save his life shall lose it; and whosoever will lose his life for my sake shall find it. . . . Love your enemies, bless them that curse you, do good to them that hate you, and pray for them which despitefully use you, and persecute you. . . ."

We must love Christ with the same love Christ had for God. He gave himself to whoever would receive him, demonstrating that God is no respecter of persons.

As we look around us, may we have the eyes of Christ so we can see persons in need and then joyfully reach out and minister to them. May all our deeds be prompted by Christlike love. Amen.

Jesus and Prayer
Scripture: Luke 18:1

Jesus believed in the power of prayer. He set down some rules for praying:

1. Men ought always to pray. (See Luke 18:1.)
2. Pray for laborers. (See Matthew 9:37-38.)
3. "When thou prayest, thou shalt not be as the hypocrites are: for they love to pray standing in the synagogues and in the corners of the streets, that they may be seen" (Matthew 6:5).
4. "When thou prayest, enter into thy closet, and when thou hast shut thy door, pray to thy Father which is in secret; and thy Father which seeth in secret shall reward thee openly" (Matthew 6:6).
5. "When ye pray, use not vain repetitions, as the heathen do: for they think that they shall be heard for their much speaking. Be not ye therefore like unto them: for your Father knoweth what things ye have need of, before ye ask him" (Matthew 6:7-8).
6. "If ye shall ask any thing in my name, I will do it" (John 14:14). "Ask, and it shall be given you; seek, and ye shall find; knock, and it shall be opened unto you: For every one that asketh receiveth; and he that seeketh findeth; and to him that knocketh it shall be opened" (Matthew 7:7-8).
7. "If a son shall ask bread of any of you that is a father, will he give him a stone? . . . If ye . . . know how to give good gifts unto your children, how much more shall your heavenly Father give the Holy Spirit to them that ask him?" (Luke 11:11, 13). Jesus' life demonstrated the power of prayer.

We rejoice, our Father, in the way Jesus encouraged each person to pray privately, not relying so heavily on institutional prayers by clergy. May we each day take seriously this high privilege of approaching the heavenly throne. Amen.

What Jesus Believed
Scripture: Matthew 5:17-20

Jesus believed in the abundant life: "I am come that they might have life, ... more abundantly. ... [I am] not come to destroy men's lives, but to save them."

He believed in the overcoming life: "Be of good cheer; I have overcome the world." The world will never satisfy us.

He believed in going about doing good. He said he came to seek and save the lost. He said he came not to be ministered unto but to minister.

He believed in forgiveness. If I believe in the fatherhood of God, then I must acknowledge all his children as my brothers and sisters.

He believed that mighty faith removes formidable mountains. Jesus said that it was God, not himself, who did the miracles.

Jesus believed that he came to save persons' lives. "The Son of man is not come to destroy men's lives, but to save them." How do we deal with persons who are full of prejudice? Jesus would have been on the same level as the Samaritans if he had agreed to let the sons of thunder (James and John) destroy them by bringing fire down on them. Could these have been the same Samaritans as those to whom Philip later preached and who were baptized by the Holy Spirit when John and Peter laid their hands on them? We can respond to prejudice with prejudice, to hatred with hatred, to envy with envy; but then we will never be able to pray for those with whom we have dealt so arrogantly.

Brief though Jesus' life was in the flesh—and he knew it would be brief—we thank thee for inspiring us by his example of patience. May we never be so busy or so hurried as to miss opportunities to be kind and considerate of others. In Jesus' name we pray. Amen.

Jesus, God's Only Begotten Son
Scripture: John 17:1-5

The night Jesus was born, the angelic choir sang, "Glory to God in the highest, and on earth peace, good will toward men." At the end of his brief life in the flesh Jesus prayed, "I have glorified thee on the earth."

Jesus said to Nicodemus, "God so loved the world, that he gave his only begotten Son, that whosoever believeth in him should not perish, but have everlasting life." Nicodemus was a man who kept the Law. He was a member of the seventy that ruled the nation of Israel. He was a Pharisee. He came to Jesus by night and said: "Master, we know that you are a teacher come from God; for no one can do these signs that you do, unless God is with him." Jesus said, "Except a man be born again, he cannot see the kingdom of God." Nicodemus asked, "How can a man be born when he is old?" Jesus answered, "Except a man be born of water and of the Spirit, he cannot enter into the kingdom of God. That which is born of the flesh is flesh; and that which is born of the Spirit is spirit. Marvel not that I said unto thee, 'Ye must be born again.'"

Nicodemus had a small world. He did not love Samaritans, publicans, Galileans, harlots, lepers, persons possessed of demons.

God loved so much that God gave God's Son. Jesus died to save us all. We can have life everlasting through belief in him. No one else can promise us that. "I am come that they might have life," he said, "and that they might have it more abundantly."

May we show in the expressions on our faces, by the words we speak, and by the deeds of our hands, our Father, that we are self-giving Christians who enjoy making radiant our love for Christ as our Lord. Amen.

"The Crop Is Heavy"
Scripture: Matthew 9:35-38

Jesus said, "The crop is heavy" (NEB). The crop is heavy today. The church itself presents a great evangelistic opportunity. How many church members have prayer and read the Bible daily in their homes? Do they practice spiritual discipline and invite people to Christ? Is the church acting redemptively as the body of Christ?

Another concern is children. The number of children in our church schools is decreasing, but there is a record number of children in the United States today (42 million under ten years of age). We need people and churches to become more concerned about children. The church has an obligation to teach parents to become Christian educators.

Our third concern is the challenge of the inner city and suburbia. Inner-city residents today are mostly racial or ethnic minorities. Suburbia's challenge is secularism and social status. Downtown churches attract all kinds of people. Rich and poor kneel together there at the Communion table.

The church must strive harder to challenge high school youth. I asked a young man enlisting for two years in the Peace Corps why he wouldn't enlist for three years as a short-term missionary. He couldn't answer that. The 500 Peace Corps members in the Philippines total more than all missionaries of all the denominations serving there.

When General MacArthur went into Japan, he asked for a thousand missionaries. We sent 236. A few came from the mainline churches, but most of them came from the sects.

May the recurring need for each generation to provide laborers to harvest humankind for thee, our Father, appeal to us afresh as we engage in this urgent task in our time. Amen.

"We Have Seen Strange Things Today"
Scripture: Luke 5:18-26

"As he went on his way Jesus saw a man blind from his birth" (John 9:1, NEB). Just think—he had never looked on his mother's face. He had never seen beautiful flowers. "Blind from his birth."

His disciples put the question: "Rabbi, who sinned, this man or his parents? Why was he born blind?" They wanted to have a seminar. They wanted to have a workshop—a panel discussion. They didn't want to do anything for the man.

"'While I am in the world,' Jesus said, 'I am the light of the world.' With these words he spat on the ground and made a paste of the spittle; he spread it on the man's eyes, and said to him, 'Go and wash in the pool of Siloam.'" The man went away and washed, and when he returned he could see!

The basis of what I have to say in this message is in Luke 5:26: "You would never believe the things we have seen today." What had they seen? They saw some men bringing a man on a bed to Jesus. I think perhaps someone had taken these men to Jesus. Something had happened to them, and they knew what had happened to them. They wanted it to happen to this man. I think they said, "If we can just get him to Jesus, it will be wonderful. Something will happen."

Did you take anybody to Jesus last year? Somebody who was in great need? Have you done it this year? As I was preparing this message, I thought of how we are so critical of the church. Why don't we take somebody to Jesus?

When we read this beautiful story of the men's bringing their needy friend to Jesus for healing, help us to discover anew that someone may be waiting for us to bring him or her into the Christian fellowship and for encouragement. In Jesus' name. Amen.

"Who Brought You?"
Scripture: John 1:40-42

When I was in my middle teens, the pastor came into our home one night, and my mother said to him, "My son is a member of the church. He joined when he was a child, and he's not a Christian. He's doing a lot of things he ought not to be doing." Of course, that takes in a lot of us—leaving undone things that ought to be done. And he got down on his knees and prayed in our home for me. That night I went to the altar and repented, believed, and surrendered my life to Christ. Why? Because my mother cared. Because my mother wanted me to know Christ as my Savior. Thank God for a mother like that. My friends, I'd rather be preaching in Hong Kong or Taiwan tonight than to be preaching here. Do you know why? I'd rather be preaching to the Chinese because those Chinese Christians go out during the day to talk to the Buddhists and nonreligionists, and later in the afternoon they go to their homes and bring them to the church with them and sit with them. And when you give the invitation for those who wish to accept Jesus Christ as Savior and Lord and be prepared for Christian baptism, they come up here with them. They talk to them in the daytime; they go to their homes; they get them and bring them to the church. You try that in the United States and see what happens.

I think maybe China is going to lead the great evangelistic campaign. I don't think America can do it unless we change our ways. We are so steeped in our self-satisfaction, in our complacency.

Help us, our Father, to seek, find, and bring others into the fold of Christian love and faith. We are thankful for the example of such labors as can be seen in the outreach of Chinese Christians today. Amen.

Enthusiastic about Jesus
Scripture: Acts 1:6-8

Chinese Christians are enthusiastic about Jesus. In Hong Kong a businessman and his wife came to our service one night and had a young lady who worked in one of their business houses with them. When I gave the invitation, they came up with her and stood there with her. They were bringing her to Christ.

I wish you could see the Korean young people. I was speaking in Chonan. All the high schools there are government schools. We do not have a mission school in Chonan. They let me speak. I said I wanted to give every high school boy and girl in Korea a New Testament, and I asked the principals about it. They said, "Certainly." So I asked a good friend to give me $4,000 to buy the Testaments.

I preached in those schools in the daytime, and at night I preached in the tabernacle. They sat on the floor.

When I'd give the invitation fifteen or twenty girls would come up, then fifteen or twenty girlfriends and boyfriends. I would stand there and pray with them, and then the missionary would take them and get information about them. Why did they come? They came because the young people were going to see their friends, their Buddhist friends, their nonreligionist friends. They talked to them about Christ, they brought them to the tabernacle at night, and these people gave themselves to Christ. Then, as they counseled them, they enlisted them for preparation for Christian baptism.

May we let our enthusiasm for Christ and the Christian faith show in the radiance and joy of our daily lives and in our faithful witness. In Jesus' name we pray. Amen.

Singing and Seeking
Scripture: Luke 15:3-7

We sing gloriously, "Seeking the lost." How we love singing that: "Going afar upon the mountain, bringing the wand'rer back again." Isn't that great? Yes! "Into the fold of my Redeemer, Jesus the Lamb for sinners slain." It's wonderful to sing that. But have you been out on the mountain recently, looking for people for the Lord? I was preaching at Fort Smith, Arkansas, and when I was there a woman wrote me a letter. She said, "I want you to know that I was at the Methodist church one night. I'm not a Methodist; I am very active in the church. I teach a large Sunday school class, but I had lost the assurance that Jesus was my Savior. I came to church, and you preached to lost Methodists, and you gave the invitation to Methodists who had lost their experience to come forward. I wanted to come," she said, "but I didn't." Then she said, "Going home in my automobile that night I prayed and asked Christ to come into my heart and forgive my sins and give me the assurance that I was saved—that I had salvation. He came into my heart. I knew my sins were forgiven. I knew I was saved."

She wasn't a Methodist. She belonged to another group. Now do you know the reason she was at church that night? This is what is so marvelous. She said, "A member of the church invited me several times to come. She insisted that I come, and I came because of her invitation. And this is what happened to me." You can do that.

May we never underestimate the power we have as individual Christians in inviting others to hear the preaching of the gospel. May we know that our service to the kingdom may be just that—and an important service it is! Amen.

"He Came to Dwell among Us"
Scripture: John 1:1-14

"The Word became flesh." God came to dwell among us. Jesus came "to dwell among." One time he said to a man, "I must stay at your house today." This man was a collector of taxes. No one ever went to his home. No one befriended him.

Who am I? Well-educated? Wealthy? Who am I, really? Just a sinner saved by the grace of God through faith in Jesus Christ. Little wonder that the self-righteous religious people of his day didn't like it when Jesus invited himself into the home of Zacchaeus. They disapproved of such an association. Thank God Jesus wanted to eat with such a man—a sinner. He was going home with this man, he was going into his house, and he was going to stay with him! Jesus openly said that he chose the company of a man the Pharisees regarded as a sinner.

If your pastor went to certain places, you might disapprove also. You want him to come to your house, your office. If he doesn't come, then you say, "Look, he's going over there to be with those people."

We are not inclined to dwell with people unlike ourselves, but Jesus came to live among all kinds of persons—and he did. When he sat in Zacchaeus's house, there is no record of what he might have said to his host. Maybe he just sat there. That's all that was necessary. He was breaking barriers. He never went to be with Pharisees except by their invitation, but he very likely would have gone to be with them had they invited him.

Help us to be generous, our Father, in choosing those with whom we associate, knowing from Jesus himself that every person is a child of yours and that some of your children need our Christian friendship more than others. Amen.

Coming to Christ
Scripture: Galatians 2:20-21

I was preaching in Jacksonville in the Beach Church. I had preached for the pastor's father when he was a little boy. I preached on giving your body to Christ. "If you want Christ to live in you," I said, "come to the altar and pray." They came—half a dozen, eight, or ten. There was a young sailor. He said, "I've never been in a service like this. I've never seen anything like this."

When we got through the service, most of the people left. We stayed there until about one o'clock. You don't have to quit at twelve. The only emotion or excitement you have in church on Sunday morning is checking watches.

A woman came in with two boys—one twelve and the other thirteen. She was weeping. She said, "I want my boys to be Christians." I talked to them. She said, "They used to go to Sunday school here, but I took them out because of what the teacher was saying." You be careful what you teach, hear! Teach the Bible.

"I've been teaching them at home, but I want them to be converted and give themselves to Christ." The preacher made arrangements to teach them about church membership. I never will forget that experience—a mother concerned about the souls of her two boys.

Are you bringing people to Christ? Now, my friends, what's the use of your having all this Christian experience that you're having if you're not going to use it? What do you want? You say, "Salvation." What for? So you can tell others. You can be fishers of people.

Give me the courage and desire, our Father, to find someone who needs to meet Christ—and then let me lead that person into the Christian fellowship where Christ may indeed be found. Amen.

"Who Lives There?"
Scripture: Matthew 9:1-7

The men who brought a paralyzed man to Jesus heard Jesus say, "Your sins are forgiven." He said it because he saw the faith of the men who brought him. This man was physically paralyzed. A lot of people are paralyzed by fear, greed, selfishness, pride, jealousy, disobedience, lust, drink, sex.

In Oklahoma I saw a lot of little shotgun houses—one room, another room, another room—all in a row. I said to the preacher, "Who lives there?" "I don't know," he said. "Well, let's go see. Let's find out."

In the first house we found a dear old fellow who was blind. An elderly friend was reading to him. He didn't have a radio so I said, "Brother, I'm going to get you a radio." I went up to the liquor store and went in to see the manager. I told him what I was doing, and I told him how much I hated liquor but I loved him, and I said, "I want you to give me a radio." He said, "I'll do it." He went back and got a radio.

A telegraph operator got sick with tuberculosis. He moved to Tyler, Texas. He stayed in bed all day. He'd get up at six o'clock, eat supper, and go to see the people who had moved into the community recently. He would say to them, "I have come to tell you about the plan of salvation." Look around you and ask, "Who lives there?" Then find out by visiting.

Put in our hearts, O God, a loving curiosity to find out who the people are who live around us. Then inspire and encourage us to visit them in Christian love to let them know we care about them. In Jesus' name. Amen.

The Church's Evangelistic Opportunities
Scripture: Matthew 9:35-38

As Christ's laborers we should develop outreach opportunities beyond the local church—like conducting services at County Fairs, erecting chapels close to state parks, offering ministries at shopping centers, on the streets, in jails. Are we going to go where the people are? Some young preachers are even preaching at drag races where there may be as many as eight or ten thousand people.

Is family evangelism on our agenda? If the family deteriorates, the church deteriorates; the nation deteriorates.

Many forms of communication are available to us to spread the gospel—newspapers, radio, television.

Another task is to get the church Christ-centered and committed, rather than merely church-centered. I'd like for us to talk about Christ. We ought to talk to nonparticipating members about Christ.

In Fort Wayne, Indiana, I asked the preachers to give me a list of their nonparticipating members—people who don't come and don't pay. The preachers didn't go with me to visit them, but they provided laypersons to go with me. Many had dropped out of the church because they went to the lake for the summer and had gotten out of the habit of attending church.

Consider scheduling services at times other than on Sunday. One pastor—a friend of mine—has services on Monday nights for persons who cannot attend on Sunday. Another provides services on Saturday. Sunday morning services no longer accommodate the schedules of many people. Study your membership. How many members cannot attend Sunday worship because of their work?

Our Father, give us holy imagination to find ways to offer public worship opportunities to more persons for whom the church carries responsibility. May we not get rigidly committed to traditional ways of doing things that leave out so many who need the church's ministry. Amen.

Work the Parish
Scripture: James 1:27

If you want people to visit door-to-door, you must enlist them one-by-one. Do not ask for volunteers.

When you visit from house to house, you don't know what you're going to find. You may visit Roman Catholics who are outside their church. They are divorced and married again without the church's blessing. Some are leaving the church because the church as they know it is too autocratic.

A church that has two or three services on Sunday morning reaches more people and gets more participation (multiple choirs, multiple sets of ushers, etc.). Maids, cab drivers, waitresses, and others who have to work and serve the public on Sundays go to the Roman Catholic churches to pray because most Protestant churches are open only when they are working. Examine your church roll to find members who cannot come on Sunday morning. Can alternate worship services be developed?

Take special interest in high school youth. Give youth the example of honest-to-goodness Christian living. Give them opportunities to serve. They will start a Sunday school in an underprivileged community. They will do evangelistic visiting.

Ask your Sunday school workers and teachers how many visits they made this year to absentees and sick members. Suppose I'm ten years old, and I come to your Sunday school next Sunday morning. What happens? You'll put my name down. Will you come and visit me and meet my parents? New persons who register their attendance at worship services will know you care if you visit them in their homes that same day.

Help us to see the opportunities the church has every Sunday, our Father, to make contact with new persons—new to the congregation, new in the community. Rid us of excuses for not going to visit them in the spirit of Christ. Amen.

Dealing with Temptations and Storms
Scripture: Matthew 4:1-11

When Jesus came back from the wilderness, he came back in the power of the Spirit because he was going to live according to the word of God; he was going to worship God and serve him only.

We do not have victory because we have so many gods. Jesus said, "The victory is mine," because he knew that the one God he trusted and obeyed would give him the victory. It didn't make any difference what Pilate or the Roman government did to him; it didn't make any difference what the Pharisees and the self-righteous people did to him. His faith was in God, and he was going to obey God. As Paul said, "He humbled himself and became obedient unto death" (Philippians 2:8).

Let's look at what happened one day. Jesus said to his disciples, "Let's go across the lake." So they got into the boat. Jesus was tired. He went to sleep in the boat. A squall came down. The wind was blowing. The waves were lashing the boat, and the disciples were afraid. They awakened Jesus and said, "Don't you care whether we live or perish?" Jesus spoke to the waves, and they became quiet; then he spoke to the wind, and there was a calm. Then the disciples did become fearful and Jesus said, "Why are you such cowards? Have you no faith even now?" (Mark 4:40, NEB).

As the storms of life beat down, we can be victorious over them if our faith is in Jesus Christ. Some think that because they are Christians they are exempt from the storms of life. But no one escapes the storms. God doesn't send them. We stir them up ourselves.

We are grateful, our Father, that you do not play favorites. All of us are caught up in the totality of life—storms included. Help us to find that by putting our trust in you we can weather all kinds of anxieties and distresses. In Jesus' name we pray. Amen.

Jesus at the Door of Your Church!
Scripture: Matthew 20:25-28

Suppose Jesus were to come to your church next Sunday morning. The fellowship committee members would greet him at the door and ask, "What's your name?" "Jesus of Nazareth." "Oh, you're a Jew. We don't have anything to do with Jews." If you despise a man because he is a Jew and only because he is a Jew, you despise Jesus Christ because he was a Jew. Then a committee member might ask, "Where do you live? What's your address?" His answer, "Foxes have holes, and birds of the air have nests; but the Son of man has nowhere to lay his head."

"Don't you have a split-level house, Jesus? Or do you have a ranch house? Haven't you got five bedrooms and four baths? What kind of car do you drive, Jesus?" "I walk, or I ride a donkey." "Oh, you don't have a Mustang? What's your vocation, Jesus? What do you do?" "Oh, I'm trying to be a servant to all the people. I'm trying to bring life to all people."

What would you do with Jesus? He couldn't give your church any status. He couldn't support the budget. You couldn't go around proudly saying, "Jesus is a member of my church" —this fellow who is homeless, who hasn't got an automobile, who doesn't own or even rent a house. What could he do for your church?

You want status. You want someone who can support the church. The man from Gadara who was put into his right mind by Jesus wanted to accompany his benefactor, but Jesus told him to go home and witness to what had happened to him. Are people astonished that something has happened to you that transformed you into a Christian?

Help us, our heavenly Father, to become bona fide Christians. May our presence in the world and in the church remind others that we have been with Jesus. In his name. Amen.

Are You Having Any Victories?
Scripture: Matthew 13:53-58

What demons vie for the control of life? Perhaps the greatest demon is self. We profess that we believe in God and go out to live for self. The demons of gossip, hate, prejudice, things, prosperity possess us. When we put our faith in Christ, he drives them out.

Jairus, the president of the synagogue, asked Jesus, the Galilean peasant-carpenter, to come and put his hands on his little twelve-year-old daughter and heal her. And Jesus responded. En route, a woman sick for twelve years touched the hem of his garment and heard Jesus say that her faith had made her whole (Luke 8:40-56).

Are you full of fear, or do you have faith in Jesus Christ? Do you believe that faith brings the victory? We are either dominated by fear or faith. Both are contagious. We are bound to have disease. Our bodies just deteriorate. Don't worry about it. Take it as it is. If your faith is in God, let God do the worrying. If your faith is in self, you are in fear. Faith brings peace; fear brings discord.

Christians don't have funerals. They have reincarnation services. Jesus couldn't do anything when he returned to Nazareth because his home folks did not believe in him. He failed only when people did not have faith in him. Our faith ought to be in him—not self, not the church. Are you having any victories? You can in Christ.

Christians have a healthy attitude toward the body. When Saint Paul learned that the Corinthian Christians were tempted to exploit their bodies in sinful ways, he wrote to them, "Do you not know that your body is a shrine of the indwelling Holy Spirit, and the Spirit is God's gift to you?" (1 Corinthians 6:19, NEB)

May we be able to accept the natural limitations of our temporary life in the flesh, our Father, knowing that mortality is subject to adversity. But may we just as surely know that our essential nature is of the Spirit, which is indestructible, and can enjoy health and vitality even when our bodies decline. Amen.

"As Obedient Children"
Scripture: 1 Peter 1:13-21

We had a woman in our church whose name was East. And we had a pastor, George Stewart, who couldn't remember names. This woman would come up after every service on Sunday morning, and she'd say, "Doctor, can you call my name?" He knew her name was a direction, so he'd say, "Well, this is Sister North." The next Sunday morning she came up and said, "Do you remember my name?" "Oh, yes, it's Sister South." And he'd always name a direction, but he never got her name right.

In the First Epistle of Peter we read this description of a Christian's lifestyle: "You must therefore be mentally stripped for action, perfectly self-controlled. Fix your hopes on the gift of grace which is to be yours when Jesus Christ is revealed. As obedient children, do not let your characters be shaped any longer by the desires you cherished in your days of ignorance. The One who called you is holy; like him, be holy in all your behavior, because Scripture says, 'You shall be holy for I am holy.' If you say 'our Father' to the One who judges every man impartially on the record of his deeds, you must stand in awe of him while you live out your time on earth. Well you know that it was no perishable stuff, like gold or silver, that bought your freedom from the empty folly of your traditional ways. The price was paid in precious blood, as it were of a lamb without mark or blemish—the blood of Christ. Predestined before the foundation of the world, he was made manifest in this last period of time for your sake. Through him you have come to trust in God who raised him from the dead and gave him glory, and so your faith and hope are fixed on God" (NEB).

The scriptures tell us, our Father, that you know each of us by name. We cannot fathom this, but we rejoice that it is true. May we be as eager to call you by the name of "Father" as you are to call us by our names. In Jesus' name we pray. Amen.

By the Way We Live
Scripture: John 13:34-35

I was in Salisbury, North Carolina, and the Methodists were having a committee meeting that afternoon to consider recommending a young man for membership in the conference. Finally someone asked him, "How did you get called to preach?" He said, "We had a pastor when I was a high school boy, and he had a son my age. We were great friends. I was called to preach by the way his father lived in the parsonage." That's the greatest compliment I ever heard of a preacher. It wasn't what he said in the pulpit. It's how we live that convinces people. Are we living as Christ would live?

A man went to a bargain sale to get something his wife wanted. The women there were pushing and shoving, and he decided that he would have to do something to get what his wife wanted. So he began to push and shove. A woman turned around and said, "Why don't you behave like a gentleman?" He said, "I have for the last two hours, and now I'm behaving like a lady."

Holiness has to be lived at the bargain counter. Did you ever see the saints at a bargain sale stand back and say, "Just come up and get what you want. I'll wait."

Then I remember the thief on the cross. He saw the jeering crowd, the envy of the jealous priests, the gambling soldiers, and the crowd going to and fro. And the one thief said to Jesus, "Are you not the Christ? Save yourself and us!" The other thief said, "Do you not fear God?" and then he said to Jesus, "Remember me when you come into your kingdom." He wanted to be with Jesus. He said, "Remember me when you come into your kingdom." And Jesus said, "Today you will be with me in Paradise" (Luke 23:39-43).

May we not be troubled, our Father, because we are always being watched by others who expect to see in us a demonstration of a higher quality of life than they see in those who are not professing Christians. Amen.

How the Gospel Is Spread
Scripture: Acts 4:13-20

I was preaching in Georgetown, South Carolina, not far from Georgia. There is a paper plant there where thousands of persons work. I went around the stores talking with people. They would say to me, "Do you know Mr. So and So? He's a carpenter out at the plant. Do you know him? He lives the Christian life." I said, "Yes, I know him." I had met him at the church. I'd go to another store. Same thing. This carpenter, working in a plant with a thousand other people lived so attractively and winsomely and graciously as a Christian that his radiance was recognized by everyone around him.

When we are filled with the Holy Spirit, we remind people of Christ. This hymn becomes our prayer:

> Have thine own way, Lord!
> Have thine own way!
> Hold o'er my being absolute sway.
> Fill with thy Spirit till all shall see
> Christ only, always, living in me.*

In Jesus people saw God. A Christian is one who is Christ incarnate. Wherever he or she goes, people see Christ. When Simon Peter made his speech in Jerusalem on the day of Pentecost he said, "God gave us Christ and Christ gives us the Holy Spirit so that we can be witnesses for him." That's how the gospel is to be spread. If we have been baptized by the Holy Spirit and Jesus has given us the Holy Spirit, then we go out to spread the gospel. People were attracted to Jesus, and people will be attracted to Jesus through us—not to us. They ought to be able to see Christ in us.

Help us to understand, our Father, that our witnessing for Christ is more effective and persuasive by the demonstration of our lives than by the proclamation of our lips. Amen.

*From the hymn "Have Thine Own Way, Lord" by Adelaide A. Pollard.

You Need Christ Now
Scripture: Matthew 16:13-20

Of what do we need to repent?

1. We need to repent of unbelief in Christ. Jesus said, "If you shall ask any thing in my name, I will do it" (John 14:14). When I found that verse I wrote down many things I wanted to ask for in the name of Jesus, but I discovered some things that I could not ask for in his name.

2. We need to repent of our fears. Some of the chief rulers believed on Christ but would not confess him because of the Pharisees, "for they loved the praise of men more than the praise of God" (John 12:43).

3. We need to repent for quenching the Spirit. The first sin we have record of in the early church is recorded in the Book of Acts. Ananias and Sapphira had quenched the Spirit by lying that they had not kept back part of the price of the land, which they promised to give to the church.

Jesus said, "Men ought always to pray" (Luke 18:1). We find time to pray when we get into trouble and need God. We say we don't have time to go to church, and yet we have time to go to many other places.

4. We need to repent of blasphemy. The late Bishop Gerald Kennedy of The Methodist Church said, "Blasphemy is to believe that a person is hopeless in the providence of God."

5. We need to repent of robbing God. We rob God of time—the time we spend in unprofitable conversation, pleasures, and amusements. And what about our money? Minimally, we should pay God the portion that the Bible requires (that is, 10 percent).

6. We should repent of denying Christ and the cross. We need to repent of professing Christ as our personal savior and then doing nothing for him.

If we find it hard, our Father, to acknowledge our sins that separate us from your love, help us now to enthrone Christ, who will bring divine love into our hearts and cast out fear. Amen.

All Things New
Scripture: Revelation 21:1-5

You can have the new birth. Jesus said, "Except a man be born of water and of the Spirit, he cannot enter into the kingdom of God" (John 3:5). You cannot explain the miracle of the birth of a baby; neither can you explain the miracle of the new birth.

A soldier who always knelt down to pray irritated another soldier who threw a muddy boot at the praying soldier. He hit him on the head and stunned him. Then he turned over and calmly went to sleep. The next morning when he awoke, his muddy boots had been cleaned and polished. When he asked who performed that service he was told it was the one he had hit the night before with his muddy boot. He went to him and said, "I must have your Christ."

In the early church, the Jerusalem apostles called Simon Peter to explain why he had eaten with Gentiles. "I was in the city of Joppa praying," he said, "I saw a vision. . . . I heard a voice." He told how he went to the home of Cornelius, a Roman soldier, saying, "As I began to speak, the Holy Ghost fell on them, as on us at the beginning" (Acts 11:5, 7, 15).

We need to see that all people need Christ today. John, in exile on the Isle of Patmos, said, "I saw a new heaven and a new earth. . . . And I John saw the holy city, new Jerusalem, coming down from God out of heaven."

The most beautiful home is the heavenly home. You and I choose to live in the new heaven and new earth by becoming new creatures in Christ. We can repent of our sins and have them washed away. Jesus Christ's sacrifice on Calvary was for every person in the world. That includes you.

> *Just as I am, without one plea,*
> *But that thy blood was shed for me,*
> *And that thou bidst me come to thee,*
> *O Lamb of God, I come, I come.**

*From the hymn "Just as I Am, Without One Plea" by Charlotte Elliott.

How Much Is Enough?
Scripture: Mark 12:41-44

I was in a church for many years and found out that a lot of members picked out the sorriest giver and said, "I give as much as he does." Remember that old rooster who rolled a turkey egg in front of a chicken and said, "I don't want to be judgmental, but I just wanted to show you what can be done."

Making a money offering is as much a part of worship as singing, praying, or preaching. Don't let the plate pass you by. If you can't put something in, take something out.

An old railroad conductor got converted and became active in the church. One Sunday he had to take up the offering. He put the plate out in front of a man, and the fellow didn't put anything in. The conductor stuck it out again, and the old fellow didn't put anything in. The conductor stuck it out the third time, and he didn't put anything in so he reached for the bell cord! Stop the train—this fellow isn't paying his fare!

Sometimes we live in a small world. We are reluctant to reach out even to one person for Christ. We aren't going to do any personal work. During Billy Graham's New York Crusade he did his best to get people to talk about their faith on the buses. They wanted Billy to do it. Jesus wants all of us to be witnesses.

Who do you include in your world? Does anyone ever come to see you and say, "I want what you've got"? We contact people all the time, everywhere we go. A young preacher and I parked the car this afternoon and started walking. We ran into a man right away. The Christian's business is to help people.

Help us to enlarge the circumference of our association with other persons, our Father, so we might more effectively attract and invite them into the abundant life of Christ. Amen.

Believing the Gospel
Scripture: Luke 7:36-50

Paul wrote that the gospel "is the power of God unto salvation to every one that believeth" (Romans 1:16).

1. Zacchaeus tried to find salvation in money. He said to Jesus, "Half of my goods I give to the poor; and if I have taken any thing from any man by false accusation, I restore him fourfold" (Luke 19:8). He wanted a clear conscience. He experienced transformation under the influence of Christ.

2. Saul of Tarsus persecuted Christians in Jerusalem and got authority to pursue those who fled to Damascus. On the road he was abruptly halted and heard the living Lord say, "Saul, why do you persecute me?" (Acts 9:4). In Damascus he found salvation.

3. The Gadarene demoniac, cast out of his community, saw Jesus and cried, "'What have I to do with thee, Jesus?'" (Mark 5:7). Jesus freed him from his troubled state.

A man told me that he and his wife had been drunkards. One morning they went to Sunday school, where friends told them about Christ and prayed with them. The preacher visited them, and they and their children were converted. This man now lives an exemplary Christian life.

When Jesus sat at dinner with Simon the Pharisee, a woman of the streets entered the house. She knelt before Jesus and lavished her affection on him. His host disparaged her action but Jesus said, "Simon, when I came to your door you did not give me any water to bathe my feet, but this woman has washed my feet with her tears and wiped them with her hair. You did not salute me with a kiss, but this woman has kissed my feet. You did not anoint me but this woman has anointed me." Then he said to her, "Your sins are forgiven. Your faith has saved you."

May we learn once again, our Father, from these familiar stories about Jesus and his dealing with persons in sin and in need. Faced with broken spiritual relations, we pray that his redemptive love will regain control of our hearts. Amen.

"Repent and Believe the Gospel"
Scripture: Mark 1:14-15

Mark tells us that Jesus came into Galilee preaching, "The kingdom of God is at hand: repent and believe in the gospel."

1. We need to repent for trying to find life in the things of the flesh instead of the spirit. We must eat to keep our bodies healthy, but we also need to care for our souls. Do you read the Bible each day? Do you worship God each day?

2. We need to repent for trusting material riches rather than being rich toward God. Do we have heavenly treasures? Do we give God's church its due? We print on our money, "In God We Trust," but I'm afraid we trust in the money instead.

3. We need to repent for giving ourselves to our own pleasures rather than to the pleasures of God. Make a list of those you know to be invalids, or shut-ins, or sick. Beside their names, write down the dates of the last time you visited them.

4. We need to repent for insisting on having our way rather than the way of God. Repent means to turn around, to change one's mind, to put God first, and to live for one's neighbor and love one's neighbor as one's self.

5. We need to repent of sin. We know when we disobey God, when we do wrong. We know what God wants us to do. He may want us to be tithers, to have family worship, to quit whatever hurts our lives and our homes. God knows what we should do, and so do we. He knows that we should quit doing, and so do we.

Here's wonderful news—God will forgive. The mercy of God is from everlasting to everlasting. We need to "turn around." We need Christ and his love in our hearts today.

When we sing, "Leaning on the everlasting arms," our Father, may we confidently do just that, knowing that as we put childlike trust in your goodness and mercy we find strength and courage for day-by-day living. Amen.

Be an Encourager
Scripture: Acts 4:36-37; 11:19-26

Joseph, a Levite born in Cyprus, whom the apostles called Barnabas (which means "One who Encourages"), sold a field he owned, brought the money, and turned it over to the apostles. —Acts 4:36 (TEV)

The apostles gave Barnabas his new name because of the life he lived. He encouraged Saul of Tarsus and succeeded in getting the church to receive him. The apostles sent Barnabas to Antioch to encourage the new Christians there to stand fast.

What a joy it is to know an encourager! I entered first-year preparatory school at Birmingham College in September 1915. I wanted an education. So I quit my job for a part-time job that paid one third of what I had been making. The slow pace of the college discouraged me. I wanted to go back to the business world.

One morning I stood in the chapel, looking out the window, trying to decide what to do. An upperclassman came and stood by my side. "Harry, we are glad you have entered school. We are going to stay by you. You have our prayers and help." He walked away. I decided to stay. He was a son of encouragement.

Dear Father, we thank you for those who have encouraged us with faith and love. Give us the spirit and encouragement for the discouraged. In the name of our blessed Lord. Amen.

THOUGHT FOR THE DAY

What a joy to know an encourager!

Harry Denman (No permanent residence)

Worldwide Communion
Scripture: Acts 1:1-8

We hear them telling in our own tongues the great things
God has done. —Acts 2:11(NEB)

This was said in Jerusalem by people "from every
nation under heaven." The church was a worldwide Christian
fellowship on the day of Pentecost, and it is so today.

On the streets of Budapest, Hungary, persons have
smiled, greeted me, and pointed to the cross I wear on the
lapel of my coat. We could not communicate with our tongues,
but we did communicate with our hearts of love. On a
transatlantic flight I saw a passenger with a Bible. I showed
him mine. We knew we were in the same fellowship.

Because the fellowship of one hundred and twenty told
the great things God had done through God's Son Jesus
Christ, the fellowship increased by thousands. The fellowship
extended a helping hand to a lame beggar, and he rejoiced
because of Christ's healing power. Some who belonged to the
fellowship were imprisoned and beaten, but every day the
fellowship went steadily on teaching in the Temple and in
private homes, telling the good news of Jesus, the Messiah.

*O Savior and Lord of the world, we pray that our fellowship
may have oneness with thee and with one another. We pray in thy
name, desiring thy joy within us in full measure. Amen.*

THOUGHT FOR THE DAY

The business of the Christian fellowship is to tell the
good news of Jesus, the Messiah.

Harry Denman (United States)

Making Christ Known
Scripture: John 1:14-18

God's only Son, he who is nearest to the Father's heart, he has made him known. —John 1:18 (NEB)

The Gospel writer John said of Jesus that he made God known. He did this with his deeds. Jesus said, "If I am not acting as my Father would, do not believe me. But if I am, accept the evidence of my deeds even if you do not believe me, so that you may recognize and know that the Father is in me, and I in the Father."

The black attendant in the men's restroom in the bus terminal in Cincinnati, Ohio, said to a white man, "Are you a Christian?" He asked the white man this question because the white man had found a beautiful wristwatch in the rest room and had turned it over to the black attendant to give to the owner when he returned. In reply to the black man's question the white man said, "I am trying to be; pray for me."

The white man said to the attendant, "Are you a Christian?" The black man said, "I am trying to be; pray for me." The two men stood there and prayed for each other.

The attendant said to the white man, "You are the only person who ever turned a lost article over to me."

O God, I pray that today my living will make Christ known to others. In his name I make this prayer. Amen.

THOUGHT FOR THE DAY

Our deeds make Christ known.

Harry Denman, Evangelist (Alabama)

Scripture Index

OLD TESTAMENT

NEW TESTAMENT